**books**online

Read this book online today:

With SAP PRESS BooksOnline we offer you online access to knowledge from the leading SAP experts. Whether you use it as a beneficial supplement or as an alternative to the printed book, with SAP PRESS BooksOnline you can:

• Access your book anywhere, at any time. All you need is an Internet connection.
• Perform full text searches on your book and on the entire SAP PRESS library.
• Build your own personalized SAP library.

The SAP PRESS customer advantage:

Register this book today at *www.sap-press.com* and obtain exclusive free trial access to its online version. If you like it (and we think you will), you can choose to purchase permanent, unrestricted access to the online edition at a very special price!

Here's how to get started:

1. Visit *www.sap-press.com*.
2. Click on the link for SAP PRESS BooksOnline and login (or create an account).
3. Enter your free trial license key, shown below in the corner of the page.
4. Try out your online book with full, unrestricted access for a limited time!

Your personal free trial **license key**
for this online book is: qied-p4xa-6gym-bv53

Using SAP®: A Guide for Beginners and End Users

SAP PRESS

SAP PRESS is a joint initiative of SAP and Galileo Press. The know-how offered by SAP specialists combined with the expertise of the Galileo Press publishing house offers the reader expert books in the field. SAP PRESS features first-hand information and expert advice, and provides useful skills for professional decision-making.

SAP PRESS offers a variety of books on technical and business related topics for the SAP user. For further information, please visit our website: *www.sap-press.com*.

Nancy Muir and Ian Kimbell
Discover SAP, Second Edition
2010, 440 pp., paperback
ISBN 978-1-59229-320-9

Manish Patel
Discover SAP ERP Financials
2008, 544 pp., paperback
ISBN 978-1-59229-184-7

Greg Newman
Discover SAP ERP HCM
2009, 438 pp., paperback
ISBN 978-1-59229-222-6

Martin Murray
Discover Logistics with SAP ERP
2009, 385 pp., paperback
ISBN 978-1-59229-320-1

Olaf Schulz

Using SAP®: A Guide for Beginners and End Users

Galileo Press

Bonn • Boston

Galileo Press is named after the Italian physicist, mathematician and philosopher Galileo Galilei (1564—1642). He is known as one of the founders of modern science and an advocate of our contemporary, heliocentric worldview. His words *Eppur si muove* (And yet it moves) have become legendary. The Galileo Press logo depicts Jupiter orbited by the four Galilean moons, which were discovered by Galileo in 1610.

Editor Eva Tripp
English Edition Editor Meg Dunkerley
Translation Lemoine International, Inc., Salt Lake City, UT
Copyeditor Emily Nicholls
Cover Design Nadine Kohl, Graham Geary
Photo Credit iStockphoto.com/Skynesher/000009040043
Layout Design Vera Brauner
Production Graham Geary
Typesetting SatzPro, Krefeld (Germany)
Printed and bound in the United States of America

ISBN   978-1-59229-408-4

© 2012 by Galileo Press Inc., Boston (MA)
1st edition 2012

Library of Congress Cataloging-in-Publication Data
Schulz, Olaf.
[SAP-Grundkurs für Einsteiger und Anwender. English]
Using SAP : a guide for beginners and end users / Olaf Schulz. -- 1st ed.
p. cm.
Includes bibliographical references.
ISBN-13: 978-1-59229-408-4
ISBN-10: 1-59229-408-1
1. SAP ERP. 2. Integrated software. 3. Business--Data processing.
I. Title.
QA76.76.I57S3814 2012
005.5--dc23
2011035201

SUSTAINABLE FORESTRY INITIATIVE   Certified Fiber Sourcing
Label applies to the text stock   www.sfiprogram.org

Contents at a Glance

Dear Reader,

Being a beginner at anything, including SAP, can be a frustrating and trying experience. That's why we've provided you with this new book, which makes getting started with SAP easier than ever before. Whether you need SAP perspective and knowledge for your new job or your employers want to introduce you to the SAP system, or you aspire to a career in the study of the SAP world—this book makes getting started easy.

This beginner's book takes you through the various parts of the system—it tells you what you need to know about SAP and gives you an overview of the main components of the software. It's the first resource of its kind, and includes simple step-by-step instructions that help you learn the ropes quickly and easily. I have every confidence that this resource will be a useful tool that you can refer to whenever you have a question or are looking for guidance.

We appreciate your business, and welcome your feedback. Your comments and suggestions are our most useful tools to help us improve our books for you, the reader. We encourage you to visit our website at *www.sap-press.com* and share your feedback about this work.

Thank you for purchasing a book from SAP PRESS!

Meg Dunkerley
Editor, SAP PRESS

Galileo Press
Boston, MA

meg.dunkerley@galileo-press.com
www.sap-press.com

Contents

Part II   Basic Principles of System Operation

About This Book

This SAP introductory book is aimed at anyone who wants to familiarize himself or herself with the SAP system or get an overview of the most important functions and components. The book describes the characteristic principles of the software, how you navigate in the SAP system, and which central functions are available for the various business areas—logistics, accounting, and human resources.

If you're already familiar with the SAP system and want to specialize in one of the various SAP components, or if you're looking for detailed information, this book is probably not the best resource for you. In this case, you should refer to a book that deals with your specific field of interest, and take a look at *www.sap-press.com*.

Structure of the Book

The book is divided into three parts and 19 chapters:

Part I outlines the history of the SAP enterprise and provides an overview of its products and special features.

Chapter 1, Brief History of the SAP Enterprise, describes the history of SAP AG from its foundation to the present.

In **Chapter 2**, How Does SAP Software Work?, you learn how to adapt the software to the requirements and needs of enterprises.

Chapter 3, Overview of the Most Critical SAP Products, provides an overview of the products of SAP Business Suite—that is, SAP ERP, SAP SCM, SAP PLM, and SAP SRM.

Part II forms the centerpiece of this book. It explains step-by-step how you operate the SAP system.

Chapter 4, Organizational Structures and Master Data, illustrates the significance of master data for all business processes, and how you can map the enterprise structure in SAP systems using organizational units.

Chapter 5, Logging on to the SAP System, describes how you establish a connection from a workplace computer to an SAP system.

Chapter 6, Navigating in the SAP System, discusses the navigation in the program interface.

Chapter 7, Maintaining the System Layout and User Data, shows you how to adapt the SAP system to your requirements.

Chapter 8, Creating Evaluations and Reports, deals with evaluating and reporting processes. The data that is stored in the SAP system is often used for evaluations, which then form the basis for the decision-making process in the enterprise.

Chapter 9, Printing, describes the print process in the SAP system, how to print documents, and the creation of screenshots from the SAP system.

Chapter 10, Automating Tasks, teaches you how to have the SAP system work for you by automating tasks via batch jobs.

Chapter 11, Working with Messages and Business Workplace, shows you how to use the SAP system to perform different office administration tasks. The Business Workplace enables you to send short messages, manage documents, and deploy workflows.

Chapter 12, Using Help Functions, describes the different help functions: the SAP online help, the F1 and F4 help, and many more.

Chapter 13, The Role and Authorization Concept, provides general information on authorization control and the role concept in SAP ERP.

Part III of this book provides an overview of the most critical SAP components.

In **Chapter 14**, Materials Management, you learn how purchasing processes are mapped in the MM component in the SAP system. You are provided with information on the required master data, the organizational structures, and the procurement process, including purchase order, goods receipt, and invoice verification.

Chapter 15, Sales and Distribution, discusses sales processes and illustrates the sales process with the SD component in the SAP system. It introduces master data, organizational structures, as well as sales order, goods issue, and invoicing.

Chapter 16, Financial Accounting, gives you an overview of the central functions of the FI component in SAP ERP. It discusses the general ledger, as well as accounts receivable and accounts payable.

Chapter 17, Controlling, describes the basic principles and functions of the CO component in SAP ERP. This includes controlling tasks, overhead cost controlling, product cost controlling, and profitability analysis.

Chapter 18, Human Resources, deals with the tasks and processes of the HR in the SAP system, for example, organizational management, recruitment, personnel administration, and time management.

In the case study in **Chapter 19**, you can reinforce your understanding of the basic SAP processes by reproducing a continuous process in the SAP system.

The **Appendix** of this book provides critical information for quick reference: abbreviations, a glossary with the most important SAP concepts, an overview of transaction codes, menu paths, key combinations, buttons, and function keys.

More content is available on the book's catalog page at *www.sap-press.com/ H3213*. There you can download solution notes for the exercises, additional information, and various overviews from the appendix for printing.

Working with this Book

You can use this book both as a general introduction and as a reference book. Each chapter of Part II and Chapter 19 in Part III contain exercises in which you can apply what you've learned. You can also carry out the exercises directly in an IDES standard system. Allow yourself plenty of time and make sure that you understand all of the steps. This way, you become acquainted with the SAP system. Remember: Never carry out the exercises in a live SAP system; if you're unsure, ask your supervisor or administrator.

Reading this book does not require previous knowledge of SAP, just basic PC knowledge and an understanding of the processes in business enterprises.

Beginners should read the book from the beginning because the individual chapters are based on each other. Each topic provides background information about concepts and processes. Finally, the processes in the system are described click by click and with numerous screenshots.

SAP's IDES System

You can maximize your success with this book if you have access to an SAP ERP test or training system. All the examples in this book are based on the IDES system, which means that you don't have to implement customizing settings in order to reproduce examples or carry out exercises.

IDES (International Demonstration and Evaluation System) is the SAP ERP training system of SAP AG where you navigate in a virtual enterprise. It maps an entire enterprise structure and provides master data for all areas. SAP customers have free access to the IDES system.

If you cannot use an IDES environment in your enterprise or training center, other systems are available. For example, Consolut GmbH provides free access to an IDES system at *http://www.consolut.com/en/s/sap-ides-access/ discover-sap-ides.html* (subject to change).

Acknowledgments

It is not easy to write a book on this kind of subject, especially since it covers such a wide range of topics, all of which aims to be useful to all readers.

While writing this book, I received support from many people. First of all, I want to thank my wife, Nicole, for her support, and Eva Tripp, editor at SAP PRESS, for the excellent cooperation and infinite patience. My thanks also go to Renata Munzel and Frau Anja Junold for their constructive reviews of the chapters on financial accounting, controlling, and human resources. Also, I want to thank my brother Ulrich and my friend Peter Clausius for their help with the English review.

Part I

The SAP Enterprise

1 Brief History of the SAP Enterprise

SAP produces software to support the processes of businesses from different industries and of various sizes. Since it was founded in the 1970s, SAP has become the largest European and fourth largest global software manufacturer. This chapter outlines the most critical milestones in the development of SAP from the early stages up to today.

This chapter discusses:

- Where SAP began
- How SAP became the enterprise it is today
- What the SAP R/3 and SAP ERP products are made of

1.1 Getting Started: From RF to SAP R/3

SAP's history begins in Weinheim, Germany, in the early 1970s. In 1972, five former IBM employees—Hans-Werner Hektor, Dietmar Hopp, Hasso Plattner, Klaus Tschira, and Claus Wellenreuther—founded the enterprise *Systemanalyse und Programmentwicklung* (System Analysis and Program Development), which was later renamed *Systeme, Anwendungen und Produkte in der Datenverarbeitung* (Systems, Applications and Products in Data Processing). In the early stages, they programmed at their customers' data centers because they didn't have their own systems yet. The very first product was created on computers that belonged to their first customer, Imperial Chemical Industries (ICI).

The Realtime Financials (RF) system was the first product of SAP that supported financial business processes. The computers of the time can't even be compared with today's IT systems. The software was operated on large computer systems, punch cards were used as data carriers, and memory capacities were limited to only a few kilobytes.

Former Data Carriers—Punch Cards (Source: SAP AG)

RF formed the basis of further software parts, called modules. Later, RF was also referred to as SAP R/1. The letter "R" stands for real time, and even decades later this letter is still included in the names of SAP's core products.

> **INFO**
>
> **Real-Time Processing**
> Real-time processing means that actions are immediately executed in the system and have immediate effect on the processes concerned.

SAP's software had the following three features from the outset:

- **Real-time processing**
  The processing was supposed to be made in real time, that is, an input is immediately available in the entire system.

- **Standard software**
  The software was supposed to be standardized to a large extent. In other words, every enterprise obtains the same software, which is then customized during the implementation project.

- **Integration**
  The various modules or components are supposed to be integrated, which means that the data from one application is also available to other applications.

You can find more information on these properties in Chapter 2, How Does SAP Software Work?

> **EXAMPLE**
>
> **Integration**
>
> The settlement for a completed procurement process (the Materials Management (MM) component in SAP) is implemented in financial accounting (the Financial Accounting (FI) component in SAP). In this process, the relevant departments use the documents that were created or stored in the SAP system during the operation.

Two years after SAP was founded, it established itself for more than 40 additional customers from different industries. *SAP GmbH Systeme, Anwendungen und Produkte in der Datenverarbeitung* was founded in 1976. In the following year, SAP headquarters were relocated from Weinheim to Walldorf, Germany.

In 1979, SAP redesigned its applications and revised the technologies in system and database development; these were included in the SAP R/2 system (the successor of SAP R/1). The next leap in SAP development was the initial public offering; in 1988, SAP GmbH became SAP AG.

In 1991, SAP AG presented the first applications of the SAP R/3 system at the CeBIT trade fair in Hanover, Germany. SAP R/3 is a system with new client-server architecture and a graphical user interface. The three layers of this client-server architecture (database layer, application layer, and presentation layer) are represented by the figure "3" in the product name. Relational databases are used internally, and the system can be used in different platforms. Chapters 2 (How Does SAP Software Work?) and 3 (Overview of the Most Critical SAP Products) provide additional information about this.

> **NOTE**
>
> **Relational Databases**
>
> Information is stored as tables for relational databases. The tables are linked with one another. So, the information doesn't need to be stored multiple times in the system. Connections—or relations—emerge between the tables. Relational databases that are well-known today include MaxDB of SAP, Microsoft SQL Server, mySQL, Oracle, and DB2 from IBM.

The client-server architecture is based on a three-layer concept which describes the system's technical task allocation: The presentation layer is a user PC (front end) in the network, on which the screens are displayed. If one user PC fails, it won't affect the other users. The applications are "only" presented. The system's programs and the user's inputs are processed at the application layer. Various user PCs are connected with a server. One or more servers access the databases, which can be installed on separate machines. Chapter 2 discusses the client server principle in more detail.

The R/3 system was extremely successful. The hardware required by a client server system was more efficient and less expensive; at the same time, a greater number of users could work with the system. SAP R/3 consisted of a technical basis, SAP's "operating system" so to speak, and the applications, which were broken down into various modules (or "components," as we refer to them today) for the different enterprise areas.

From the functional perspective, SAP R/3 provided software for all steps in the value chain of an enterprise. These steps (i.e., purchase, dispatch, and invoicing) are mapped by the SAP software. All essential departments of an enterprise were now able to use the SAP system for their work: accounting, controlling, sales and distribution, purchasing, production, stockholding, and human resources.

> **INFO**
>
> **Enterprise Resource Planning**
> A system that supports enterprise processes is referred to as an ERP system. ERP stands for Enterprise Resource Planning. The goal is to utilize these resources as efficiently as possible and effectively control the enterprise.

1.2 SAP from the Turn of the Millennium to the Present

In 2000, there were over ten million SAP users around the world. The software, which covers the classic enterprise areas, is still available. But in addition to that, the Internet era that dawned in the 1990s brought new technologies, which involved new options for communication between customers and enterprises, such as web sales. In addition, the cooperation of businesses changed, and they increasingly communicated via web technologies.

SAP R/3 Enterprise (Release 4.7) was the last SAP system to include the real time "R" in its name. In 2003, the product name SAP R/3 was replaced with mySAP ERP and then SAP ERP. A stronger emphasis was placed on the purpose of SAP software—*enterprise* resource planning.

SAP ERP 6.0 is the current release that is used in 2011, and as the basis of this book. New functions are imported via Enhancement Packages (EHP). The core of the system is still comprised of the applications from R/3 times; the range of products, however, contain more solutions that further refine the functional scope of SAP ERP or offer support for processes that are not covered in SAP ERP. Chapter 3, Overview of the Most Critical SAP Products, provides a more detailed description of these solutions.

An important innovation was the implementation of SAP NetWeaver as a technology platform. Among other things, SAP NetWeaver includes those functions which were previously located in the SAP basis. The keyword for SAP NetWeaver is *integration*—there is the option to access the SAP system via the Internet to support processes using different software applications and to gather information. You'll find a brief overview of SAP NetWeaver in Chapter 3.

In past years, SAP has focused on expanding into new markets. Various software products are directed toward the target group of small and medium businesses (SMB). In addition, SAP's acquisitions (such as Business Objects in 2007 and Sybase in 2010) have attracted attention.

SAP Main Building at the Enterprise's Headquarters in Walldorf (Source: SAP AG)

INFO **SAP Figures**

To illustrate SAP's market success, let's talk numbers: Today, SAP has a workforce of approximately 47,000 employees located in Germany, the US, and India. SAP is a global enterprise with more than 97,000 customers in 120 countries. Its headquarters are still located in Walldorf, Germany.

In this chapter, you've learned about the history of the SAP enterprise and its most essential product, SAP ERP. Some important characteristics of the SAP software were already discussed, including the separation of client, server, and database, as well as integration. The following chapters discuss how the SAP system functions in more detail.

2 How Does SAP Software Work?

Chapter 1 already introduced you to some characteristics of SAP systems. In addition to features like standardization, real-time processing, and integration, these also include adaptability and extensibility.

> **This chapter describes:**
>
> - Basic principles of SAP software
> - Characteristics of standard software
> - How you can adapt the SAP system to your enterprise
> - Characteristics of client-server architecture
> - How business processes are mapped and integrated continuously
> - What real-time processing is

2.1 What Is "Standard Software"?

SAP provides standard software. This means that this software in its standard version (or with minor modifications) can map many business processes in various industries. Using standard software has a lot of advantages. The customer can benefit from continuous optimizations, enhancements, and new technologies. Because the developers work closely with their customers, other users' requirements are considered for new versions.

The opposite of standard software is individual software, which is developed for one customer and is supposed to meet only one customer's specific requirements. In this case, this single customer has to pay the development costs and all subsequent costs on his own.

SAP provides predefined packages, so-called industry solutions, for use in specific industries. Currently (in 2011), about 24 industry solutions are available, for example, SAP for Utilities (IS-U), SAP for Automotive (IS-A), and SAP for Defense & Security (DFPS). See Chapter 3 for more information on these.

Industry solutions are standard software with an extended functional scope to map the processes of the industry enterprise.

2.2   Adapting the SAP System to an Enterprise

The previous section referred to SAP as standard software. Of course, the requirements and processes vary from business to business. SAP products can be adapted to each customer's requirements and business processes. SAP software consists of modules or components with different functions; the customer can select those that suit his needs. The SAP system is adapted during the implementation project.

This adaptation of the system is enabled by Customizing, which allows you to set up the system without programming (called "configuring"). For example, when you implement a new system, the system maps the structure of the business—called the organizational structure—including clients, company codes, and so on. (You can find more information on organizational structures in Chapter 4.) In the Financial Accounting component, for example, you as the customer define how taxes on your business are determined, because SAP products are used in countries where tax rates vary and taxes are determined differently.

The adaptation of the SAP system in Customizing is also the reason why the screens in your system may not be identical to those shown in this book.

You can implement Customizing in the SAP system via the Implementation Guide, which maps the setting options in a tree structure sorted by areas. The next two figures show screens from Customizing of the SAP system.

Customizing maps the structure of the enterprise and its individual areas and departments in the SAP system through the organizational structure. The figure shows how the organizational structure of an enterprise is set up in the SAP system and which organizational units are linked together. Customizing of the organizational structures provides a Customizing table; you can use it to assign plants to a purchasing organization within the organizational structure, for example.

Customizing also maps the business's processes. The next figure shows how you can make various settings in the SAP system via the Implementation

Guide. In this example from the organizational structure area, a plant is assigned to a company code.

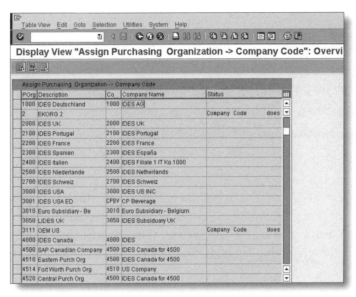

Customizing of Organizational Structures (Example Purchasing Organization— Plant)

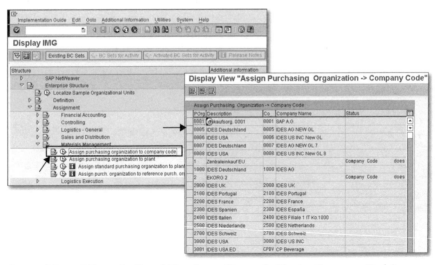

Customizing of Organizational Structures (Example Plant—Company Code)

Customizing Activities

- Creating organizational structures
- Mapping business processes
- Implementing basic system settings
- Adding selection lists
- Creating material types that are not included in the standard version
- Defining approval procedures
- Defining whether fields are supposed to be hidden
- Configuring areas for automatic number assignments

With Customizing, settings are made in the system without writing one single line of program code. But programming may be necessary if the requirements can't be met with Customizing. In the SAP system, you can implement developments using the programming languages ABAP and Java, as described in the next section.

2.3   What If the Standard Is Not Sufficient?

If the standard system and the Customizing options are not sufficient to meet your business requirements, you can extend the system with custom developments or products by SAP partners. You can integrate these non-SAP products by SAP partners via the technical platform SAP NetWeaver (see Chapter 3).

Programming for the SAP System

Programming requirements can be implemented using the development environment that is provided in the SAP system, or with ABAP (Advanced Business Application Programming Language) or Java. ABAP programmers use the ABAP Workbench, a development environment from SAP NetWeaver (see Chapter 3).

2.4   Orientation Toward the Process

Business processes are defined sequences of steps in the enterprise. When you order goods, you trigger a process: a purchase requisition may be implemented, the incoming goods posted, and finally, the invoice verified. The SAP system focuses on the business process because it needs to be mapped continuously within the system.

It is critical that you as the user visualize the process when working in the system. Make sure you understand what the process is supposed to achieve, where it starts, and where it ends before you begin.

The next figure shows the sales process from the perspective of the SAP system, and makes it easy for you to understand the individual substeps: The customer inquires about the availability and price of a specific product. He then places an order with your enterprise. Your enterprise executes the order and creates and posts the invoice.

Sales Process as Mapped in the SAP System

For enterprises that use SAP software, it is common that multiple departments are involved in a business process. For example, the sales process involves the sales department, the warehouse, and invoice verification (which is usually integrated with accounts receivable accounting as a part of financial accounting). The SAP system ensures that the individual processes integrate seamlessly and can be processed.

The system records all processes, steps, and user activities so that they are continuous, transparent, and reproducible at any time. The basic principle "Don't post without documentation" also applies to IT systems, because business processes have to be effective and auditors must be able to trace all processing steps and documents.

2.5   Real Time

Because the SAP system is highly integrated, changes must be accessible to everyone involved. Otherwise, a colleague from another department may work with inaccurate or obsolete information. That's where the real time principle comes into play. *Real time* is the amount of time that is required to complete a system activity, and means that changes are immediately available to all users across the system. The result is that all pieces of information are kept up-to-date in the business, and completed process steps can be directly used as a basis for others.

> **Real Time**
>
> You add a contact partner to the vendor master record in the SAP system. After this information has been saved, the change is immediately effected in the entire SAP system. Every user who has the respective authorization can access the master record and thus view the new entry.

2.6   Central Data—Decentralized Processing

In most businesses, data is not stored on the employees' PCs, but instead on a central computer. This is called client-server architecture, and lets you access a central computer (server = provider) from your workplace computer (client = customer).

SAP uses a three-layer client-server architecture, which has the following layers:

- Client (presentation layer—your workplace computer, for example)
- Server (application layer)
- Database (database layer)

So if, for example, you use the SAP system on your workplace computer and call customer data, this request is transferred from your computer to the server. The database server then processes this data (by editing, deleting, or requesting the data). The result of the task is finally transferred from the server back to the client so that you can view and process the data on your screen.

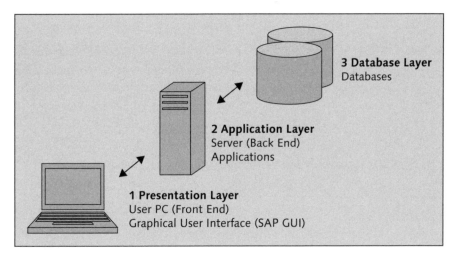

2

The Three-Layer Client-Server Architecture

This concept is central to many professional business applications (ERP systems) that are used by more than one person. Using client-server architecture has numerous advantages:

- You can use different hardware and operating systems on the server and on the client.
- If one client fails, the other users can continue working.
- Central data backups are possible.
- The data retention can be centralized.

However, client-server architecture also has disadvantages:

- If the server fails, none of the clients can work.
- The network infrastructure must be stable and secure.

With client-server architecture, it doesn't matter whether the client accesses the server applications via a Local Area Network (LAN) or via an Internet connection.

This chapter introduced the most important basic principles of SAP systems and described the characteristics of standard software. When a business purchases a complete software package, the package is then adapted to its requirements and specific processes using Customizing. Custom solutions can be programmed if the Customizing options are not sufficient. Chapter 3 provides an overview of the SAP products.

3 Overview of the Most Critical SAP Products

SAP offers software for different sized enterprises and business requirements. Before you get to know the practical parts of the SAP system in upcoming chapters, first you need to understand SAP's most critical products. Many software solutions are available for special requirements beyond those that are presented here, but this chapter covers the largest and most important.

This chapter discusses:

- Which SAP software is available for financial accounting, human resources, and logistics
- SAP Business Suite applications
- The technology that supports these solutions
- What SAP NetWeaver is

3.1 Complete Package: SAP Business Suite

Since the early years, SAP has extended and diversified its software offerings to cover different business requirements. Rather than a single application, the SAP Business Suite is SAP's core product, and consists of various solutions. You can purchase (or license) these solutions individually or as a complete package.

The SAP Business Suite consists of the following parts:

- SAP ERP
- SAP Customer Relationship Management (SAP CRM)
- SAP Supplier Relationship Management (SAP SRM)
- SAP Product Lifecycle Management (SAP PLM)
- SAP Supply Chain Management (SAP SCM)

SAP NetWeaver is the technical basis for all of these products.

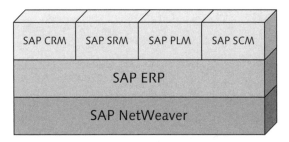

Parts of the SAP Business Suite

The following sections discuss these individual parts and their most important functions.

3.2 The Central Component: SAP ERP

SAP ERP forms the core component of the SAP Business Suite. You can use SAP ERP to map operative and administrative business processes across departments.

SAP ERP contains the following applications:

- Accounting (SAP ERP Financials)
- Human resources (SAP ERP Human Capital Management)
- Logistics (SAP ERP Operations and SAP ERP Corporate Services)

Within these applications, you can find the components (formerly known as modules) that you already know from SAP R/3. The following table shows some of these components; the most essential ones are detailed in Part III of this book.

Application	Function	Component (acronym)
Accounting	Financial Accounting/External Accounting	FI
	Controlling/Managerial Accounting	CO
	Financial Supply Chain Management	FSCM
	Treasury	TR

The Most Essential Components of SAP ERP

Journals and magazines only published in electronic format may not have page numbers or the numbering may not be by volume and issue. Give as much information as you can to identify the article you have used.

CHARAVARYAMATH, Chandrashekhar and SINGH, Baljit (2006). Pulmonary effects of exposure to pig barn air. [online]. *Journal of occupational medicine and toxicology*, 1:10.

For newspaper articles, give the date of the newspaper instead of the volume and issue.

DERBYSHIRE, David (2006). Adverts endorsed by stars are rated only just above junk mail. [online]. *The Daily Telegraph*, 20 July, 5.

Web pages
Include the author(s), year, title, [online], day and month updated or posted (if available) and the URL. The updated or posted day and month are helpful because the source may change.

CRICK, Bernard (2011). *George Orwell: voice of a long generation*. [online]. Last updated 17 February. http://www.bbc.co.uk/history/british/britain_wwtwo/orwell__01.shtml

Web pages do not always have individual authors. You can use the corporate author.

NETDOCTOR (2014). *Brufen (Ibuprofen)*. [online]. http://www.netdoctor.co.uk/seniors-health/medicines/brufen.html

If you cannot identify an author or corporate author, reference the web page by title.

Big Lottery Fund. (2012). [online]. http://www.biglotteryfund.org.uk/

Online recordings of TV, radio and film
For an online recording from TV or radio, include the programme title, part title if applicable, broadcast year, [online], broadcast channel, broadcast day and month.

> *Panorama.* Wikileaks: the secret story. (2011). [online].
> BBC1. 14 February.

For an online recorded feature film, provide film title, year of release, [online], director, broadcast channel and broadcast date.

> *Changeling.* (2008). [online]. Directed by Clint Eastwood.
> Sky Movies Premier. 7 November 2009.

More examples

For examples of how to reference and cite other sources such as conferences, government publications, images, DVDs and social media, see the "Guide to Referencing and Citations" on the Help on Referencing web pages on the Library Gateway.

Referencing software

You can use RefWorks bibliographic software to create a database of your references by importing the details of your sources. Citations and reference lists can then be produced in Microsoft Word.

There is also a tool in Microsoft Word which you can use to enter the details of your sources and create citations and bibliographies.

Help

More information is available on the Help on Referencing web pages on the Library Gateway
libguides.shu.ac.uk/referencing

Application	Function	Component (acronym)
Accounting (Contd.)	Enterprise Controlling	EC
	Enterprise Controlling	SEM
	Project System	PS
Human resources (HCM)	Personnel Administration	PA
	Recruitment	PR
	Personnel Planning and Development	PD
	Payroll	PY
	Training and Event Management	PE
	Time Management	PT
	Organizational Management	OM
	Travel Management	TM
Logistics	Purchasing	MM
	Production Planning and Control	PP
	Sales and Distribution	SD
	Customer Service	CS
	Warehouse Management	WM
	Transportation and Distribution	LE
	Quality Management	QM
	Real Estate Management	RE
	Plant Maintenance	EAM (PM)
	Environment, Health, and Safety	EH&S

The Most Essential Components of SAP ERP (Cont.)

The following figure shows Graphical User Interface of the SAP system (SAP GUI) directly after logon. Here, you can clearly identify the enterprise areas covered by SAP ERP.

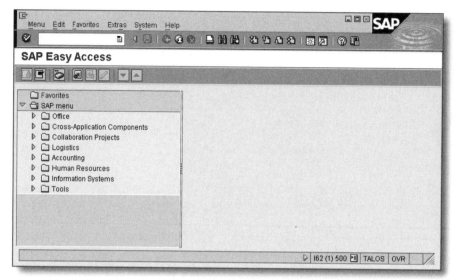

The Graphical User Interface of the SAP System

The following sections briefly discuss the processes that can be mapped in SAP ERP and the associated SAP components. Keep in mind that you typically can't consider each area of a business separately, since many functions are linked together.

Accounting

SAP ERP Financials contains software for both financial accounting and controlling. New tools like SAP Financial Supply Chain Management (for cash flow management) have been added since the early versions of SAP R/3 were released. In addition, SAP has completely revised general ledger accounting in the system (new general ledger).

You can use the financial accounting component (SAP FI) to map financial reporting requirements that are applicable in many countries, languages, and currencies. Important areas of accounting include the following:

- Financial accounting (external accounting)
- Controlling (managerial accounting)
- Corporate Governance
- Treasury
- Financial Supply Chain Management

The tasks of financial accounting, which are supported by SAP FI, center on business accounting. All business transactions are entered, documented, and allocated to accounts. Based on this data, you can create the legal balance and the profit and loss statement at the end of the fiscal year.

The SAP component for managerial accounting or controlling (SAP CO) focuses on business success. Business processes are supposed to be optimized for profit maximization. Cost accounting, performance accounting, and investment are utilities in managerial accounting. The information gained from these processes forms the basis for important business decisions and the business's orientation. Legal provisions are not binding for the business in managerial accounting, as they are in financial accounting.

Beyond that, you can use SAP to meet further financial requirements: SAP ERP contains functions that help businesses comply with national and international rules and regulations. Here you must distinguish between legally binding and voluntary measures. These measures are summarized under the concept of Corporate Governance, which basically entails a responsible business management and control.

Functions are also available to create and plan financial means and to ensure payments. This area is referred to as Treasury.

Another increasingly important task of financial accounting is the safeguarding of liquidity (in other words, the solvency of the business). Receivables management plays a critical role to ensure the liquidity. Tasks required for this goal range from credit standing check of customers and processing of clarification cases, to electronic invoicing and online payment transactions. The transparent mapping of cash flows is also referred to as Financial Supply Chain Management (SAP FSCM).

Human Resources

Another important area, in which the SAP system is used, involves human resources. SAP ERP Human Capital Management (SAP ERP HCM) has replaced Human Resources (HR) in SAP R/3.

SAP ERP HCM enables enterprises to:

- Manage employees (personnel administration)
- Create payrolls
- Plan qualification measures and trainings

- Record and settle working times
- Manage applicant data

Personnel administration involves the management of employees. Data is presented in the form of infotype records, such as organizational assignments, personal data, addresses, planned working time, basic pay, and bank details.

With the Payroll tool you can create salary certificates for employees and transfer the results to accounting.

Personnel Development helps you plan and implement education and training measures for employees. The development requirement of the employee is derived by comparing the current qualification with the job profile. Training and Event Management is an integrative part of SAP ERP HCM, and allows you to plan, implement, and manage trainings and other business events.

Time Management is the management of attendance times, flextime, annual leave, and absences. The information is entered online in the system by those employees responsible, Employee Self-Service applications, or time recording systems.

The system supports the entire recruitment process, from entering applicant data to final staffing assignments. Applicant data can be entered either by the applicants themselves (via an Internet portal) or by employees of personnel management.

In Organizational Management, employees are assigned to their corresponding positions in the business. The system provides organizational units to map organization structures in the system.

Logistics

The SAP system supports all business areas that belong to the supply chain, which includes all business processes that concern suppliers and customers, as well as the production of products:

- Purchasing (materials management)
- Production and product development
- Sales and customer service

Materials Management (SAP MM) involves goods or services that must be procured (purchased) and then managed and paid. The process starts with the processing of the purchase requisitions, which are sent to Purchasing from various departments of the business and then trigger the purchase order itself. Materials Management is also responsible for inventory management of materials with material valuation for the financial statements. Information about the material that is still in stock must be gathered in inventories. Another important task within Materials Management is invoice verification, where invoices for purchased goods or services are checked for correctness. MM is also responsible for the maintenance of material master data. You will find more detail on Materials Management in Chapter 14.

The materials procured in Materials Management can be used for production, for example. Production Planning and Control in the SAP system (SAP PP) includes the sales and operations planning as well as production planning itself (both for discrete manufacturing—that is, manufacturing of general goods—and for process manufacturing, which is the manufacturing of countable units, such as fluids in the chemicals industry). This process includes capacity and requirements planning, production orders, Kanban (a method of production flow control that works according to the pull principle), make-to-order production, repetitive manufacturing, and assembly processing.

In Sales and Distribution (SAP SD), the SAP system supports all processes associated with the sale of goods or services. In this context, employees must process quotations and sales orders, determine the availability of goods, and create scheduling agreements. Sales and Distribution includes the check of credit limits in sales, determination of prices and conditions, and invoicing. If a business exports a high volume of goods, then foreign trade and customs processing is another important topic.

The logistics process concludes with the Customer Service area (SAP CS), which is used for customer care. It includes the management and processing of customer service orders, such as warranty, maintenance, and repair.

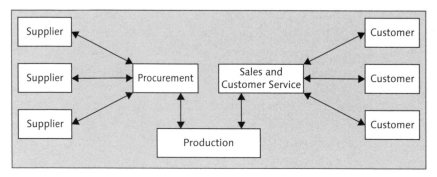

Supply Chain

EXAMPLE **Supply Chain**

The processes in Purchasing, Product Development, and Sales and Distribution can be mapped using SAP. In this example, a mechanical engineering business manufactures different types of pumps. Because the storage costs need to be kept as low as possible, only customer inquiries with quantities of up to ten pieces can be handled immediately. Larger quantities are produced in separate production plants. A safety stock of three pieces is kept in stock for each pump type for guarantee cases.

In line with the incoming sales orders, materials are procured from the suppliers and further processed in the in-house production plants to produce the end products. The ordered pumps are delivered to the customer and invoiced. All business processes described here between the supplier and the customer of the mechanical engineering business belong to the logistics area. Data can be automatically transferred from logistics to financial accounting through integration.

Beyond the core business processes described here, SAP ERP also includes other components, which SAP summarizes in SAP ERP Corporate Services. These include, among others, Quality Management (QM) and Environment, Health, and Safety (EHS), which are not further discussed in this book.

3.3   Maintaining Customer Relationships: SAP CRM

CRM—short for Customer Relationship Management—is the active management of customer relationships. SAP CRM supports all phases in which employees of a business communicate and contact customers:

- Marketing
- Sales
- Service

The functions of SAP CRM cover a wider scope and are used to map more complex processes than the components of SAP ERP.

Information on customers, which is usually only available to sales employees with direct customer contacts, is stored in the system. This data is also relevant for employees from the marketing and product development areas. This data can then be used as the basis for promotions, or to help product development better cater to customer requests. Without an IT system, important information gets lost (for example, if an employee with close customer contact leaves the business). The sales, marketing, and service areas can access central information on the customers and potential customers to respond to their needs. You can also use SAP CRM for scheduling and resource control. In SAP CRM, reporting and analytical functions increase in importance. These functions are required to gain insight on customer behavior that can then be used for future promotions.

> **NOTE**
> **Mobile Applications in the CRM Area**
> CRM applications have been increasingly used in the last few years on mobile devices such as RIM Blackberry or Apple iPhone.

3.4   Optimizing Supplier Relationships: SAP SRM

The purchasing department of a business is invested in collaborating with good suppliers for a long time. Of course, it is always best to procure the required goods or services as cost-effectively as possible. But there may be reasons not to decide on the supplier who offers the lowest prices. This may be the case if, for example, a more expensive supplier can ensure fast and easy delivery despite possible bottlenecks, and offers better delivery service.

The purpose of SAP Supplier Relationship Management (SAP SRM) is to optimize business relationships with existing and potential suppliers. It lets you strategically plan and control relationships with these suppliers by integrating them closely with the purchasing processes. SAP SRM supports contract and supplier management, supplier selection, supplier qualification, purchase order, source determination, creation of invoices, and credit memos.

3.5   The Entire Lifecycle of a Product: SAP PLM

SAP Product Lifecycle Management (SAP PLM) supports the "lifecycle" of a product, from the initial product idea, to drafts and alignment of production, to customer service.

SAP PLM consists of all functions associated with these tasks, such as the management of plants, equipment, and product documentations. With product development projects, for example, it is important to keep an overview of all product master data and product structures, recipes, and specifications. The component also supports quality control and project and resource management. If you deploy a product portfolio management, you can control various projects.

With regard to the cooperation with colleagues and development partners, SAP PLM lets you exchange information like project plans, technical drawings, product structures, product documentations, maintenance instructions, and so on.

Using SAP PLM

EXAMPLE

SAP PLM is frequently used in the automotive industry. An example would be the following:

A car manufacturer designs the successor *Type 2* of a compact car, since the current model, *Type 1*, has good sales figures. Prototypes are tested and optimized until the new model is ready for series production. At the same time, provisions are made for the production and market launch. *Type 2* then replaces its predecessor, *Type 1*, and the demand among the customers of this brand is high.

After several years, the demand for the current *Type 2* has decreased. To make this model more attractive for potential customers, minor changes are made to this model and special promotions are started. Prototypes of the successor model, *Type 3*, already exist.

Type 3 replaces *Type 2*, but the buyers of *Type 2* still receive services and replacement parts from their car dealers. The product lifecycle ends when the production of replacement parts for *Type 2* ceases.

3.6   For all Supply Chain Elements: SAP SCM

SAP Supply Chain Management (SAP SCM) includes functions for the entire supply chain, from the supplier to the customer. The software offers advanced functions for complex business processes in logistics.

SAP SCM is an extremely powerful software solution with diverse individual components. Due to its wide functional scope, the following list only provides a short overview of SAP SCM:

- **Warehouse management**
  SAP SCM consists of a solution for warehouse management whose options go far beyond the Warehouse Management component (WM) in SAP ERP. SAP Extended Warehouse Management (SAP EWM) is deployed for all processes in warehouse management.

- **Transportation management**
  SAP SCM also provides a separate solution in the transportation area called SAP Transportation Management (TM). In contrast to Logistics Execution System (LES) in SAP ERP, this solution was also developed for transport service providers.

- **Tracking of logistics processes**
  SAP Event Management (EM) was designed for tracking and status management tasks.

- **Support of RFID processes**
  Radio Frequency Identification (RFID) allows for the non-contact identification and localization of objects (which are provided with an RFID label) using RFID readers. This facilitates data entry. In this context, the SAP component, SAP Auto-ID Infrastructure (AII), represents a link between the RFID reader and the SAP system.

- **Supplier collaboration**
  By means of SAP Supply Network Collaboration (SNC), you can achieve closer cooperation of external suppliers by letting them respond to customer stocks and requirements independently.

- **Planning and optimization of the supply chain**
  SAP Advanced Planning & Optimization (APO) consists of a very widespread task area with functions for production planning, sales planning, availability checks, transportation planning, and so on.

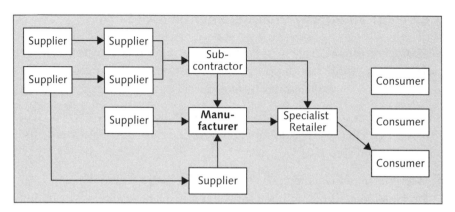

Advanced Supply Chain

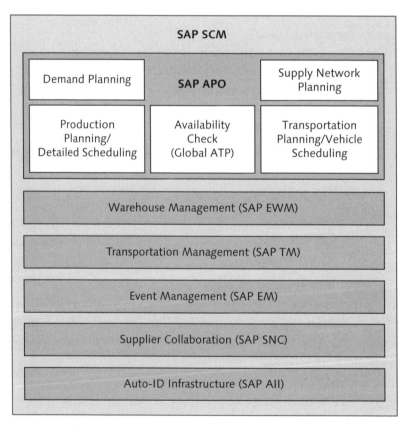

Overview of SAP SCM Components

If you take a close look at the usage areas of SAP SCM, you may notice some overlap of SAP ERP components. For example, there is a component for warehouse management within SAP ERP and SAP SCM respectively; the latter, however, has more refined options than the former.

3.7   Industry Solutions

Besides the standard solutions, SAP also offers solutions for different industries. This is because the processes that an energy supplier needs to map are different than those of a mechanical engineering business. Industry solutions combine standard processes with special requirements and functions. SAP offers packages for the following areas, among others:

- Manufacturing industry
  - SAP for Automotive
  - SAP for Aerospace and Defense
- Processing industry
  - SAP for Oil & Gas
  - SAP for Chemicals
- Financial service providers and public administration
  - SAP for Banking
  - SAP for Healthcare
  - SAP for Defense & Security
- Services industry
  - SAP for Utilities
  - SAP for Retail
  - SAP for Consumer Products

A total of 24 industry solutions are currently available at the time of publishing (2011).

3.8   Special Software for Medium-Sized Enterprises

In addition to the solutions for large businesses—such as the SAP Business Suite, SAP also offers solutions for small- and medium-sized businesses, which are briefly discussed in the following sections.

SAP Business One

With SAP Business One, SAP addresses customers for whom SAP ERP or the software products of SAP Business Suite are too complex or too expensive. SAP Business One can be used to map core functions like financials, human resources, and materials management. This product can "grow" together with the enterprise and be implemented at relative low costs within a couple of days.

SAP Business All-in-One

SAP Business All-in-One is a solution for medium-sized businesses that offers different industry-specific features. So, different solutions from SAP Business Suite are used as required. SAP NetWeaver is the technological platform for SAP Business All-in-One.

SAP Business ByDesign

SAP Business ByDesign is an on-demand solution, which means that the business that uses the solution only selects the functions it actually requires. The application server, which the customers use, is hosted by SAP and is available via a secured Internet connection. The server on which the applications are located is supported and managed at SAP's data centers. The user can access the required functions via an Internet browser (for instance, Microsoft Internet Explorer). The users' access to the servers is done via a VPN connection that is secured in multiple levels.

> **NOTE**
>
> **Virtual Private Network**
>
> A Virtual Private Network (VPN) is a secure connection via the Internet. The data packages are transferred in encrypted form between sender and receiver.

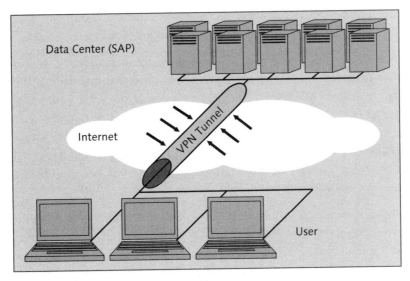

SAP Business ByDesign—System Infrastructure

SAP Business ByDesign basically covers all business processes mentioned in this chapter: financials and accounting, logistics, human resources, customer relationship management, and so on.

3.9   The Technical Basis: SAP NetWeaver

SAP NetWeaver forms the technical basis for SAP applications and business processes—it is the operating system, so to speak, that runs all the applications you use. SAP NetWeaver is responsible for the following tasks:

- User integration
- Information integration
- Process integration
- Application basis (application server)

But what exactly does this mean?

The functions that are part of user integration allow them to utilize functions and information they require for their work. One option would be to access the SAP system from different channels—that is, via mobile devices (smartphones) or via a portal (usually an Internet connection). This means that you have access to the system using various frontends. You can use both SAP GUI for Windows and an Internet browser to access an SAP system.

In SAP NetWeaver, the information integration includes components for master data management, reporting, and analysis (business intelligence and knowledge management). Master data management ensures that redundant and incorrect data is eliminated. The SAP NetWeaver Business Warehouse component (SAP NetWeaver BW) is a data warehouse, meaning it's where you can collect and format information from different systems and make it available for reports and evaluations. BW is one of the few SAP NetWeaver components which you as the user may contact directly.

Process integration means, on the one hand, that information from different areas can be connected through interfaces. On the other hand, the term refers to the option to automate business processes beyond system and enterprise boundaries. You can fulfill your tasks without any problems, even if IT systems of different manufacturers (non-SAP systems) are used or if other enterprises are integrated with the processes.

The application server is the technical basis for all other SAP products. Besides communication with applications, its tasks include basic functions, such as user management, data exchange, monitoring, and transportation. In addition, SAP NetWeaver lets customers expand their systems themselves: They can develop their own software applications using the programming languages ABAP and Java (J2EE).

Accordingly, SAP NetWeaver primarily forms the technical basis for an SAP system and the required applications so that business processes can be mapped across areas. This way, all participating departments are integrated. SAP NetWeaver can be used in heterogeneous IT environments (ones in which you can use software products of different manufacturers). Other manufacturers and software companies that provide add-ons for the SAP system can then integrate the software with the system landscapes.

This chapter provided an overview of the SAP products. As you've learned, SAP offers software solutions for all business sizes. Here, a distinction is made between industry-specific and industry-neutral solutions. The components of SAP ERP originate from accounting, human resources, and logistics. Products are offered for which you don't need to provide any system infrastructure because you can access the systems via the Internet. SAP NetWeaver forms the technical basis for all of the described products and solutions, and provides components so that you can optimally integrate the system with the enterprise structure and expand it as necessary.

The next part of this book focuses on the concrete work in the system and describes the basic operation of SAP.

Part II

Basic Principles of
System Operation

4 Organizational Structures and Master Data

Before you can work with the SAP system, you need some background knowledge. There are some basic settings in the SAP system that remain more or less unchanged over a long period of time and that form the foundation for your daily work. These include organizational structures (which are created in Customizing) and master data. If you work in a department as a user, you must "tell" the system for which area of the business a specific action is performed. To do this, you must know about the organizational units.

In this chapter you will learn:

- To map enterprise structures in the system
- Which master data you need for your work with SAP

4.1 Organizational Structures

Every enterprise has its own structure and business processes in purchasing, sales and distribution, and accounting. The structure of the organization reflects these processes and can be presented in an organization chart. Every department maps its structure in this organization chart. Frequently, not all levels and functional areas of the business are presented in the overall organization chart. Instead, each chart could be limited to individual areas, such as purchasing, with its corresponding structures (i.e., sales).

The next figure shows one such part of the organization chart with units from logistics. This example presents the fictional bicycle manufacturer, *Sportbikes International*. The Sportbikes International companies are pooled in a holding. Production happens at two plants in Germany and one plant in England. The subsidiaries' warehouses are subdivided into the two areas finished products and quality assurance (QA). A purchasing department undertakes the procurement for all production plants across the group through centralized purchasing; an expert team is responsible for procuring finished products, and another group of employees for purchasing services.

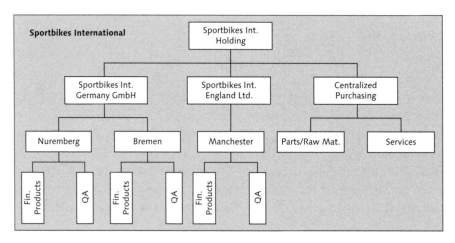

Example of an Enterprise Structure from the Logistics Perspective

Such organizational structures are mapped and assigned using organizational units in the SAP system. Before you, as the user, can work with the SAP system, you must link your various tasks in the SAP system with the corresponding organizational units. You can create and assign the organizational units through Customizing (see Chapter 2). Once this assignment has been made, it is very difficult to implement changes (for example, problems arise during company takeovers or mergers).

To transfer the business structure to the system, you need several organizational units, which will be discussed in more detail. The organizational units originate from the purchasing area. Other areas in the enterprise—financial accounting, human resources, sales and distribution, and so on—use different organizational units that are customized for their respective needs. Because complete enterprises are mapped in SAP ERP, specific central organizational units must be available to several (user) departments. For example, a plant is the decisive organizational unit for financial accounting, sales and distribution, and materials management (purchasing). Among other things, financial accounting monitors and performs incoming and outgoing payments that result from sales orders (sales and distribution) and purchase orders (purchasing). These are discussed in more detail in the chapters on the respective SAP components (see Part III). This book provides information particularly on the organizational units of Materials Management (MM), Sales and Distribution (SD), Financial Accounting (FI), Controlling (CO), and Human Capital Management (HCM).

The following sections detail the most important organizational units of the individual business areas of Sportbikes International that are relevant for the purchasing department. If you transfer the structure of the sample business, Sportbikes International, to the SAP organizational units, you get a result like the one shown in the following figure.

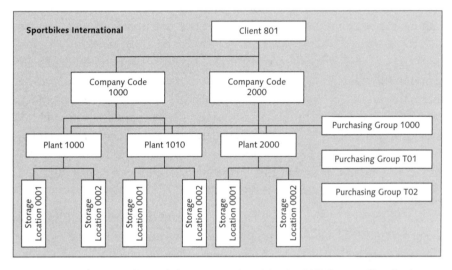

Organizational Units of Sportbikes International in the SAP System (Purchasing Area)

The client (801) represents the group or the corporate headquarters, and it is the topmost organizational unit. Company codes 1000 and 2000 are located below the client and represent the companies (subsidiaries) in Germany and England. In Germany, there are two production plants, 1000 and 1010, that have corresponding storage locations. In England, plant 2000 has its own storage locations. Purchasing organization 1000 handles all purchasing, and for this reason, it is not assigned to a company code. Purchasing groups T01 and T02 are intended for purchasing teams with different task areas; purchasing groups are not assigned to any other organizational element directly.

Keys of the Organizational Units Used

In this example, the keys (801, 1000, and so on) were assigned randomly. In real life, however, you should use useful, assignable keys (for example, existing internal numbers and names like company number, plant number, warehouse number, or cost centers). Many different approaches and variants exist here, but some basic rules for keys of specific organizational units are discussed in the next sections.

The following section describes the organizational units from the Sportbikes International example in detail. The respective organizational units are created for an area (such as financial accounting, purchasing, sales and distribution, and so on) and are then available to all relevant application areas. For example, the purchasing department orders materials for a plant, and the internal valuation of these materials is included in the financial statements created by financial accounting. Part III of this book (Chapters 14 through 18) provides further organizational units that are required for areas such as financial accounting or HR. So, the sales organization sells the additionally purchased or produced materials to the customers in sales and distribution.

- **Client**
  You enter or select the client when you log on to the SAP system. Since the client represents the group (and is therefore the highest organizational unit in the system) then all settings that are made for the client also apply to the subordinate units. The key for the client always has three digits and is numeric, for instance, 801.

- **Company code**
  Accounting is mapped at the level of the company code, which is representative of an independent balancing unit. A client can contain various company codes, but a company code is unique across the client. The key for the company code has four digits and is alphanumeric.

- **Plant**
  Since a plant produces goods or sells services, it is a central organizational unit of logistics. A plant can also be used in these roles:
  - Production location (materials management, production planning)
  - Sales office (sales and distribution)
  - Issuing storage location (sales and distribution)

A plant must be assigned to one single company code. It is always unique across the client; in other words, a plant number can only be assigned once. However, a company code and a plant with the same key can exist in one client. The key for the plant has four digits and is alphanumeric.

- **Storage location**
  The storage location lets you differentiate material stocks (stock types) within a plant. For the storage location, only the quantities of materials are relevant and not the values. These are considered at the level of the plant or the company code. A storage location is directly assigned to a plant. The key of the storage location is unique within a plant, so the same key can exist at another plant. The key for the plant has four digits and is alphanumeric.

- **Purchasing organization**
  The purchasing organization maps the business's purchasing department in the system. You can map either a central or a decentralized purchasing department, depending on the requirements. A client can also contain various purchasing organizations, and a purchasing organization can be assigned to a company code. But this can also be cross-company code—in other words, it doesn't have to be assigned to a specific company code. The assignment of plants, for which procurement is to be made, must be made by all means. When mapping a central purchasing department, the purchasing organization is not assigned to any company code. The key for the purchasing organization has four digits and is alphanumeric.

- **Purchasing group**
  A team of employees usually forms a purchasing group. The purchasing group itself is not assigned to any other organizational unit. The key for the purchasing group has three digits and is alphanumeric.

Organizational units are not only a mandatory requirement to map the business in the system, but they are also required if you perform processes in the system. If goods are procured, the system needs to know to which user the documents must be assigned. In plain words: Who procures for which company code and for which plant? The example in the next figure shows the organizational units involved in the transaction to create a purchase order in the SAP system. (Transactions in the SAP system are functions that can be called by the user via an alphanumeric code, known as the transaction code; you'll find more information in Chapters 5 and 6.)

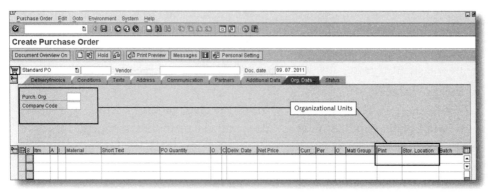

Organizational Units in the Purchase Order (Transaction ME21N)

Transaction ME21N, the purchase order, shows an example of using organizational units. Here you specify which purchasing organization and purchasing group is responsible for procurement, for which company code the purchase order is to be made, and for which plant procurement is to be made. Organizational structures are defined and assigned (mapped) via Customizing in the SAP system.

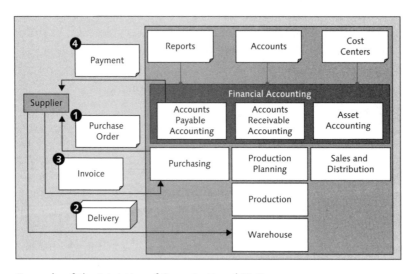

Example of the Joint Use of Organizational Units

The figure and the table illustrate which organizational units are relevant for the individual components.

	Company Code	Purchasing Organization	Sales Organization	Plant	Storage Location
Purchasing (MM)	×	×	–	×	(×)
Accounts Payable Accounting (FI)	×	–	–	–	–
Sales and Distribution (SD)	×	–	×	×	–

Examples of the Interlocking of SAP Components and Organizational Units

Organizational Units in Processes

When you enter a purchase order, you must fill in the corresponding fields:

- For which company code do you procure?
- Which purchasing organization and which purchasing group procure?
- For which plant do you procure?
- At which storage location is the material to be stored?

When you enter an order in sales and distribution, you must specify the following:

- Which sales organization is responsible?
- Which sales area is responsible? Which plant delivers the goods (delivering plant)?

Now that you've learned the principles of organizational units in the SAP system, let's move to master data in the upcoming section. If you want to learn more about the individual organizational units in the various SAP components, go directly to Chapters 14 through 18.

4.2   Master Data

Master data is information that remains unchanged for a long time and is repeatedly required in business processes. Once the data has been created, it is available to various users in different areas. For example, a master record can be the address of a customer or information on a material. Master data plays a critical role both in SAP implementation and in daily work.

Good maintenance of master data is key to optimizing the SAP system. When you create a purchase order, for example, you only need to enter the supplier number to automatically call the address and additional information.

Examples of Master Data

- Creditor (supplier): name, address, etc.
- Debtor (customer): name, address, customer number, terms of delivery, etc.
- Material (article): material number, short text, size and weight, valuation, etc.
- Services: service type, description, service number, etc.
- Employee: name, address, personnel number, department assignment, etc.

Besides master data, transaction data is also available. Transaction data can be changed; it is created, edited, and valid for a limited period of time for a specific transaction only.

Examples of Transaction Data

- Invoice: document number, amount, material, quantity, etc.
- Purchase requisition: material, quantity, preferred supplier, etc.
- Purchase order: document number, supplier, material, quantity, conditions, etc.
- Standard order: debtor, conditions, delivery date, material, quantity, etc.
- Material document: delivered quantity, material, storage location, etc.

The next figure illustrates the difference between master and transaction data.

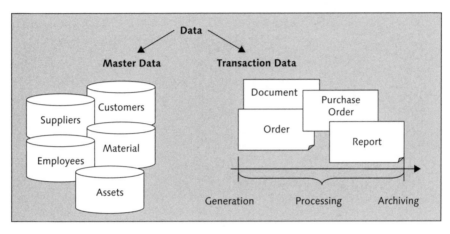

Master Data and Transaction Data

Because many applications and users can access the same master data if they have the relevant authorizations, redundancies (or multiple data retention) are avoided. However, redundancies can be unavoidable if systems of different manufacturers are deployed in the business.

The most important master data in the SAP system are presented in Part III of this book, in the context of specific SAP components.

The following example describes how to create a material master record in the SAP system. A material master record contains information on the material, which is relevant for accounting or logistics processes. In other components, a material is often referred to as an article. If you want to reproduce the example in the system yourself, first read Chapters 5 and 6, which outline the logon and navigation in the SAP system.

1 In the SAP Easy Access menu, select **SAP menu ▸ Logistics ▸ Materials Management ▸ Material Master ▸ Material ▸ Create (General)** to call Transaction MM01, and then double-click on the menu item **MM01 – Immediately**. Alternatively, you can start the transaction directly via the command field.

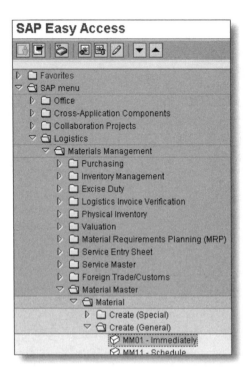

2 The system displays the initial screen of Transaction MM01. Enter the following test data:

– **Material:** ZZTM02

– **Industry Sector:** Mechanical engineering

– **Material type:** Raw material

3 Then click on the **Select View(s)** button. A material master record is displayed that is subdivided into various views; these are assigned to the respective user department. Click on the views, **Basic Data 1**, **Purchasing**, and **Accounting 1**.

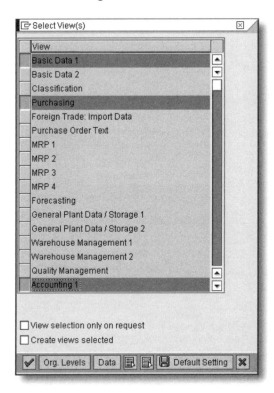

4 Click on the **Organizational Levels** button, and maintain the plant in which the material is to be held: Enter 1000 in the **Plant** field, and confirm with ⏎ or click on the **Next** button ✔. Alternatively, you can choose plant 1000 via the **Help** field 🗗, which is located on the right of the field.

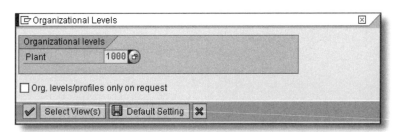

5 The system now displays the **Basic data 1** tab of the new material master record. Enter the following values in the fields listed:

- **Material** (short text): TFT monitor 22 inch widescreen
- **Base Unit of Measure**: PC
- **Material group**: 103
- **Gross Weight**: 12
- **Weight Unit**: kg
- **Net Weight**: 10

These individual master data represent important properties of the material, which are required for procurement and for internal valuation.

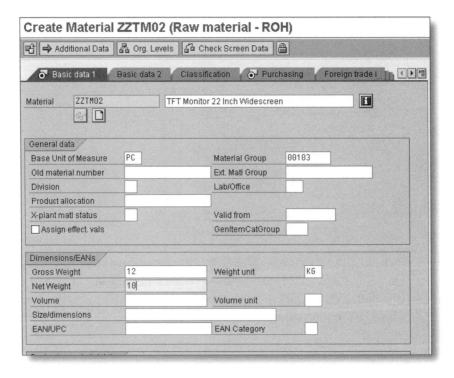

6 When you click the ◄► button, you navigate to the **Purchasing** tab. Here you maintain relevant purchasing information, such as base unit of measure, material group, purchasing value key, goods receipt processing time, underdelivery tolerance, and overdelivery tolerance. You can also open the tab by clicking the title. Then enter the value 000 in the **Purchasing Group** field.

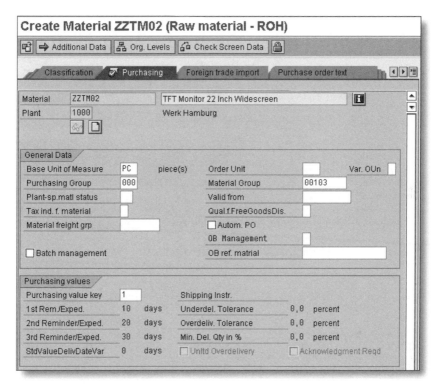

7 Click on ◄► to go to the **Accounting** 1 tab, or open it by clicking the title. As the name suggests, you maintain data on this tab that is important for accounting, that is, how the material is valuated internally. For this purpose, you must enter the valuation class, valuation price, and the price control. Enter the following values:

- **Valuation class**: 3000
- **Price Control**: V (moving average price)
- **Moving Price**: 150 EUR

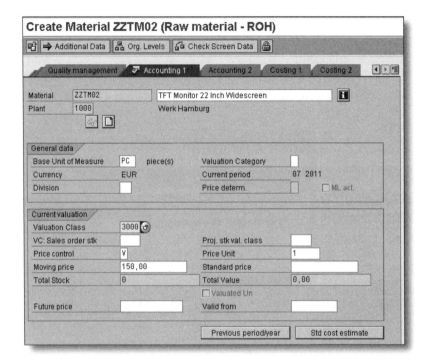

[8] Save the master record by clicking the 💾 button **(Save)** in the upper part of the screen.

Done! You have now successfully created a material master record.

NOTE

Material Master Quality

Enter the master data with care. In many cases insufficient attention is paid to the master data quality. Remember that virtually all business processes in the SAP system access master data. If a field value is missing, the process can't be executed correctly.

This chapter taught you two basic elements in the SAP system: The structure of an enterprise is mapped in the SAP system using organizational units. All organizational units are defined and assigned in Customizing. The chapter also outlined the difference between master and transaction data: Mater data usually remains in the system for a long period of time and is available to all applications and all authorized users in the system. Transaction data is created in the various business cases and changes frequently.

Chapter 5 details how to log on to the SAP system.

4.3   Try It!

Exercise 1

You are supposed to create an organizational structure for Engineering Massachusetts Holding Ltd. The focus is on the producing and procuring units. The company has three production locations: one in Boston, one in Springfield, and another one in Pittsfield.

The production location in Boston is financially independent, but Springfield and Pittsfield belong together. Each location has a warehouse for raw materials and a warehouse for finished products. Within the business, one centralized purchasing department procures for all locations.

Outline how you could map this structure in the system using the following organizational units.

Organizational Unit	Key
Client	805
Company code Boston	1000
Company code Springfield and Pittsfield	2000
Plant Boston	1010
Plant Springfield	2010
Plant Pittsfield	2020
Finished goods warehouse	0001
Raw materials warehouse	0002

Exercise 2

What's the difference between master and transaction data? Name three examples from different business areas for each.

5   Logging on to the SAP System

The previous chapters provided basic knowledge of the SAP system and described organizational structures and master data. This chapter begins with a description of SAP system operation.

From this chapter you will learn:

- To connect with the server using SAP Logon
- How the SAP screen is structured
- To log on and off from the SAP system
- Which information is provided in the status bar

5.1   SAP Logon

You probably have several links to applications you use frequently on your desktop, such as Microsoft Office applications like Microsoft Word or Outlook. After your SAP administrator completed the installation of SAP GUI, you'll find an icon for SAP Logon on your desktop, too.

SAP Logon

Establishing a Connection to the SAP System

Using the SAP Logon, your Windows PC establishes a connection to the SAP system via the network when you carry out the following steps:

1 Double-click on the **SAP Logon** icon on your desktop to start SAP Logon, or go to the Windows Start menu and follow the menu path: **Start ▶ Programs ▶ SAP Front End ▶ SAP Logon**.

2 The configured SAP systems are displayed in the **Systems** tab of the opened SAP Logon. To log on to the required system, select the name (in this case, **Prod** for production system) and click on the **Log On** button.

3 A logon screen is displayed if SAP Logon can establish a connection to the SAP system.

NOTE

Different SAP Systems in the Enterprise

Most businesses deploy various SAP systems besides the one that you use in your daily work. The figure also shows the **Development** system and the **Test** system.

To log on to the SAP system, you need the following information:

- Number of the client
- User name
- Password

In SAP Logon, you not only have the option to log on to the system, but you can also change the parameters or add a connection to a new SAP system. To define a new system in SAP Logon, you need some SAP system parameters.

NOTE

Settings in SAP Logon

The SAP administrator for your business can provide the parameters for an SAP system. Not every user is authorized to change these parameters or add new systems on his desktop PC. Under Windows, you need write authorizations for the *saplogon.ini* file in the Windows system directory.

Changing Connection Settings for the SAP System

After you've logged on to SAP Logon, you can check or change a connection. Perhaps you need to access another system for specific reasons or the parameters of a test system are changed. To check or change a connection, do the following:

1 You can adjust the settings of a selected system via the **Change Item** button. You need the respective authorization on your desktop PC.

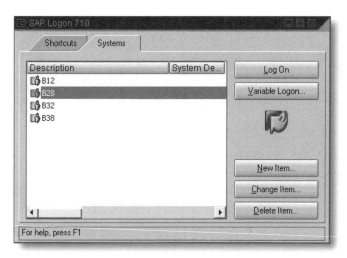

2 Various parameters for the system connection are available. The following fields are mandatory and must be filled in:

- **Description**: alphanumeric; provides information for the user
- **Application Server**: IP address or DNS name
- **System number**: two-digit, numeric
- **System ID**: three-digit, alphanumeric

Whether the **SAProuter String** field must be filled depends on the network infrastructure. Here you need to enter the IP address or the DNS name.

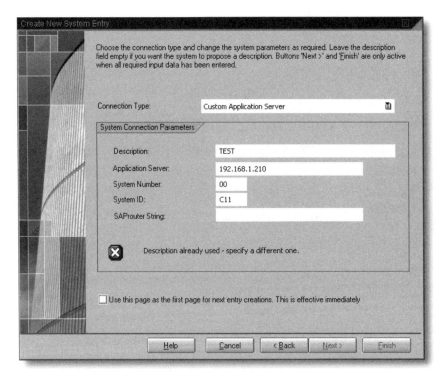

3 After you've changed the parameters, click on **Finish**.

The connection information is now stored in your SAP system. The following sections show how to log on to the SAP system.

5.2   Logging on for the First Time

The steps for your initial logon vary from subsequent logons. Initial logon can mean that you want to log on to the system for the first time (for example, if you have a new employer) or once you receive a new password.

The initial logon requires the following information, which is usually provided by the SAP administration team:

- Client
- User
- Password

The client (three-digit numeric key) is mandatory. Your user account is client-dependent. For example, if you want to log on to the test system, you need a different client than for the logon to the production system. An enterprise may have various clients for different tasks.

> **NOTE**
>
> **Password Rules**
>
> There are the following essential rules for passwords in the SAP standard:
>
> - You can use letters, numbers, and special characters.
> - The password must have a length between three and 40 characters; the standard system requires a minimum length of six characters.
> - The first character of the password must not be a question mark or exclamation point.
> - The first three characters must differ from those of the user and must not be three identical characters.
> - None of the first three characters can be a blank space.
> - The password must not be SAP* or PASS because these are reserved for SAP.
> - The password must differ from the previous five passwords.

The password is case-sensitive and it is not visible once you enter it. For initial logon, or if you've forgotten your password, the administrator provides you with an initial password. You can use this password only once and must immediately change it after successful logon.

You require the following information for initial logon:

- Client
- User
- Initial password (You receive this password from your system administrator and you must change it after initial logon!)

To log on to the system and change your password for the first time, proceed as follows:

1 Start SAP Logon by double-clicking on the icon on your Windows desktop or via the Start menu (see the section about establishing a connection to the SAP system).

2 SAP Logon is opened. Check that you are on the **Systems** tab.

3 Select the desired **System Entry**. Then click on the **Log On** button.

4 When your desktop PC successfully establishes a connection to the SAP system via the network, the logon screen is displayed.

5 Enter the logon data that you received from your system administrator or trainer in the logon screen. Enter "EN" in the **Language** field to ensure that your user interface is in English after logon. If you do not write any information in the **Language** field, the system defaults to English.

6 Make sure that you enter the logon data exactly as you received it! The system is case-sensitive and doesn't permit any errors, especially if security is concerned. If you are sure that you've entered all data correctly, click on the **Next** button 🗸 , or press ↵ .

7 You've logged on to the system successfully! Next the system prompts you to enter a new password. Confirm the message by clicking on the **Ok** button.

8 Enter the new password twice, once each in the **New Password** and **Repeat Password** fields. The characters are not visible during entry.

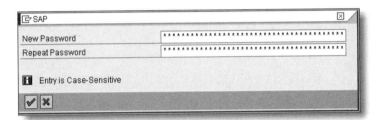

9 Confirm your entry by pressing the ⏎ key or clicking on the **Next** button 🗹. The new password is now defined in the system.

TIP

Defining the Logon Language

Chapter 7, Maintaining the System Layout and User Data, describes how to define the logon language in the system so that you don't have to specify it each time you log on.

5.3   Logging on to the System

If you want to log on to the SAP system after the initial logon (perhaps when you start your usual workday in the morning), proceed as follows:

1 In SAP Logon, select the system to which you want to log on. Then click on the **Logon** button.

2 Enter your client's name in the **Client** field.

3 Enter your user name in the **User** field.

4 Enter your **Password**.

5 Specify EN in the **Language** field.

6 If all entries are correct, click on **Next** ⊘.

> **NOTE**
>
> **Incorrect Password**
>
> If you've entered the password incorrectly three times in a row, logon is closed. Fortunately, you can restart logon immediately. If you've entered the password incorrectly five times, the user is locked. In the standard version, it will be unlocked at 0:00 a.m. The lock expires after a maximum of 24 hours. The locked user can be unlocked by the SAP administrator at any time, though a new initial password must be assigned. An incorrect password is displayed in the status bar:
>
> ⊗ Name or password is incorrect. Please re-enter

The next section discusses the user interface of the SAP system, which you can view after the logon.

5.4   The SAP User Interface

SAP GUI is the user interface in which you work; it displays the applications that run on the server on your desktop PC. After successful logon to the system, the following screen is displayed.

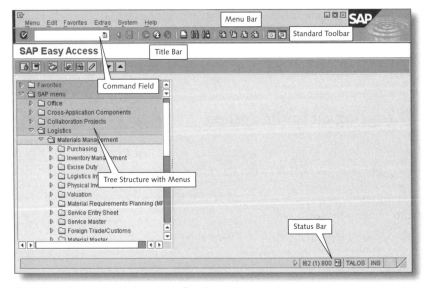

SAP Easy Access (Initial Screen after Logon)

You can conveniently navigate to the desired application via the user menu, SAP Easy Access menu.

The SAP screen contains many buttons and fields. The following section details the various areas of the SAP user interface that will help you better orient yourself to SAP in your daily work. The elements that you can click on in the SAP screen are indicated in **Bold** in this book.

Menu Bar

The menu bar is located at the top of the screen. Which menus are displayed depends on the respective application (transaction) and the level at which you are located within the application. The menu items **System** and **Help** are always available in the menu bar regardless of the transaction you're working on.

Menu Bar

You can call the menu items by clicking on them. They may contain submenus. With , you can activate a menu that offers the following functions:

- Restore
- Move
- Change size
- Minimize
- Maximize
- Close
- Create session

You can find the buttons for minimizing, maximizing, and closing the window on the right-hand side of the menu bar; these are listed in the following table. They are comparable with the buttons you already know from Microsoft Windows.

Button	Name	Use
	Minimize	The application window is minimized and displayed at the bottom of the screen. Its size is restored by clicking it.
	Maximize	The application window is displayed in its full size.
	Close	The open application window is closed.

Icons in the Menu Bar

Standard Toolbar

The standard toolbar is located below the menu bar. It contains icons (buttons with symbols) for the most important functions, such as **Save** and **Cancel**. The buttons are displayed in all screens; inactive buttons are grayed out, and you can only use the buttons that are displayed in color. If you move the mouse pointer over the button without clicking on it, the system displays brief information about the function, which is also referred to as tooltip.

Standard Toolbar

Some functions can also be called via the function keys, which are located at the top of your keyboard ([F1] through [F12]). Remember that some function keys have different settings, depending on the application. The following table lists the most essential buttons and function keys.

Button	Key/ Key Combination	Name	Use
	[↵]	Next	Confirms the entered/ selected data; *not* a save function.
	[Ctrl]+[S]	Save	Save changes; same function as SAVE in the EDIT menu.

The Most Essential Buttons of the Standard Toolbar

Button	Key/ Key Combination	Name	Use
	F3	Back	Go back to the previous screen.
	⇧ + F3	Exit	Close a transaction without saving the data or changes.
	F12	Cancel	Cancel transaction; same function as CANCEL in the EDIT menu.
	Ctrl + P	Print	Print a document or list.
	Ctrl + F	Search	Find a value in a list.
	–	Create a new session	Open a window with a new session.
	–	Create a link	Create a new link in SAP GUI.
	F1	Help	Displays descriptions on a field on which the cursor is positioned.
	Alt + F12	Adjust local layout	Enables user-specific settings of the display options.

The Most Essential Buttons of the Standard Toolbar (Cont.)

For information on working with sessions, refer to Chapter 6, Navigating in the SAP System. To learn more about links and adaptations of the local layout, read Chapter 7, Maintaining the System Layout and User Data. The help function is described in Chapter 12, Using Help Functions.

Title Bar

The structure of the title bar always depends on the transaction you use. It can also contain other buttons in addition to the respective transaction name.

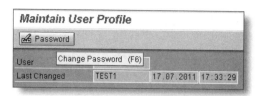

Example of a Title Bar

Command Field

You can navigate in the SAP system without a mouse by using the SAP Easy Access menu via the keyboard. This way, you can start transactions by directly entering the transaction code. You can enter transaction codes in the command field (see also Chapter 6, Navigating in the SAP System).

Command Field

Status Bar

The status bar is located at the bottom of the screen and extends over the entire screen width. On the left side, you can see an area that displays system messages. The right side displays four fields that provide current information on the system's status.

By clicking the ▣ button in the first status field, you get various pieces of information on the system and client you're working with. The status bar indicates which program and transaction are currently active. You also find information on the response and interpretation time of the SAP system.

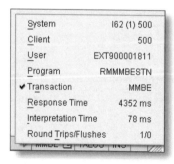

Information in the Status Bar

The following table describes the most essential information that is available in the status bar.

Name	Explanation
System	System and client to which you are currently logged on
Client	Client
User	Logon name
Program	Program that is currently active
Transaction	Name of the transaction that is currently active
Response time	Time in milliseconds in which the SAP system responds
Interpretation time	Time in milliseconds in which commands to the system are executed
Round trips/flushes	Connections to one or more SAP systems

Description of the Status Bar

In the second status field, you can view the name of the server to which you are connected (here, I62).

The third status field shows whether you are in overtype mode (OVR) or in insert mode (INS). If OVR is set, you overwrite the existing data on the right side of the cursor when you enter data; if INS is set, you add or insert data. You can toggle between the modes by clicking on this field.

The next section describes how to exit the SAP system.

5.5   Logging off from the SAP System

You have several options for terminating SAP GUI. One option is to proceed as follows:

1 Click the button at the top left, and select the **Close** menu item, or press Alt + F4 .

2 Click **Yes** to confirm the message "Unsaved data will be lost. Do you want to log off?"

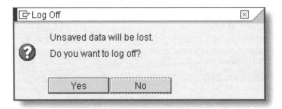

Or you can log off as follows:

1 Click the **Close** ⊠ button at the top right.

2 Click **Yes** to confirm the message "Unsaved data will be lost. Do you want to log off?"

The message that unsaved data will be lost is displayed at every logoff for security reasons.

This chapter described how to log on to and log off from the SAP system. With SAP Logon, you can configure a connection to an SAP system or start the connection setup. To log on to an SAP system, you require a client, user, and password. Specifying a logon language is optional. SAP GUI is installed on your PC, and enables interaction with the system.

Chapter 6 presents the options available for navigation and data entry in the SAP system.

5.6   Try It!

Exercise 1
Describe how to establish a connection to the SAP system.

Exercise 2
Which information is mandatory for logging on to the system and which information is optional?

Exercise 3

Which of the following are valid passwords?

a) SAP*

b) q7

c) meier#1

d) demo#2010

e) swordfish

Exercise 4

What do you enter in the command field to terminate a session without query?

6 Navigating in the SAP System

Chapter 5 taught you how to log on to and log off from the SAP system. After logon, you use the applications that belong to your task area. You fulfill different tasks by editing all screens that belong to the respective action and filling the necessary fields with content.

6

This chapter discusses:

- How to navigate in the SAP system
- How to use transaction codes
- How to enter data in the system
- Which options are available to call an application

6.1 Overview of the Navigation Options

Directly after you've logged on to the SAP system, it displays the initial screen shown in Chapter 5.

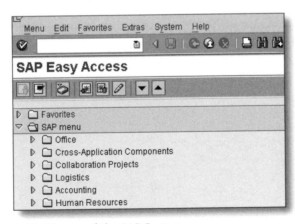

Initial Screen of the SAP System

The SAP system provides you with three options to navigate to the desired application:

- Via the SAP Easy Access menu
- Via transaction codes
- Via favorites and links

You can customize the SAP Easy Access menu to your specific needs and set whether transaction codes are shown in the menu tree or in favorites. To make these modifications, select **Extras ▶ Settings** in the menu bar. You can also use the key combination ⟨⬆⟩ + ⟨F9⟩ to set the following:

- Display transaction codes in the SAP Easy Access menu
- Show or hide the SAP logo
- Display favorites at the end of the menu
- Hide the SAP Easy Access menu and display favorites only

To display the transaction codes in the SAP Easy Access menu, proceed as follows:

1 Choose **Settings** under **Extras**.

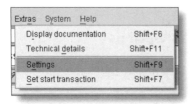

2 The **Settings** window is now open. In this window, activate the **Display Technical Names** checkbox to map the transaction codes in the tree structure of the SAP Easy Access menu.

Here you can also set whether the favorites are displayed in the SAP Easy Access menu (via the **Display favorites at end of list** checkbox).

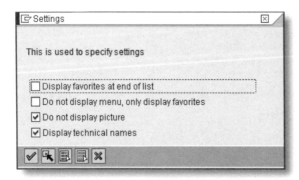

The following two sections provide more information on the navigation options via the SAP Easy Access menu and via transaction codes. Favorites and links are discussed in Chapter 7, Maintaining the System Layout and User Data.

6.2   Navigating via the SAP Easy Access Menu

After you've logged on to the SAP system, it displays the SAP Easy Access menu as a tree structure on the left-hand side of the screen.

The SAP Easy Access menu offers a user-specific entry point and navigation options in the SAP system. In this context, "user-specific" means that the tree structure displays only those transactions with which you may work according to your role (see Chapter 13, The Role and Authorization Concept, for details on roles).

Via the SAP Easy Access menu, you can expand the tree structure, which contains the individual folders (nodes), by clicking on the ▷ button. You can close it again with ▽ .

The folders themselves are identified with the buttons, ⌂ (opened folder) or ☐ (closed folder). The executable transactions are marked with a building block ◊.

SAP Easy Access Menu—Nodes and Transactions

To start a transaction via the SAP Easy Access menu, proceed as follows:

1 Open the respective subordinate folder by clicking on ▷ . An opened folder is indicated by a triangle pointing downward ▽ . This folder may contain subordinate folders.

2 Start the desired transaction by double-clicking the 🗹 button, which opens the initial screen of the respective transactions.

NOTE

Presentation of Menu Paths in this Book

Like other SAP books, this book does not provide screenshots of the SAP Easy Access menu whenever it is described how to reach a specific transaction, but instead lists the individual steps of the menu path. In this example, the path is **Logistics ▶ Sales and Distribution ▶ Sales ▶ Order ▶ VA01 – Create**.

TIP

How to Close All Folders in the SAP Easy Access Menu (Tree Structure)

If you want to close several folders and subfolders in the SAP Easy Access menu, you can close them all in one step. For this purpose, select **Menu ▶ Refresh** or `Ctrl`+`F1`.

6.3 Navigating via Transaction Codes

Transaction codes help you quickly access the desired application without navigating via the SAP Easy Access menu. Transaction codes are alphanumeric codes assigned to every application in the SAP system. You must know the transaction code of the desired application in order to navigate to it. The appendix of this book provides an overview of the most critical transaction codes.

TIP

Overviews For Download

You can download all overviews provided in the appendix free of charge by entering your personal code (provided on the first pages of this book) at *www.sap-press.com*.

To use transaction codes in the command field, proceed as follows:

1 Click on the command field after logon. The blinking cursor indicates that this field is active and ready for input.

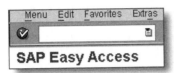

2 Now enter a transaction code. Confirm your input by clicking the green checkmark ✅ or pressing the ⏎ key.

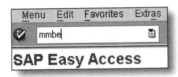

Transaction codes without preceding parameters can only be entered in the initial screen of the SAP Easy Access menu. If you are already in another transaction, you must enter a parameter in addition to the transaction code.

You can show or hide the command field by clicking on the triangle ◁.

Command Field

The following table lists the most important parameters.

Parameter	Explanation
/nend	Logs off from the system, with confirmation.
/nex	Logs off from the system, without confirmation.

Parameters Used in the Command Field

Parameter	Explanation
MMBE	Example of a transaction code without additional parameters. It starts Transaction MMBE. This is only possible in the SAP Easy Access menu in this form.
/nMMBE	Closes the current transaction and starts a new one, such as Transaction MMBE here. Enter /n and the desired transaction code without any space.
/oMMBE	Starts a transaction in a new session, such as Transaction MMBE here. Enter /o and the desired transaction code without any space.
/n	Terminates the current transaction.
/i	Deletes the current session.
/o	Shows a list of current sessions.
/*MMBE	Starts a transaction and skips the initial screen, such as Transaction MMBE here. Enter /* and the desired transaction code without any space.

Parameters Used in the Command Field (Cont.)

To describe the navigation via transaction codes in more detail, let's work through an example in the system. We ultimately want to determine the line items of your customers (debtors) for the current day in company code 1000. Proceed as follows:

1 Log on to the SAP system as described in Chapter 5. In the SAP Easy Access menu, open the customer line item list via the menu path: **Accounting ▶ Financial Accounting ▶ Accounts Receivable ▶ Account**. Alternatively, you can enter Transaction FBL5N directly via the command field.

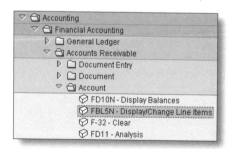

2 Under **Account**, you can find Transaction FBL5N (Display/Change Line Items). A building block icon displayed in front of the transaction means that the transaction can be executed. Double-click on the ⏱ button, and the initial screen of Transaction FBL5N opens.

3 Enter the following information:

– **Company Code**: 1000

– **Open on Key Date**: Current date (DD.MM.YYYY)

4 Click the **Execute** button or press the F8 key.

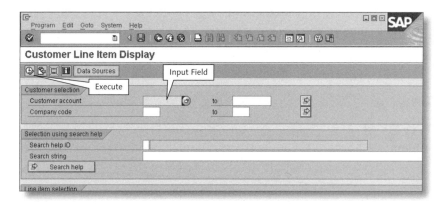

5 Now the system shows the line item list. You can view in the list which sales were made to the respective customer.

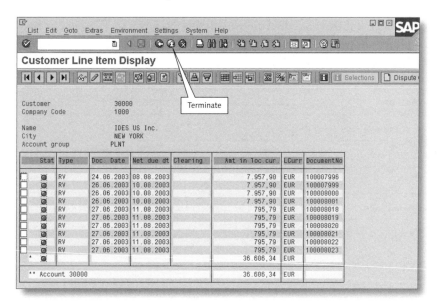

6   Click on the **Close** button 🔙 to close the customer line item list. The system takes you back to the SAP Easy Access menu.

The transaction code is displayed in the SAP Easy Access menu and also in the status bar at the bottom right of the screen.

6.4   Entering Data in the SAP System

You have various options in the SAP system to enter data and communicate with the system. A previous section, Logging on for the First Time, already presented some essential elements of the SAP user interface:

- Menu bar
- Standard toolbar
- Title bar
- Status bar
- Command field

This section now presents an overview of the central user interface elements that you'll encounter in a transaction. You can use either mouse navigation or various keys of your keyboard to navigate between these elements.

You can execute specific functions (such as copy and paste) by pressing a specific key combination on your keyboard at the same time (for example, Ctrl+C and Ctrl+V). You usually use the keys, Ctrl, ⇧, or Alt in combination with a letter. The appendix provides a comprehensive overview of useful key combinations.

Action	Key Combination
Cancel actions step by step	Esc
Select all	Ctrl+A
Cut	Ctrl+X
Insert	Ctrl+V
Navigate in the list of selectable entries	←, ↓, ↑, →

Overview of the Most Essential Key Combinations in the Navigation

Action	Key Combination
Copy	[Ctrl]+[C]
Search	[Ctrl]+[F]
Go to menu	[Alt]
Navigate to next element	[↹]
Navigate to previous element	[⇧]+[↹]
Navigate to next screen area	[Ctrl]+[↹]
Navigate to previous screen area	[⇧]+[Ctrl]+[↹]
Undo	[Ctrl]+[Z]

Overview of the Most Essential Key Combinations in the Navigation (Cont.)

After you've entered your data, you must save it so that the system adds the new or changed information to the database.

Tab

Via tabs, you can conveniently navigate in complex contents by switching switch between the individual tabs. If you click on the title of a tab, it is displayed in the foreground.

Example of a Tab

Screen Area

Screens that include various input options are often subdivided into several areas. A screen area, also known as a field group or group box, combines various input options for a specific topic.

Example of an Area

Field

You can enter information in the SAP system via input fields (white) and display fields (gray).

Example of an Input Field

In some cases, fields must be filled; required entry fields like these are labeled with a checkmark (☑). The system displays an error message if you miss a required entry field.

You don't have to fill in optional fields which are frequently information fields.

If you are not sure which inputs are expected in the field, use input help F4. You can also enter the field values manually.

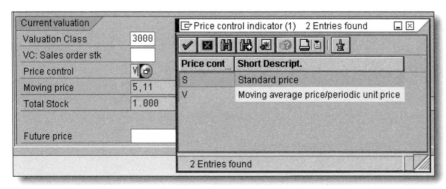

Selection List in the Input Help

You can copy the fields' content to the clipboard and thus avoid transfer errors by doing the following:

1 Fill in the corresponding field (for example, the customer name, John Smith).

2 Select the entry by pressing the left mouse button. Use the key combination Ctrl + C to copy it.

3 Navigate to the field in which you want to insert the content, and press Ctrl + V to insert the information.

Button

You can use buttons such as  Help to execute numerous functions like create or save. Some buttons are labeled; others bear a symbol or icon. If you position the cursor over a button, its function is shown. You can also use the key combination Ctrl + Q to get this tooltip.

Tooltip of a Button

Function Keys

Your keyboard has a row of keys labeled F1 to F12. The next table provides an overview of the most important function keys. Remember that some function keys have different settings, depending on the application.

Action	Function Key
Back	F3
Cancel transaction	⇧ + F3
Cancel	F12
Adjust local layout	Alt + F12
Help	F1

Function Keys in the Standard

Checkbox

Using checkboxes, often called indicators, you can select various different options by clicking on the box. After you click on them, a checkmark appears in the box. It is possible to select several checkboxes.

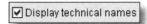

Example of Checkbox

Radio Button

By selecting a radio button, you can select one single option out of several. After you've clicked on them, they are labeled with a black dot.

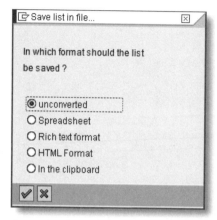

Example of a Radio Button

Dialog Window

If you need to make further inputs or if the system wants to display specific information, a dialog window opens. The original window remains open in the background.

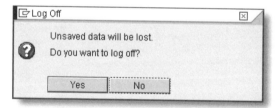

Example of a Dialog Window (Here, a Warning Message During Logoff)

6.5   Input Help

When searching for specific criteria, SAP provides the input help at specific points. You can call it with the function key F4. If no input help can be displayed, a selection list is presented.

Let's use Transaction MMBE as an example to show how the input help can be deployed:

1 Start Transaction MMBE (Material Stock List).

2 Leave the cursor in the **Material** field and press the F4 function key. A search window opens in which you can enter the various criteria that you want to search. Press ⬦ to run the search.

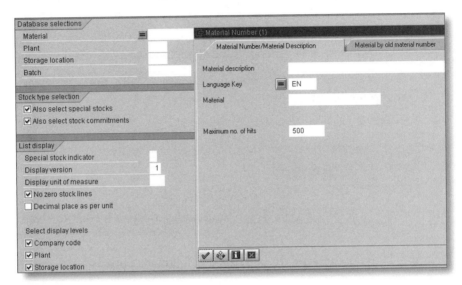

6

> **NOTE**
>
> **Search Patterns**
>
> It is not necessary to enter the entire search term. If you don't know the entire term, you can use a search pattern. For example, if you search for the material short text "blank", you can use the following search patterns:
>
> - *lank*: Finds all criteria that contain "lank".
>
> - *lank: Finds all criteria that begin with any letter combination and end with "lank".

6.6   Working with Sessions

SAP provides the option to open and work with several sessions at the same time in the system. This allows you to work with up to six transactions in addition to the current one.

Using Various Sessions

You are currently creating a master record for a vendor when a coworker urgently requires the warehouse stock of a material and asks for your help. You don't have to cancel the creation of the master record before you check the warehouse stock in another session.

Take the following steps to generate another session:

1 You are located in any transaction, for instance, MMBE. Click on **System** in the menu bar.

2 Select **Create Session**.

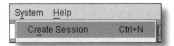

Alternatively, you can click the  button in the standard toolbar to create a new session.

To toggle between the sessions, you have the following options:

- Press the key combination Alt + ⇆ . The system toggles between the sessions. The inactive sessions are indicated in gray.

- Click on the desired session in the Windows taskbar.

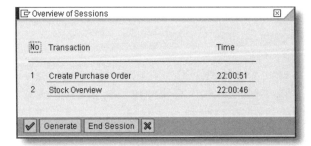

Sessions in the Windows Taskbar

- Enter the /o parameter in the command field and select the desired session from the session list.

No	Transaction	Time
1	Create Purchase Order	22:00:51
2	Stock Overview	22:00:46

✓ Generate   End Session ✗

Session List

How Many Sessions are Permitted?

The SAP system administrator can set the number of permitted sessions between two and 16 sessions. Six sessions are permitted by default.

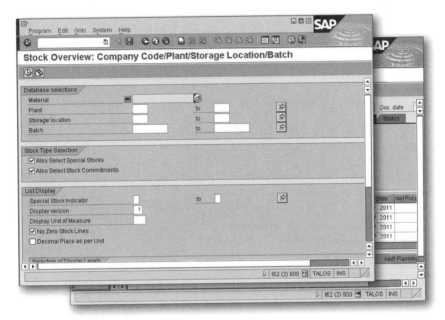

Various Open Sessions

There are three different options to close a session:

- Choose **System ▶ Delete Session** in the menu bar.
- Click the **Close** button ⊠ in the menu bar.
- Enter the parameter /i in the command field.

Performance

Open sessions have a negative effect on the system performance (or the speed of the user PC). Always make sure to close sessions that you're not using.

In this chapter, you learned how to navigate in the SAP system and work with transactions, or applications, of an SAP system. These can be started via the SAP Easy Access menu or by entering a transaction code in the command field. You can use parameters in combination with the transaction code. You also learned the various data input options and how to work with sessions.

6.7   Try It!

Exercise 1

What is a session?

Exercise 2

What do you enter in the command field to start Transaction ME21 in a new session?

Exercise 3

Name three options to toggle between sessions.

Exercise 4

Which happens if you enter the parameter /o in the command field?

Exercise 5

Which settings can you make in the SAP system in the menu under **Extras** ▸ **Settings**?

7 Maintaining the System Layout and User Data

Just like you can organize your workplace, you can also make custom settings in the SAP system to make work more convenient for you. These personal settings affect only the user with which you are logged on to the system. Other user accounts remain unaffected by these settings.

7

In this chapter you will learn:

- To create links
- To adapt the SAP system interface to your requirements
- To work with favorites
- To prepopulate fields to reduce input work

7.1 Creating Links on the Desktop

If you primarily work with one or only a few transactions and don't want to navigate via the SAP Easy Access menu each time, you can create a link to a transaction on your Windows desktop. To do so, take the following steps:

1 In the SAP Easy Access menu, select the transaction that you want to link on your Windows desktop (here, MMBE, Stock Overview).

2 Go to **Edit ▶ Create shortcut on the Desktop** in the menu bar, or press Ctrl + F3.

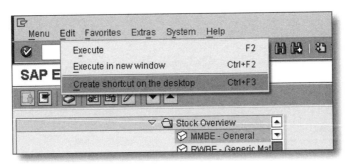

The system displays a message informing you that the shortcut was created successfully.

3 The shortcut was created on the Windows desktop. The next time you log on, you can directly use the transaction by double-clicking the shortcut.

7.2   Maintaining Your Own User Data

You can define user-specific settings like logon language, printer settings, and parameters in user settings. Take the following steps to maintain your own user data:

1 Start Transaction SU3 via the command field, or select **System ▶ User Profiles ▶ Own Data** from the menu bar.

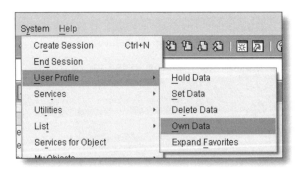

2 After you've called the transaction for maintaining your own user data, the system shows the **Address** tab. Here, you can maintain a variety of information:

- In the **Person** area, you can maintain your personal data like **Title**, **Name**, or **Department** in the respective fields. Use the 🖬 button to save each field change in this transaction.

- In the **Defaults** area, you can change the language that is used in the system after logon, among other things. Select **EN English** in the **Logon Language** selection field. In addition, you can also maintain further information in the **Address** area, such as telephone numbers and email addresses. Remember to save each field change via the 🖬 button.

3 You can also change your password using the ✅ button at the top left of the screen.

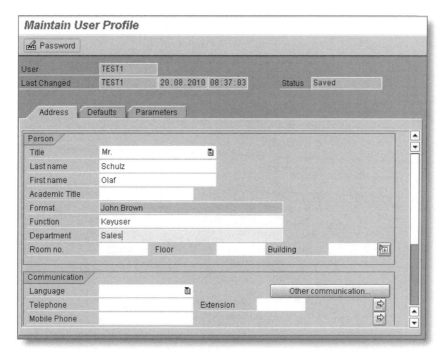

4 Now click on the **Defaults** tab, where you can determine the presentation of figures and dates. You can specify the following information:

- **Start menu:** Here you can assign an enterprise-specific area menu to your user. In this area, you can combine transactions for your task area. These parameters are usually set by the SAP administration team.

- **Logon language:** If no language is selected in the logon screen, the language specified here is used. If you define a language here (for example, EN for English), you don't need to specify a language during logon.

- **Decimal notation**: With this selection field, you define how the SAP system displays decimal numbers. For example, you can choose between 1.234.567,89 (a period for thousand separators and a comma for decimal digits, which is standard in Germany), 1 234567,89 (with a blank for thousand separators and a comma for decimal digits) or 1,234,567.89 (with a comma for thousand separators and a point for decimal digits, which is standard in the U.S.).

- **Date Format**: In this selection field, you define the date format, for instance, DD.MM.YYYY or MM/DD/YYYY.

- **Time Format**: In this selection field, you specify which time format is used. For example, choose between 11:10:15 (hours, minutes, seconds) or 11:10:15 PM. This last format—AM (ante meridiem) and PM (post meridiem)—is common in the U.S. The time zone must be set if an international business has employees in Germany and in the U.S., for example.

- **Output Device**: LOCL and LP01 are names in the SAP system for a default Windows printer (see Chapter 9, Printing), which is the one installed on the workplace computer.

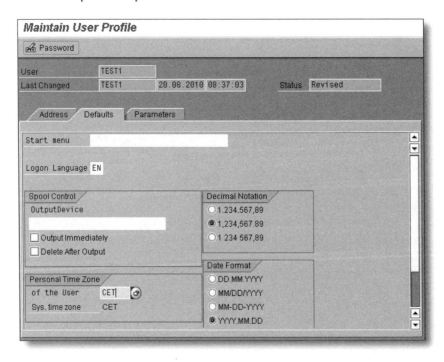

5 In the **Parameters** tab, you can set the default values for fields in transactions. These fields are populated with default values in the respective transactions to save the user the trouble of unnecessary inputs. The section Prepopulating Parameters for Fields describes how this works. If you primarily work in company code 1000, then you can prepopulate fields in transactions with this key.

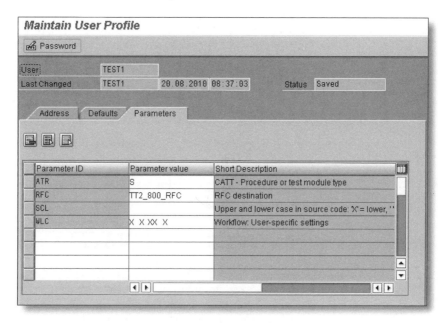

The following section shows how you can adapt the layout of the SAP system on your PC.

7.3   Adapting the Local Layout

In the SAP system, you can change the look and feel of the user interface—that is, the SAP GUI—according to your requirements. These settings of the local layout only refer to the SAP GUI of your user. This section shows how you can adapt the presentation of SAP GUI, the cursor, and the system messages.

You can go to the layout menu if you click the 🖳 button (**Local Layout**) in the standard toolbar.

Adapting the Local Layout

First learn how to make some settings to change the presentation of the SAP window. You can enable/disable the tooltips via buttons, influence how messages are displayed, and determine which properties the cursor may have. Proceed as follows:

1 In the standard toolbar, click on **Local Layout** and then select **Options**.

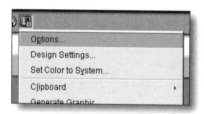

2 The **Options** menu opens. Click on the button 🖺 (**Selection**) and navigate to the **Options** menu item in the **Options** tab.

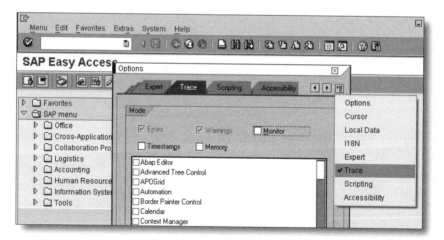

3 You have the following setting options in the **Options** tab:

- In the **Quick Info** area, you specify how quickly a short help text is displayed if you move the mouse pointer over a button without clicking on it.

– In the **Messages** area, you can define whether the system displays dialog windows on the screen in addition to the information in the status bar, or whether an acoustic signal is output. You specify this by activating the corresponding checkbox next to the option.

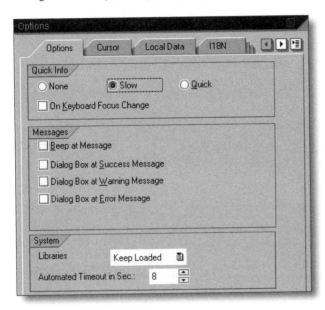

4 It is also possible to change the properties of the cursor. To do so, click on the **Cursor** tab or on the button 🖹. You now have the following setting options:

– In the **Cursor Position** area, you can set the position of the cursor. Set the **Use Accelerator Keys** flag to automatically set the cursor in a field after key commands have been used.

– With the **automatic Tabbing at End of Field** checkbox you define that the cursor is automatically positioned in the subsequent field as soon as the current field is filled completely. If you activate **Note Cursor Position in Field on Tabbing**, you can use the ⇆ key to go to the next field and ⬆+⇆ to go to the previous field. If you activate **Position Cursor at End of Text**, the cursor is positioned behind the last character when you click any point within the field.

– In the **Cursor Width** area, you can choose whether the display of the cursor is narrow or wide. The **Block Cursor in Overwrite Mode** checkmark represents a block cursor. The width of the cursor depends on the setting.

- In the **Others** area, you can choose the **Cursor in Lists** checkmark to mark one option only. If this field is deactivated, the system selects a complete column or an entire field.

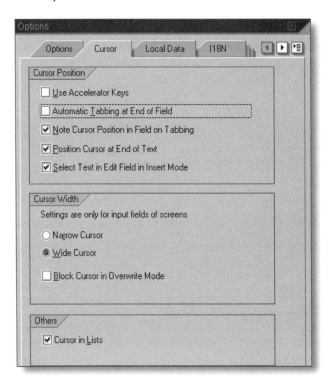

5 After you've made all changes, click on **OK** to accept them and close the tab (not shown in the figure). You can get more information on the respective tab via the **Help** button.

The following table lists some examples for useful key combinations:

Key Combination	Result
Alt + F12	Calls the function for adapting the local layout.
Ctrl + ⇧ + P	Creates a screenshot without dialog window but with status texts.
Ctrl + /	The cursor is placed in the first OK code field.

Overview of the Most Important Key Combinations

Key Combination	Result
Ctrl + ⬚	The cursor is placed in the first field or element that must be focused.
Ctrl + +	Creates a new session.
Ctrl + :	Creates an SAP link.

Overview of the Most Important Key Combinations (Cont.)

Besides the previously described settings, you can also change the color settings for the user interface in the layout menu by following these steps:

1 Again, call the layout menu via the button ▣, and select **Design Settings**.

2 Click on the **Color Settings** tab to define a color scheme in the selection field in the **Theme Setting** area. This changes the appearance of the SAP GUI.

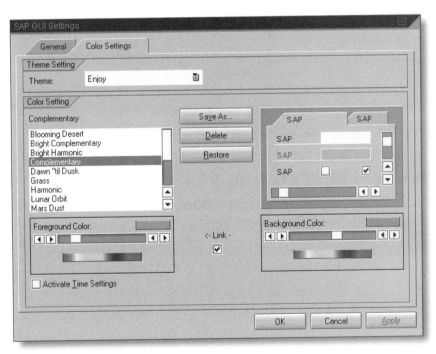

3 In the **General** tab, you define the font and activate or deactivate the sound.

> **NOTE**
>
> **Using GuiXT**
>
> GuiXT is a product developed and sold by Synactive. You can use this product to adapt and change the appearance and the behavior of the screens and transactions beyond the standard settings. The basic features are already provided together with SAP GUI. Other available functions are subject to change. The GuiXT add-on must be selected when SAP GUI is installed so that the functions are made available.

7.4   Creating Favorites

You already know about favorites from using Internet browsers, where you identify pages you frequently open as "Favorites". SAP offers the same concept for SAP GUI. You can identify the following objects you frequently use as favorites in the SAP Easy Access menu:

- Transactions
- Internet pages
- Files or programs located on your computer or the network drive.

The latter is useful if you require a document, such as a PDF regularly. You can access this file via your favorites as necessary using Windows Explorer.

The following section presents these options.

Adding Transactions to the Favorites

You can add a transaction via drag-and-drop to your favorites. To do so, you can perform the following steps:

1 Open the SAP Easy Access menu, and search for the transaction you want to add to your favorites.

2 Position the mouse pointer exactly on the transaction and keep the left mouse button pressed.

3 Keeping the left mouse button pressed, set the mouse pointer exactly on the **Favorites** folder and release the left mouse button again. The transaction was added to your favorites.

Alternatively, you can add transactions to your favorites via the menu bar. Proceed as follows:

1 In the SAP Easy Access menu, select the transaction you want to add to your favorites.

2 Click on **Favorites** ▶ **Add**. The transaction selected was added to your favorites.

A third option is to add transactions via the right mouse button to the **Favorites** folder. Proceed as follows:

1 Right-click the **Favorites** folder. The context menu opens.

2 In the context menu, select **Insert Transaction**. Then enter the transaction code to add it to your favorites.

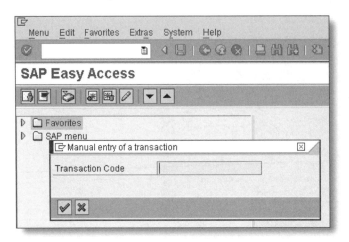

Adding Websites to the Favorites

You can also save a link to a website on the Internet in your favorites by taking the following steps:

1 Right-click the **Favorites** folder. Select **Insert other objects** from the context menu that opens.

2 Double-click **Web address or file** in the dialog window that opens.

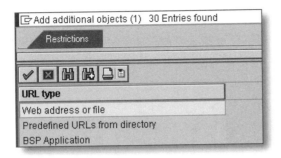

3 Input a description of the favorite in the **Text** field, and enter the URL (for example, *http://www.sap-press.com*) in the **Web address or file** field. Confirm your entries by clicking the ✔ (**Accept**) icon. The desired website was added to your favorites.

Adding Files or Programs to the Favorites

To add files or programs from your local drive or a network drive to your favorites, proceed as described in the previous section. Enter or select the file name or the path in the **Web address or file** field instead of the web address.

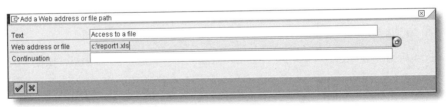

Adding a File to the Favorites

115

Deleting Favorites

You can also delete your favorites if you don't need them anymore by selecting the unwanted favorite and choosing **Delete Favorite** from the context menu (right mouse button).

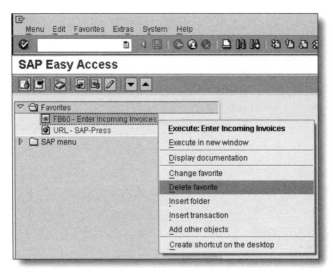

Deleting Favorites

7.5   Prepopulating Parameters for Fields

In specific cases, you must enter the same data over and over again. To spare having to do repeated entries, you can save specific parameters as default values. These default values are permanently available to you within your user, and will be prepopulated in the corresponding fields the next time you log on to the system.

Transaction VD03 (Customer Master Data) should be used to show how you can prepopulate fields with parameters. The key of this organizational unit (1000) should be used as a default value in the **Sales Organization** field.

First, you must determine the parameter ID for the desired field. Then, specify the default value for the field under **System ▶ User Profile ▶ Own Data**. The individual steps are as follows:

1 Navigate to the field in which you want to insert a default value — either using the corresponding transaction or following the respective menu path.

2 To reproduce this concrete example, open Transaction VD03 by entering the transaction code in the command field or navigating via the SAP Easy Access menu path: **Logistics ▶ Sales and Distribution ▶ Master Data ▶ Business Partner ▶ Customer ▶ Display ▶** VD03 – **Sales and Distribution**.

3 The system displays the initial screen of Transaction VD03. Click on the **Sales Organization** field. Then press the function key [F1] (field help).

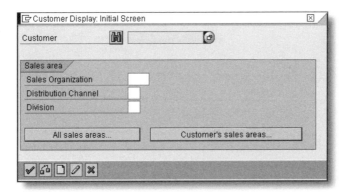

4 Click on the **Technical Information** icon ( ) to determine the parameter ID. Every field has its own parameter ID.

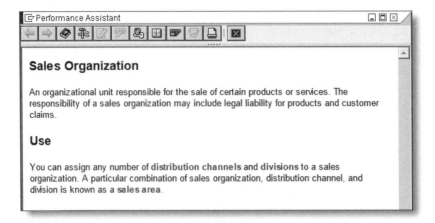

[5] Memorize the parameter ID. The parameter ID for the **Sales Organization** field is VKO.

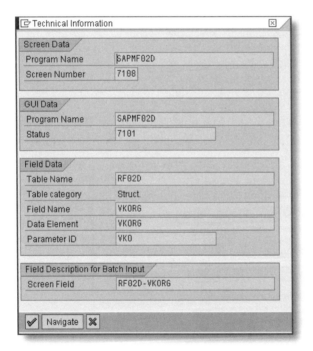

[6] Exit the transaction by clicking 🏠 **(Exit)**.

[7] Next, change your profiles. To do so, open your own user data by starting Transaction SU3 (Maintain Users Own Data) via the command field; or select **System ▶ User Profile ▶ Own Data** in the menu.

8 Click on the **Parameters** tab, and enter "VKO" in the **Parameter ID** column and "1000" in the **Parameter Value** column. If you've entered a correct parameter ID (that is, one known to the system) and confirmed it with ⏎, the system displays the short description. This way, you can also check whether the parameter ID is correct.

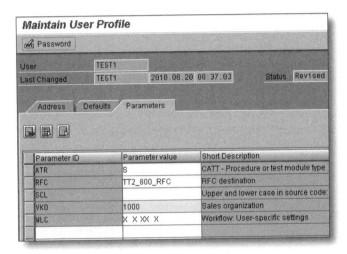

9 Save your settings by clicking the **Save** button 💾 . You've prepopulated the field for the sales organization with the parameter value 1000.

10 Test your settings by starting Transaction VD03 again. If it worked, the **Sales Organization** field is now prepopulated with the value 1000 in the initial screen of the transaction.

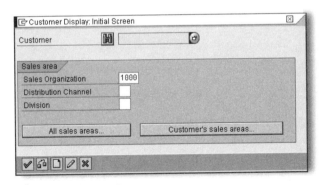

TIP

Make Use of the Clipboard

You can select the parameter ID with your mouse, copy it to the clipboard with Ctrl+C, and insert it again using Ctrl+V.

7.6 Holding, Setting, and Deleting Data

The functions, **Hold Data**, **Set Data**, and **Delete Data** save time by lowering the number of inputs in the SAP system. The settings are retained during one session only, which is different from prepopulation with parameters.

You have the following options:

- **Hold Data**
  Data can be held (that is, default values can be defined) in various transactions. So, the fields filled this way are prepopulated with the default values from the previous processing when the transaction is called again. These default values can still be overwritten.

- **Set Data**
  The **Set Data** function also automatically fills the fields with default values. In contrast to **Hold Data**, the prepopulated fields can no longer be changed after **Set Data**.

- **Delete Data**
  With this function, you reset both the Hold and the Set functions so that the fields are no longer automatically populated with default values.

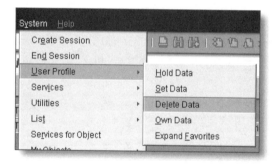

You can see how the **Hold Data** fields are filled by taking the following steps:

1 Start Transaction VA01 (Create Standard Order).

2 In the initial screen, select ST (Standard Order) in the **Order Type** field. Choose 1000 in the **Sales Organization** field.

3 Enter the article numbers for the items. Then choose **System ▸ User Profile ▸ Hold Data** from the menu.

4 Exit the transaction, and restart it. Your field entries should be prepopulated again.

This chapter described various options that make your work with the SAP system easier. For example, if you require only a few transactions for your work, you can create links to them on the Windows desktop. This way, after you've logged on to the system, you can directly navigate to the desired transaction with a simple double-click. Furthermore, SAP GUI allows you to manage your favorites, so you can store frequently required transactions or websites in your favorites menu. It is also very useful to prepopulate a parameter ID of a field with a default value. The parameter ID can be defined in your personal settings and is valid for the current user only.

7.7   Try It!

Exercise 1

Describe how to create a link to Transaction VA01 (Create Standard Order) on your Windows desktop.

Exercise 2

Name the four objects for which you can create favorites.

Exercise 3

Describe three methods of creating favorites.

Exercise 4

Describe how you can determine the parameter ID for a field. For this purpose, start Transaction XK01 (Create Vendor) in the system and determine the parameter ID of the sales organization.

8 Creating Evaluations and Reports

You daily work frequently requires you to create reports and lists. You can print and send these lists and use them for the decision-making process. SAP offers a versatile range of reporting options.

Besides the tools contained in SAP ERP, there are further powerful tools (for example, within SAP NetWeaver) which are not discussed in this book. This chapter is limited to the information system in SAP ERP.

In this chapter, you will learn:

- To call standard reports in the SAP system
- To use the SAP List Viewer for presentation
- To export reports to Microsoft Excel
- To use variants
- About further reporting tools provided in SAP ERP

8.1 Using Standard Reports in the SAP System

The reporting and analysis topic plays a central role in a business's success. The wealth of information stored in the SAP system can be evaluated and presented in reports (for example, in lists).

The different areas and departments of your business have diverse information requirements. In the HR area, the employees and managers require personal data that ranges from simple lists of employees to more complex reports. In logistics, reports can involve stock lists or lists of orders from a specific period of time. In accounting, you can display all items of a debtor (customer), the costs and revenues of a specific area, and much more.

Part III of this book provides a selection of the most important reports in the Purchasing, Sales and Distribution, Human Resources, Financial Accounting, and Controlling components.

SAP List Viewer (ALV)

The SAP system provides various options to displayed queried data. One of the most important tools for display is the SAP List Viewer (ALV). The abbreviation ALV stands for ABAP List Viewer, which is the name of the tool in older releases. Different list operations such as search, filter, and sort are available within the ALV. With the ALV grid control, SAP gives you a standardized tool for displaying lists in the system. Grid control lets you define which information is displayed in the list and choose the criteria used to filter it.

Let's use an example to illustrate how to call standard reports. You must determine in the SAP system which sales were generated by a specific sales organization within a specific period of time. The following data is used for this example: The sales organization is 1000 and the period for analysis is the previous three months. Take the following steps:

1 Open the **Logistics ▶ Materials Management ▶ Logistics Controlling ▶ Logistics Information System ▶ Standard Analyses ▶ Sales and Distribution ▶ MCTA – Customer** path in the SAP Easy Access menu. Alternatively, start Transaction MCTA by entering the transaction code in the command field.

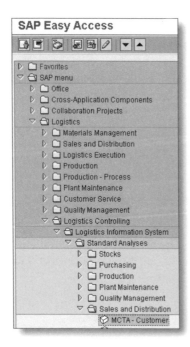

2 In the initial screen of the customer analysis, enter the sales organization in the corresponding field for which you want to create the evaluation. Enter 1000 in this example. Limit the **period to analyze** to three months (05.2011 to 07.2011). To run the evaluation and display the basic list, click the **Execute** button 🗸 or press the [F8] function key.

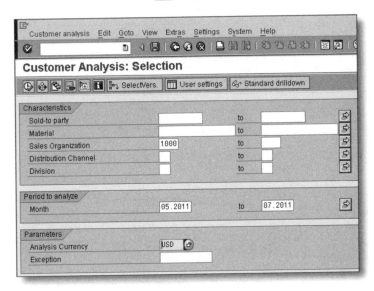

3 You can now modify the report using the buttons that are detailed in the table.

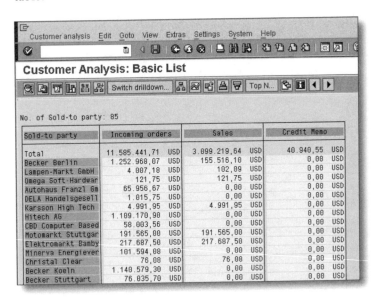

You have now successfully created a sales report. The list, which was output in ALV format, offers various navigation options. The ALV grid control has a special toolbar for this that offers the following important buttons:

Button	Meaning	Key Combination	Explanation
	First page	`Ctrl` + `Page ↑`	Navigates to the beginning of the list.
	Previous page	`Page ↑`	Navigates to the previous page in the list.
	Next page	`Page ↓`	Navigates to the next page in the list.
	Last page	`Ctrl` + `Page ↓`	Navigates to the end of the list.
	Select (details)	`F2`	Shows detailed information on the selection.
	Save in PC file	`⇧` + `F8`	Exports the list to a PC file.
	Send	`Ctrl` + `F1`	Sends a link of this list to another user.
	Graphic	`F5`	Creates a graphic.
	Sort in ascending order	`Ctrl` + `F5`	Sorts a selected column by contents in ascending order.
	Sort in descending order	`⇧` + `F4`	Sorts a selected column by contents in descending order.
	Other info structure	`Ctrl` + `F4`	Changes the list structure.
Switch drilldown...	Change drilldown	`F7`	Changes the first column.

Buttons in the ALV Grid Control

Button	Meaning	Key Combination	Explanation
舞	Analysis currency	Ctrl + F7	Changes the currency to the selected currency.
品	Drilldown by	F8	Further drilldown of a selected criterion.
Top N...	Top N values	⇧ + F6	Shows the highest values of a selected column.

Buttons in the ALV Grid Control (Cont.)

The next section describes how to find the report that meets your evaluation purposes best.

8

8.2   Finding Standard Reports

If you receive a specific report request, you can check in the SAP system for a standard report that meets your requirements. The following section presents three options to find which reports exist in the SAP standard version.

Searching for Reports

If you know the name of the report required, you can call it quickly and easily. To call reports and search them via the search help, you can activate the reporting function via the menu bar (**System ▸ Services ▸ Reporting**). Take the followings steps:

1 Open the **System ▸ Services ▸ Reporting** menu item in the menu bar.

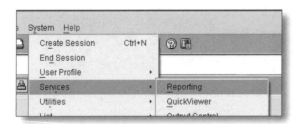

2 Then open the window **ABAP: Execute Program**; enter the name of the report in the **Program** field and execute it directly. Granted, you must first know the name to be able to use this method. Additionally, you can select the associated variants via the **Overview of Variants** button.

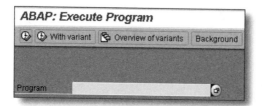

3 If you don't know the program name, you can use a search window (also known as a program directory) to determine the program name according to different selection criteria. For this purpose, open the value help via the ⬚ button in the **Program** field.

TIP

Effective Search

The less precise your selection criteria are, the more time the system requires for the search. If you only enter * in the **Program** field, it can take several minutes to obtain a result.

4 Specify your search term in the program directory and enter any part of the report name in the **Program** field. You can use the following place-holders for unknown characters:

  – Asterisk (*): character string
  – Plus sign (+): one character exactly

5 Then choose **Execute**.

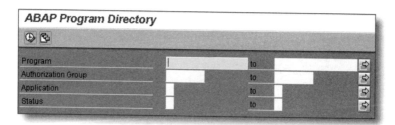

6 The system displays a list with reports. Double-click on the desired report to select it. Alternatively, position the cursor on the report name and choose **Execute**.

7 The system displays the selection screen of the report if no variant is required. If you need a variant, you must return to the initial screen via the ⊙ button or the ⌊F3⌋ function key to enter the program and variant name there. Before you do so, write down the name of the report.

⑧ Enter your selection values in the selection screen. Choose **Program ▸ Execute**. The report is displayed in a list.

Calling Reports in the SAP Easy Access Menu

You can find the reports on the individual components in the corresponding information systems. You can also directly navigate to the reports of the information system from the top level of the SAP Easy Access menu.

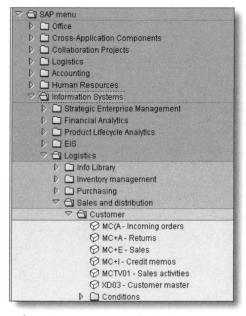

Information Systems in the SAP Easy Access Menu

8.3   Exporting Lists to Microsoft Excel

You can also process data outside the SAP system by exporting it to other programs. For example, you can export a list as a Microsoft Excel file to view and change it there.

Let's continue the example of the previous section, in which you ran a customer analysis. Now export the list created there as a Microsoft Excel file by doing the following:

1 In the SAP Easy Access menu, select **Customer analysis** ▸ **Export** ▸ **Save to PC file** (⬛+F8).

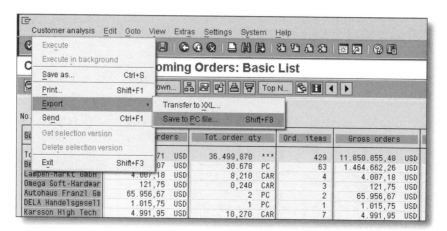

2 A dialog window opens that lets you select different radio buttons. Choose the **Spreadsheet** radio button, and then click on the **Next** button ✔ or press the ↵ key.

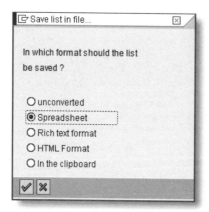

3 Another dialog window opens in which you can specify the directory (folder) where the file is to be saved on your computer and name the file. Click on the **Generate** button after you've specified the directory and file name.

4 Note that you may not have write authorizations in all directories of your business.

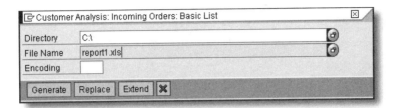

5 Next, a dialog window opens that details the number of bytes that were transferred to the file.

6 You can now further process the generated file in Microsoft Excel by starting Microsoft Excel and opening the file in the directory in which you've saved it.

8

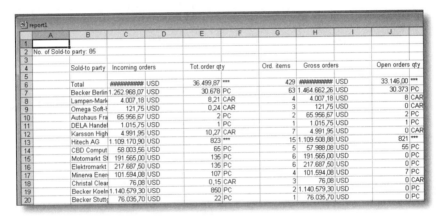

You now have the option to graphically format the selected data in Microsoft Excel charts.

8.4 Using Variants

A variant includes saved selection criteria (various search criteria in the corresponding fields that you use to restrict a search in the system). You don't need to reenter these selection criteria whenever you call the transaction, but you can save them.

If you want to save your entries in the initial screen of the customer analysis as a variant, proceed as follows:

1 In the initial screen of Transaction MCTA, choose **Goto ▶ Variants ▶ Save As Variant**.

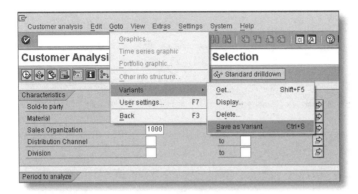

2 Enter the variant name (**Variant Name**) and a descriptive text (**Descrip-tion**) in the relevant fields of the **Variant Attributes** screen. Then click on ▣ (**Save**). After you've saved your entries, the SAP system displays the message "Variant ... was saved."

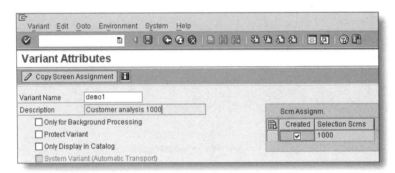

To load a saved variant, do the following:

1 Choose **Goto** ▸ **Variants** ▸ **Get** in the initial screen of Transaction MCTA.

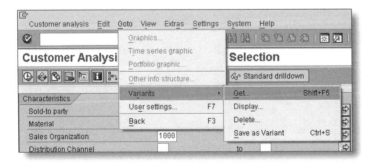

2 A variant catalog is displayed from which you can select the saved variant. The fields are then filled accordingly.

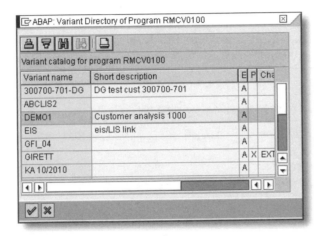

8.5   Other Reporting Options in SAP ERP

The SAP system provides numerous reports with which you can access the saved data. In the SAP standard system, many predefined reports can be executed in the ABAP programs directly.

For advanced reporting requirements, SAP ERP offers its own reporting tools you can use to define custom evaluations according to your requirements. (This also involves ABAP report generators.) The following are the most critical reporting tools in SAP ERP, with which you can create custom evaluations:

- SAP Query (including components of SAP Query, InfoSet Query, and QuickViewer)
- Report Painter/Report Writer
- Drilldown Reporting
- Logistics Information System (LIS)

The use of the appropriate tool depends on the specific report requirement. Influencing factors include data format, options for further processing, and (graphical) presentation options. This scope of this book does not cover the versatile characteristics of each tool.

Reporting Tool		Main Usage Area
SAP Query	SAP Query	All SAP components (In SAP ERP HCM, InfoSet Query is referred to as Ad-hoc Query)
	InfoSet Query	
	QuickViewer	
Drilldown Reporting		Accounting (FI, CO, TR, IM, PS)
Report Painter/Report Writer		Accounting (CO, FI)
Logistics Information System (LIS)		Logistics (SD, MM, QM, PM, PP)

Overview of the Most Critical Reporting Tools in SAP ERP

Beyond that, SAP NetWeaver Business Warehouse includes various reporting tools (see Chapter 3) that are not discussed in this book either. One example is Business Explorer (BEx for short). Not long ago, further tools, such as Crystal Reports, were added with the acquisition of Business Objects.

8.6   Try It!

Exercise 1

Create an evaluation that shows the 20 customers that generated the highest sales figures in sales organization 1000 over the last twelve months. Then export this data to Microsoft Excel.

9 Printing

Since the paperless office has not become reality yet, it is still often necessary to print documents. You can print everything that you can view on the SAP screen. Though you usually need to print lists and purchase orders or invoices, sometimes you might want to print the entire screen—that is, to make a screenshot. In this chapter, you will learn about the most important printing functions and settings.

This chapter discusses:

- How to set up a default printer

- What spool requests and output requests are

- How to print lists from the SAP system

- How to create screenshots

9.1 Overview of the Print Functions

The SAP system provides two options for outputting documents: working with immediate outputs and using the spool system. To print the document immediately, carry out the following steps:

1 Open the document (for example, the list that you want to print and click on 🖨 (**Print**). Alternatively, you can either press ⌈Ctrl⌋+⌈P⌋ or use the **List ▸ Print** menu path.

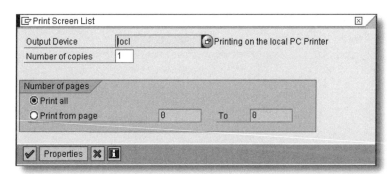

2 The system now displays a window with the print options. Maintain the other print options and select the printer. The list will be output.

If you use the spool system, the print requests are not output immediately. Instead, the print request is stored in a spool file. This file can then be sent to a printer or another output device, such as a fax machine. An output request finally initiates the print process.

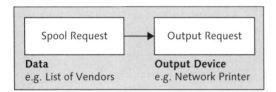

Spool Request and Output Request

- **Spool request**
  In the case of a spool request, your document is not directly output on a printer or another device after you select a print function for it. Instead, the system stores the output files of the print document in a data store until they are sent to a specific output device (via an output request). With the spool request, the print data is temporarily stored, and you can access and display this data.

- **Output request**
  For output requests, the print data of a spool request is output on a specific output device. There can be numerous output requests with different printers or print settings for one spool request.

It might seem easier to output a Word document on a printer than go through these steps. However, output control has to cover several additional requirements: the flexibility to output documents or lists again or on a different device, or the ability to send documents to a telefax gateway controlled via the SAP system in the business network. Output control also supports further processing via EDI. The spool system makes this possible by storing print data temporarily and differentiating between spool requests and output requests.

EDI (Electronic Data Interchange)

EDI is the electronic data interchange between computer systems. For example, a customer electronically transfers a purchase order to your business's SAP system, where the purchase order is further processed. Data is exchanged in the form of IDocs (Intermediate Documents) between SAP systems.

The following section describes the usage of spool requests in detail.

9.2   Using Spool Requests

The print process in the system has two phases: First, a spool request is created, at which time the system formats the data that is required for the output. Then you can generate an output request where you define when and on which device the data will be output.

Let's take a look at the print function using the list of vendors as an example:

1. Call Transaction MKVZ via the SAP Easy Access menu by following the menu path: **Logistics ▶ Materials Management ▶ Purchasing ▶ Master Data ▶ Vendor ▶ List Displays ▶ MKVZ Purchasing List**. Alternatively, call Transaction MKVZ via the command field.

2. In the initial screen of the list of vendors, enter the value 1000 in the **Purchasing Organization** field to output all vendors that are assigned to purchasing organization 1000.

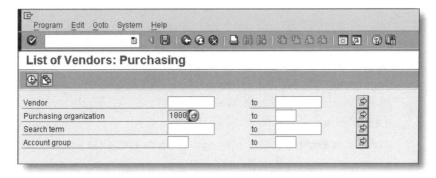

3. Proceed by clicking on ⊕ **(Execute)**. The screen displays the list of vendors.

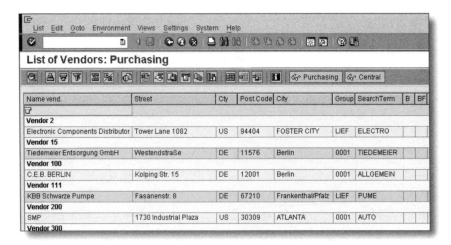

4 To print this list, click the 🖶 button **(Print)** in the menu bar, or press `Ctrl`+`P`. The system displays the **Print ALV List** dialog box. The print window may look different, depending on the application you use.

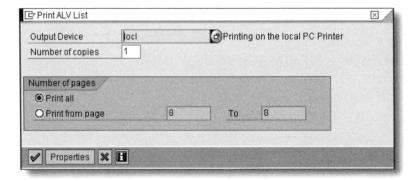

5 In this print window, you can make the settings that are necessary for your output.

- **Output Device**: Enter which printer you want to use. The 🗗 button **(Input Help)** beside the field lets you view the available printers and select one by double-clicking on it. You can create a PDF (Portable Data Format) if a PDF printer driver is installed on your PC.

- **Number of Copies**: Define how many copies you want to print.

- **Number of Pages**: The **Print All** or **Print from Page** radio buttons let you choose whether you want to print the entire document or individual pages.

6 Press the ⏎ key, or click the green checkmark ✓. The system displays a status message that confirms the creation of the spool request. Every spool request has a unique identification number.

7 Follow the **System ▸ Services ▸ Output Control** path in the menu bar to open the output control.

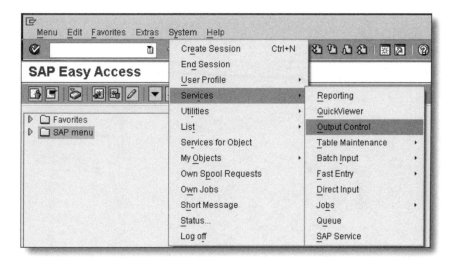

8 Click the **Further Selection Criteria** button at the top in the output control to restrict your search result.

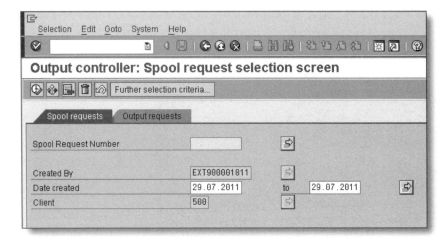

9 When you click on the **Further Selection Criteria** button, a window opens that provides the selection criteria as required. In this case, the fields of the **Standard** selection criterion are displayed.

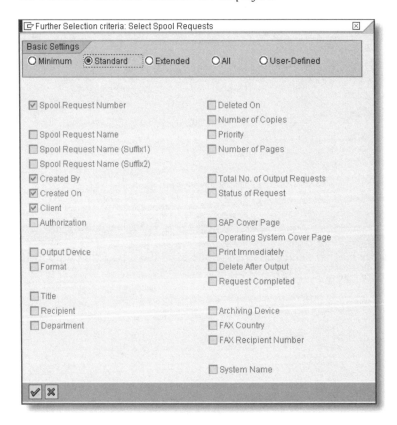

10 Press the ↵ key to return to the output control. Click on ⊕ (**Execute**) to display the output control. The system may display several requests, depending on the restriction for your selection criteria. Select the spool request that you want to output by activating the checkbox next to the spool number. Click on 🖨 (**Print**), or press Ctrl+P.

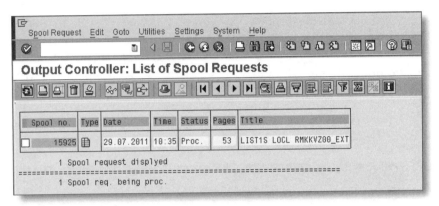

11 The system generates the output request and outputs it on the printer. You receive the message "Spool request created without immediate output," which you confirm with OK. The system then outputs your document on the selected printer.

The following section describes how you configure the default printer in the SAP system.

9.3 Changing the Default Printer

In the SAP system, the printers are defined centrally and assigned to individual users.

> **NOTE**
>
> **Printer Setup**
>
> In a live SAP system, the administrator of your SAP system is responsible for the printer configuration, not you. However, for testing purposes, it may be necessary to use an installed Windows or network printer, which you may need to manage.

It is also possible to use the default Windows printer—the one the Windows operating system proposes when you use the print function in an Office application to output a document. To set up the default printer in the SAP system, do the following:

1 Open **System ▸ User Profile ▸ Own Data** in the menu bar. Then click on the **Defaults** tab.

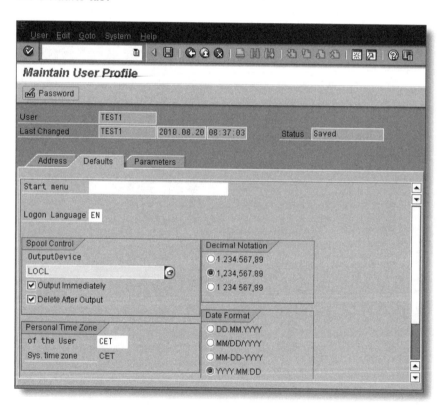

2 Enter the **LOCL** (or LP01) output device in the **Output Device** field to use the default Windows printer. You can also select the output device in the input help for the 🔘 field, and copy it by double-clicking on it.

3 Make sure that the **Output immediately** and **Delete After Output** check-boxes are activated. This way, the system will generate an output request immediately after the spool request and the output will be carried out directly after the print command. The **Delete After Output** setting ensures that print formatting (spool) doesn't remain in the SAP system.

The next section illustrates how you can create screenshots of the SAP system.

9.4   Creating Screenshots

If you have to create documentations, it is useful to illustrate your text with images from the SAP system, known as screenshots or hardcopy in the SAP system. There are two methods for creating screenshots:

- Using Microsoft Office

- Using the **Hard Copy** function in the SAP system

To create screenshots using standard Microsoft functions, carry out the following steps:

1 Open the required screen, and select a section (if applicable).

2 Copy the screenshot to the clipboard with Ctrl + Print .

3 You can then insert the screenshot from the clipboard in various applications using Ctrl + V .

- Open Microsoft Paint via the Windows start menu, insert the screenshot with Ctrl + V , and store it as a *.tif file.

- Open Microsoft PowerPoint, insert the screenshot with Ctrl + V , and save the presentation.

- Open Microsoft Word, insert the screenshot with Ctrl + V , and save the Word document.

4 Then you can further process the created screenshots in the programs mentioned in various ways.

You can also directly output a screenshot in the SAP system on a default Windows printer by taking the following steps:

1 In the standard toolbar, click on the **Adapt Local Layout** button ▣. Then click on the **Hard Copy** button. You can also use the key combination ⇧ + H in the displayed menu.

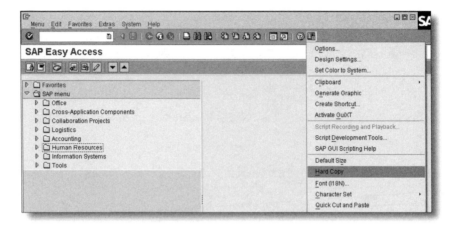

2 The screenshot is output on the printer.

This chapter introduced you to print functions in the SAP system. Printing in SAP usually requires two pieces: a spool request and an output request. You can output documents, lists, and reports.

9.5   Try It!

Exercise 1
Describe how to define a default printer in the SAP system for your user.

Exercise 2
What's the difference between spool and output request?

Exercise 3
Print a list of all sales orders (Transaction VA04).

10   Automating Tasks

This chapter shows you how to automate specific work steps so you can simplify your work. The SAP system runs specific routine tasks automatically in the background or in batch processing (also known as batch input) to save you time.

> **In this chapter, you will learn:**
>
> - What is online and background processing
> - How you can simplify work by using jobs
> - How to use batch processing with batch input sessions

10.1   Background Jobs

Background processing in the SAP system is used to automate routine tasks. Background processing occurs if the SAP system performs tasks (jobs) without user intervention. Of course, you must first tell the SAP system what programs to trigger and when. This way, background jobs are processed in the background without needing further help or attention from the user.

> **INFO**
>
> **Reports**
> In the SAP context, a report is an executable ABAP program that reads database tables and uses them to output results according to specific criteria. For example, the sales department requires an evaluation that lists all customers from a specific state that purchased goods worth $10,000 in the previous fiscal year. If such a report is executed, the task list can be displayed on the screen, printed, or saved.

Online processing is the opposite of background processing. Unlike the traditional definition in IT, the term *online* does not refer to the Internet connection here. In this context, online is used when a user starts transactions directly in the SAP system.

Background jobs are particularly suitable for recurring tasks that must be performed in the SAP system but that require no interaction between the user and the SAP system. The benefit that background jobs offer is that you can schedule the tasks to be performed at times when SAP system use is as low as possible (for example, at night). You should coordinate this time window with the SAP administration team.

The following tasks are run as background jobs:

- Printing dunnings
- Creating reports
- Transferring data via EDI (Electronic Data Interchange)

To successfully work with background jobs, you must first learn how to create a job. Determine the name of the report that you want to run in the background job, and then define the job using the Job Wizard in the SAP system. The Job Wizard guides you through job creation, including helping you to specify the job name, job class, task, start time, and output.

In this example, the system is supposed to create an up-to-date list of vendors in a background job. Take the following steps:

1 With Transaction MKVZ, you can output a list of vendors in the SAP system. Call this transaction via the SAP Easy Access menu path: **Logistics ▸ Materials Management ▸ Purchasing ▸ Master Data ▸ Vendor ▸ List Displays**. Another option is to enter Transaction MKVZ in the command field.

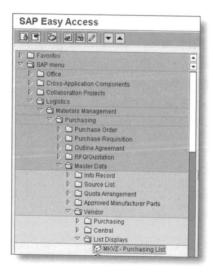

2 The initial screen of the list of vendors opens. Before continuing this transaction, however, determine the name of the report. (You will need this report name to automate the step later.) Select **System ▶ Status** in the menu bar.

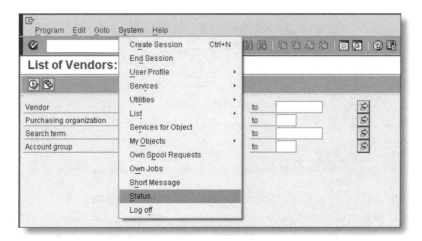

3 Name the report in the **System: Status** window. In this example, the name is RMKKVZ00. Either write down this report name or copy it to the clipboard by selecting it with the mouse and pressing Ctrl + C.

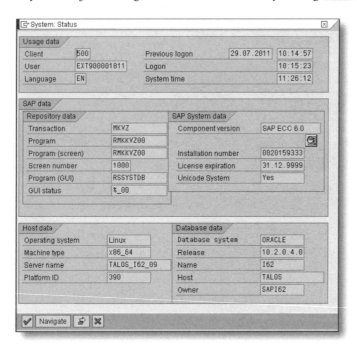

4 You will determine specific parameters (in other words, specify criteria) when you define the job in the SAP system later. For this purpose, create a variant for the list of vendors by selecting **Goto ▶ Variants ▶ Save as Variant...** in the menu bar.

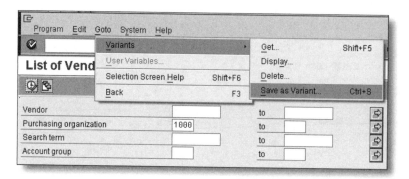

5 The **Variant Attributes** screen opens. Here you must enter a variant name and description so that you can assign and uniquely identify the variant later. To do so, maintain the fields **Variant Name** (here, "zz_vendor_1") and **Description** (here, "list of vendors").

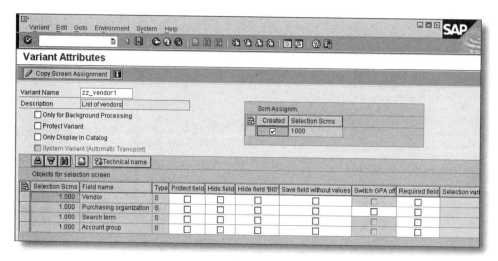

- Click the **Save** button 🔳 in the standard toolbar to save the variant. The system displays the message "Variant ZZ_VENDOR_1 saved" after saving.

6 Next, you need to schedule the background job in the SAP system. Call **System ▸ Services ▸ Jobs ▸ Define Job** in the menu bar. Alternatively, you can enter Transaction SM36 in the command field.

7 Call the Job Wizard in Transaction SM36 (Define Background Job). Similar to an Office application wizard, the Job Wizard guides you through the background job creation. To begin, click the **Job wizard** button.

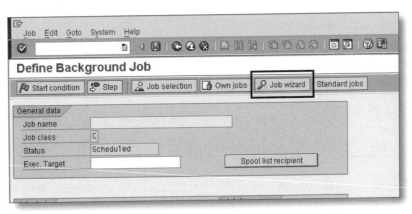

8 The initial screen of the Job Wizard opens in the subsequent step. Click on **Continue**.

9 In the next screen, enter a job name and define the job class. The job class determines the priority with which the job is processed. If available, choose **A – Prio High** here. Leave the field of the target server blank. Choose **Scheduled** in the **Job Status** field. Then click **Continue**.

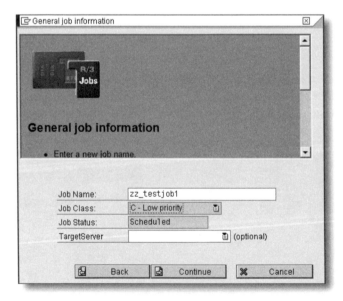

10 In the next dialog window, make sure that the **ABAP program step** radio button is selected. Click on **Continue** again.

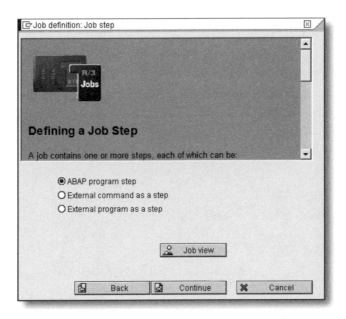

11 Next you need to specify which ABAP program to process with which variant. In the **ABAP program name** field, enter the report name (**RMKKVZ00**). If you've saved the report name in the clipboard, place the cursor on the **ABAP Program Name** field and insert the name with the key combination ⌨Ctrl+⌨V.

12 Then click on the 🔘 button **(Value Help)** next to the **Variant** field. Find your saved variant and double-click to select it. Continue by clicking on **Continue**.

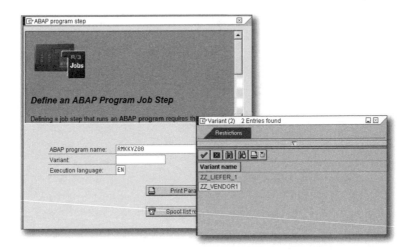

In the next screen, you can add further steps (another ABAP program). Because you don't require any further steps in this example, leave this checkbox deactivated and click on **Continue**.

Next you must specify when and how to start the job. For this example, choose the **Immediate Start** button to reproduce the result in the SAP system as fast as possible. In real life, however, you'll select a more suitable point in time. Then click on **Continue**.

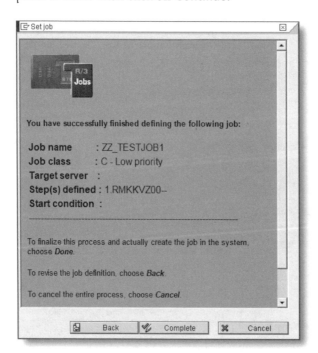

15 A message is displayed that tells you that the job can be executed immediately. In this screen you can also view how many processes run in the background. Click on **Continue**.

16 The system provides a summary of the scheduled job in the next dialog window. You can revise the job definition via the **Back** button, or terminate the entire process via the **Cancel** button. Click on **Complete** to create a job with the current definition in the SAP system. The Job Wizard is closed.

10

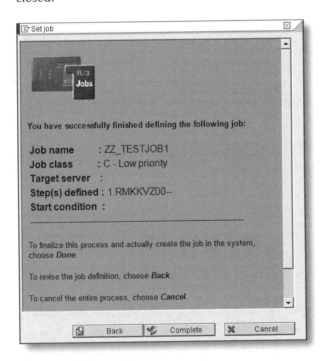

17 You then receive a status message that confirms that the job was saved (in this example, "Job ZZ_TESTJOB1 saved with status: scheduled"). Click **OK** to confirm this message.

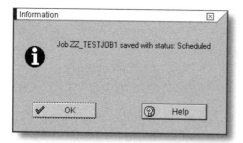

18 Now view the result by going to **System ▸ Services ▸ Output Control**.

19 Call your job again. In the output control, you can filter the search by the jobs available in the SAP system (for example, by leaving your user name and setting the creation date to the correct date; both values are proposed by the SAP system). Check the fields for accuracy, and click ⊕ (**Execute**).

20 You get an overview of all spool requests. Here you should view the list generated by the job; you can identify the job you've created based on the title. Activate the checkmark next to the spool request; if you click the ⟨image button⟩ button (**Display Content**), the system displays a preview of the list of vendors. You can also press the function key F6 to achieve this result.

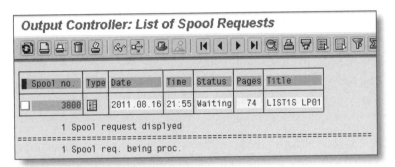

21 The system displays the list of vendors.

10

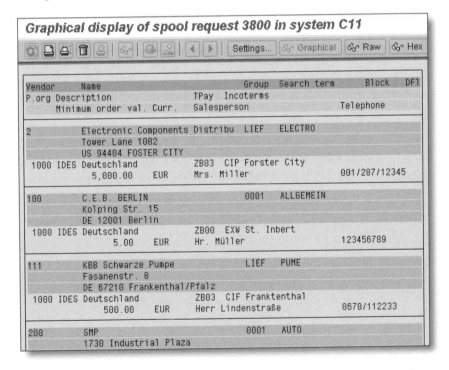

In the SAP system, you can control which jobs you've created and whether these jobs are released, active, or already completed. To do this, choose **System ▸ Own Jobs** in the menu bar.

10.2   Batch Processing (Batch Input)

The batch input technique is useful if you must process larger quantities of data (for mass data transfers, for example). You can transfer data from one SAP system (or a third-party system) to another SAP system. A batch input is often used for the non-recurring import of data from a legacy system to a newly installed SAP system.

Transactions run automatically in such a batch processing. The data required for this transaction is provided in batch input sessions, which are then processed together with the transaction. You can use batch input sessions to automatically import data into the SAP system without requiring your attention or involvement during import.

A batch input session consists of the process of one or more transactions and the associated data. In a batch input session, the transactions and data were recorded in such a way that they can be processed by the SAP system. If a batch input session is implemented, the SAP system processes the inputs of transaction codes and data (as if you were executing the transaction yourself).

The batch input consists of two key steps:

1. The batch input session is created.
2. The batch input session is processed; the contained data is then imported into the SAP system.

The main menu of the batch input session is available via the menu bar (**System ▸ Services ▸ Batch Input ▸ Sessions**) or via Transaction SM35. The next two sections discuss how to create and process a batch input session.

Creating Batch Input Sessions

This section uses an example to walk you through creating a batch input session. You learn how to create a "mini-record" of a transaction using the transaction recorder. The transaction recorder is similar to a macro recorder in an Office application. It records every step you take. From this record, you can create any number of batch input sessions for testing.

Though this example shows a transaction with only a few user interactions, you can also transfer this process to more complex applications (for example, to create materials or customer master records). For the sake of simplicity, this example uses a transaction you already know: Transaction MMBE (Stock Overview). Do the following:

1 To start the transaction recorder, select **System ▶ Services ▶ Batch Input ▶ Recorder,** or enter Transaction code SHDB in the command field. Then click on the **New Recording** button. Enter a name in the **Recording** field; either memorize this name or write it down. Enter this name in the **Transaction code** field (here, MMBE). Leave all other settings unchanged. Then click on the **Start recording** button.

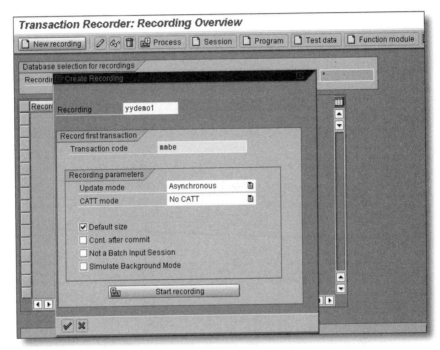

2 The transaction is being recorded now. If you have an IDES system available, you can use material T-T100 and plant 1000. Finish the transaction completely. Initially, click on ⊕ **(Execute)** to run the transaction.

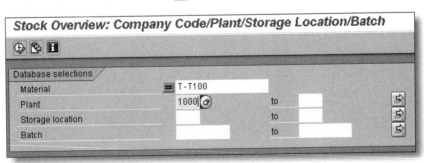

3 Exit the stock overview transaction by clicking the 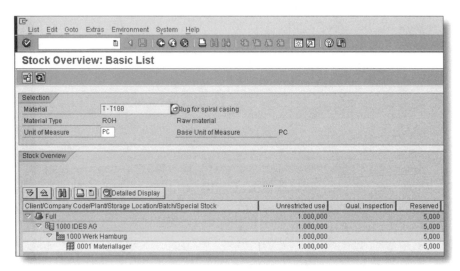 button (**Exit**).

4 The system displays a message informing you that the recording is complete. Confirm the message by clicking the **OK** button.

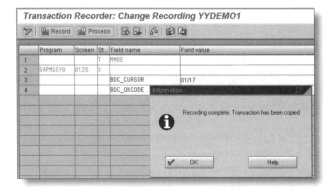

5 Click the 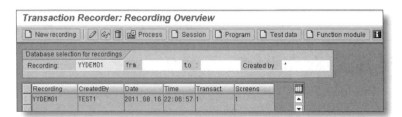 button (**Save**) to save the recording, and the **Process** button to test it. When you click the 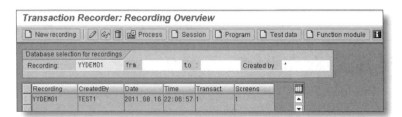 button (**Exit**), the system returns you to the recording overview. Your recording is now included in this list.

6 Select the recording, and then choose **Edit ▶ Create session**.

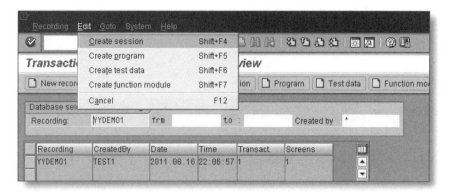

7 Enter a name for your new batch input session (here, YYDEMO1), and click the **Create** button.

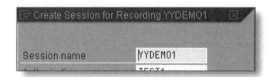

8 The batch input session was created successfully and can be started now. Select **System ▶ Services ▶ Batch Input ▶ Sessions** in the menu.

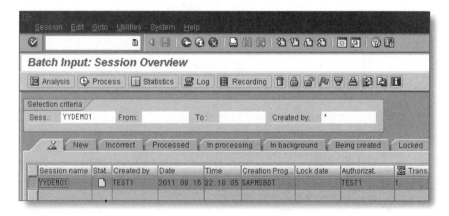

You can always test the session or create a new one at any time by starting the transaction recorder again.

Processing Batch Input Sessions

In this section, you learn how to process a batch input session. To go to the sessions defined in the SAP system and located in the session overview, proceed as follows:

1 Select **System ▶ Services ▶ Batch Input ▶ Sessions** in the menu.

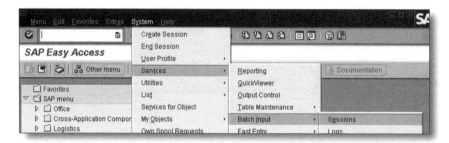

2 The batch input session overview is displayed. By clicking on ▦ you can select the row (and thus the desired session).

3 If the overview contains too many sessions, you can use the search option in the session overview to find the one you want. The **Selection Criteria** area provides various selection options for this purpose: In the **Session** field, enter the name of the session that you want to process. In the fields **From** and **To**, enter a point in time or a period of time for which you want to find sessions. With the **Created by** field, you can select the session of a specific person.

4 Check whether the selected session is marked as locked. If it is, you can unlock it by clicking on the 🔒 (**Unlock Session**) button or selecting the **Session ▶ Unlock** menu path.

5 You have the option to edit the batch input session in the session overview. The upcoming table shows how you can edit your session.

6 Select a processing mode. Processing modes for batch input sessions are listed in the following list. You can select the processing mode after you click on the **Process** button.

- **Process Foreground**: This mode displays interactions with the user and requires confirmation for individual screens. The user can intervene if an error occurs.

- **Background**: The system processes the batch input session in the background.

- **Display Errors Only**: If the batch input does not have any errors, then no user interaction is required.

7 Enter a target host in the **Target Host** field. Press the F4 function key to use the value help.

8 You can process the selected session by clicking on the **Process** button.

The following table gives an overview of the processing options available in the session overview.

Button	Function
Analysis	Analyze
Process	Process session
🔓	Unlock session
🚩	Release session
🗑	Delete session
🔒	Lock session
Log	Log

Processing Options of Batch Input Sessions

In this chapter, you learned how to work with background jobs, which can be used for recurring system tasks. You also learned how to control transactions in the process using batch input.

10.3   Try It!

Exercise 1

Give an example for when to use variants.

Exercise 2

How do you determine a report name?

Exercise 3

What's the difference between online and background processing?

Exercise 4

State three options for processing batch input sessions.

Exercise 5

Create a batch input session for displaying an evaluation on customer returns using Transaction MC+A (menu path: **Information systems ▸ Logistics ▸ Sales and Distribution ▸ Customer**).

11 Working with Messages and Business Workplace

The Business Workplace in the SAP system offers functions for efficient office communication to support your work. You can edit and manage documents, maintain calendars, and send short messages.

This chapter describes:

- How to send short messages in the SAP system
- How to use folders
- How to set up automatic replies
- How to use the calendar

11.1 Overview of the Business Workplace

The Business Workplace gives you a work environment within the SAP system that supports you with functions for managing messages, documents, and appointments. It is available to every SAP user, regardless of department.

The Business Workplace provides support for the following tasks:

- Creating workflows and editing work items
- Sending short messages
- Submitting documents
- Distributing and replying to received documents
- Creating, editing, and deleting documents
- Creating and editing folders
- Managing notes
- Using resubmission functions for documents
- Maintaining calendars
- Using out-of-office functions

This chapter introduces you to some of these functions. You can call the Business Workplace via the SAP Easy Access menu by following the **Office ▸ Workplace** path or by entering Transaction **SBWP** in the command field. The Business Workplace screen is divided into three areas:

- **Folders**

  The folders of your Business Workplace are displayed in a menu tree. You can call the contents by clicking on a folder.

- **Contents list**

  The contents of the folders (contained work items, documents, etc.) that are selected in the menu tree is displayed.

- **Preview**

  The preview displays the list entry that is selected in the contents list.

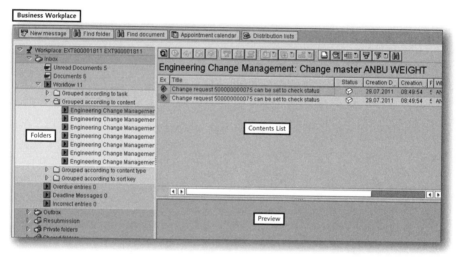

The Business Workplace

In the initial screen of the Business Workplace, you can directly use the functions that are listed in the table.

Button	Function
Neue Nachricht	Create and send a new message (⇧+F4)
Find folder	Search for a folder (⇧+F5)

Buttons in the Business Workplace

Button	Function
🗎 Find document	Search for a document with specific criteria (F5)
📅 Appointment calendar	Your calendar (⇧+F7)
📖 Distribution lists	Distribution lists (⇧+F8)

Buttons in the Business Workplace (Cont.)

In the next section you'll learn how you can send short messages in the SAP system.

11.2 Sending Short Messages

The SAP system lets you create and submit short messages. In fact, it is similar to an email system with extended functions. You can send messages to colleagues and receive messages from them. These short messages can be used within the SAP system but also on the Internet (though the latter requires appropriate server configuration). In addition, the SAP system can also send short messages to you (for example, to notify you that a specific action was performed in the background). In addition, you can direct the system to send this system information to another user. Via this message, the user can then directly navigate to the respective object in the SAP system.

EXAMPLE

Using Short Messages

You want to make an evaluation available to a colleague. Instead of exporting the evaluation and sending it as an attachment in an email, you can use a short message. You simply send a link to the object without having to export the evaluation and send it as an attachment. This way, you can make sure that the central data basis is accessed by your colleague and that you're not each using different statuses of data.

The message functions are part of the Business Workplace, but you don't have to call the Business Workplace to send a message.

Instead, follow these steps:

1 Select **System ▶ Short Message** in the menu line.

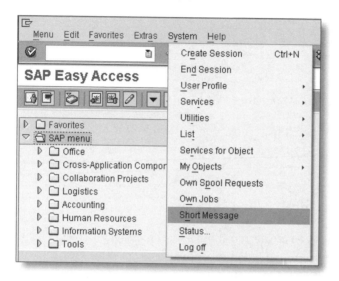

2 This opens a screen in which you can enter your short message. You have the following options:

– **Title**: Enter a subject line for your message as you would in any other email program. In our example, we entered "Sending a message from the SAP system."

– **Document Contents**: Enter your message text. The upcoming table explains the functions of the individual buttons.

– **Attachments**: If you want to add an attachment to your message, click the **Add Attachment** button 🗐 or press `Ctrl`+`⇧`+`F3`.

– **Recipient**: Enter the recipient of the short message by his user name. You can have the system search for the recipient by clicking the 🗗 button in the **Recipient** field, which gives you various search options. If you send the message to the user name, you don't have to specify a recipient type. The **Recipient** tab provides additional send options: Select the 🗷 checkbox **(Express Mail)** to have the system send the recipient a notification on his screen if he is logged on to the SAP system. Select the 🗐 checkbox **(Send as a Copy)** to send the message to other colleagues. If you activate the 🔒 checkbox **(Send as a Blind Copy)**, each recipient is hidden from all other recipients of the message.

- **Attributes**: Choose whether the document can be changed retroactively and forwarded to an external Internet address. You can also set the priority of the message (medium, high, or low).

- **Transfer Options**: Specify the date on which the document is supposed to be sent and whether the recipient can forward to others.

3 After entering values in all fields, you can submit the message by clicking on ☑ (Send).

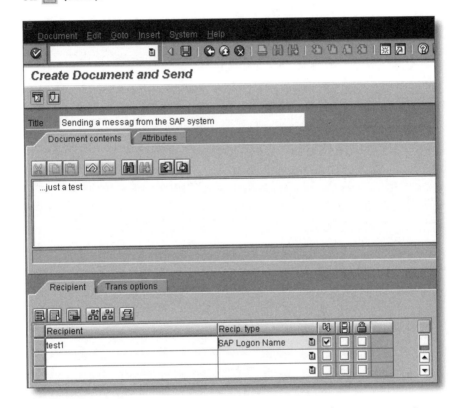

The following table lists the functions of the buttons on the **Document Contents** tab.

Button	Function
✂	Cut ($\boxed{\texttt{Ctrl}}$+$\boxed{\texttt{X}}$) selected text
🗎	Copy ($\boxed{\texttt{Ctrl}}$+$\boxed{\texttt{C}}$) selected text

Buttons on the "Document Contents" Tab

Button	Function
🖺	Insert ($\boxed{\text{Ctrl}}$+$\boxed{\text{V}}$) objects from the clipboard
🔄	Undo ($\boxed{\text{Ctrl}}$+$\boxed{\text{Z}}$) the last action
🔄	Restore ($\boxed{\text{Ctrl}}$+$\boxed{\text{Y}}$) deleted text
🔍	Find/replace ($\boxed{\text{Ctrl}}$+$\boxed{\text{F}}$) in the text
🔍	Find next ($\boxed{\text{Ctrl}}$+$\boxed{\text{G}}$)
📂	Load local file from PC
📄	Save as local file on PC

Buttons on the "Document Contents" Tab (Cont.)

11.3   SAP Business Workflow

SAP Business Workflow facilitates business processes. A workflow controls the flow of documents that are usually processed by several people and must be handled in a specific sequence. A workflow can include release or approval procedures but also complex processes, such as the creation of a master record that involves multiple departments. Workflows can also be started automatically when predefined events occur (for example, when an error is detected in a process).

EXAMPLE

Usage Options of SAP Business Workflow

A team lead assigns a task (creating a master record) to an employee. When the employee accepts the task with a workflow object, the team lead can track the processing status via the Business Workplace.

The Business Workplace provides an overview of all the activities that you have to carry out for the workflow. You can perform your tasks from the Business Workplace. The figure shows three screen areas which are used when workflows are processed.

At the top right in the Business Workplace, you can see the worklist. At the bottom right, the preview displays a work item (an object that represents a task or an action of the workflow) that is selected in the worklist.

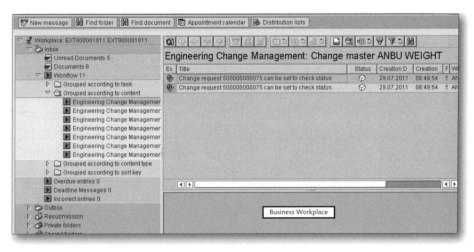

Workflow in the Business Workplace

11.4   Folders

Folders help you manage your documents and messages and organize group-specific objects. You can even link archiving systems and integrate third-party software if the provider offers software that can be licensed for SAP systems.

The Business Workplace provides several work environments to process documents and messages. To view the contents of a work environment, click on the required work environment in the folder tree; the system will display the corresponding folder content list.

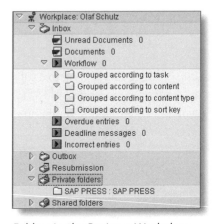

Folders in the Business Workplace

The work environments are mapped through the following buttons:

Button	Work Environment	Function
	Inbox	Contains all documents and resubmissions you've received.
	Outbox	Contains all documents sent by you.
	Resubmission	Contains documents that are resubmitted to your inbox on a defined date.
	Private folders	Here you can manage documents and messages in a folder structure that you've created for your own use.
	Shared folders	You can store group-specific or cross-enterprise documents and messages in these folders.
	Subscribed folders	Contains all folders you subscribe to.
	Trash	Temporarily contains all deleted folders, documents, and messages.

Work Environments in the Business Workplace

By right-clicking on the **Private Folders** object, you can create subfolders for your personal document administration so you can manage your documents and messages individually.

11.5   Office Organization

Office organization functions include automatic message forwarding to a substitute, resubmissions, automatic replies to the sender of a message, and a calendar. The following sections describe how you set up automatic replies and use the calendar functions.

Setting Up Auto Reply

You can use the Business Workplace to instruct the SAP system to reply automatically to incoming messages (auto reply). This function is useful if you want to automatically inform people who send you messages that you are absent from the office. Take the following steps:

1 In the Business Workplace, select **Settings ▶ Office Settings** in the menu. The **Automatic Reply** tab lets you define the activation period (start date and end date). With the **To** and **From** fields, you specify how long to enable the setting for automatic activation.

2 In the **Title** field of the **Document** area, enter the text for your subject line of the automatic reply.

3 In the text field, enter the message text.

4 After making these settings, press ⏎ or click ✔ (**Next**) to save the settings.

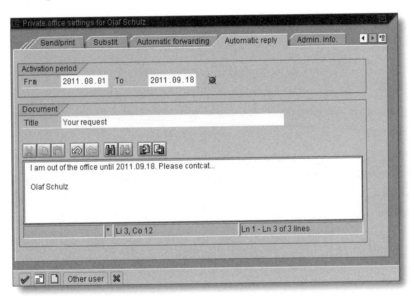

Managing Appointments

The Business Workplace also provides a calendar for your private and business appointments.

To create an entry in the calendar, carry out the following steps:

1 Start the appointment calendar by clicking on the **Appointment Calendar** button in the Business Workplace or via the **Environment ▶ Private Calendar** menu. (Alternatively, you can use the key combination ⇧+F7.) There, you have the following options:

- To adjust personal settings—for example, the presentation of the days of the week or time intervals on your calendar—click on 🖼 (Settings).

- To change the view of the current day (daily view) click on [📅Today].

- To change the view of the current week (weekly view) click on [📅Current week].

2 Choose 🗋 (Create Appointment) to create a new calendar entry.

3 A dialog window opens for the title, time frame, and notes about the appointment. When you're done, click on ✔ (Next), or press the [↵] key.

This chapter described how you can use the Business Workplace in the SAP system to send messages as well as manage documents and appointments. Chapter 12 introduces you to the wide range of help functions within the SAP system.

11.6   Try It!

Exercise 1

If you want to send a message to yourself or a colleague via the SAP system, how do you proceed?

Exercise 2

Name one real-life example of a workflow that is implemented in your business.

12 Using Help Functions

If you come to a dead end as you work in the SAP system, there are several places where you can find information that will help you. This chapter presents the various help functions of the SAP system, focusing on the ones that you can call via the F1 and F4 function keys and by using the help menu in the menu bar.

This chapter discusses:

- Getting field help via the F1 function key
- Getting input help via the F4 function key
- Information found in the help menu
- SAP library and glossary data
- The information content of the release notes
- Using the SAP Service Marketplace
- Customizing the help functions

12.1 Field Helps and Search Windows

Help is available in the SAP system. If you get stuck, you can call a field help or an input help (an overview of the entries that are expected or accepted by the system). You can also use search windows. The following sections introduce you to these options.

Help via the F1 and F4 Function Keys

If you need information on a certain field in the SAP system, you can use field help and input help (value help):

- **Field help**

  The field help, which you call using the ⬚F1⬚ function key, provides a general description of the field on which the cursor is currently placed.

- **Input help**

  If you press the ⬚F4⬚ function key, the system opens a list of the possible input values for the field on which the cursor is currently placed. You can enter the value using the keyboard or copy the required value by double-clicking on the field.

> **NOTE**
>
> **Cursor Placement**
>
> The field and input help always refer to the field on which the cursor is currently placed.

The ⬚F1⬚ and ⬚F4⬚ helps are cross-system standard functions, so you cannot assign other function codes to them.

In the example shown in the figure you're running the **Maintain User Profile** (Transaction SU3). The cursor is positioned in the **First Name** field. If you press the ⬚F1⬚ function key now, the system displays general information on the **First Name** field. Because the information in the help can be very detailed, you can scroll down in the help window to see more.

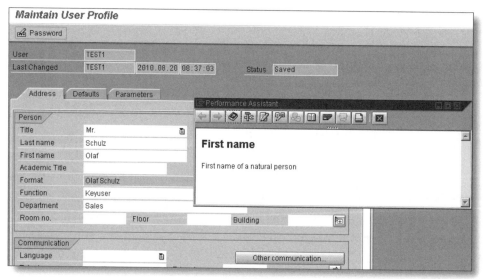

Input Help Using the F1 Key

In the example shown in the next figure, you're on the same tab as in the previous example of the F1 help. Again, position the cursor in the **First Name** field, but display the possible input values by pressing F4. You can copy the required value from the list displayed by double-clicking on it.

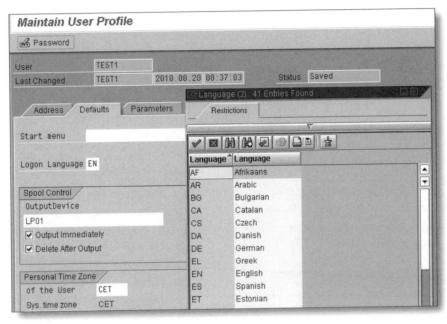

Input Help Using the F4 Key

Not every field has an input help. The next section describes how you can still determine the required value in these cases.

Search Windows

The field type determines whether a list of possible input values is available. If no input help is available, you can determine a value using search windows. Press F4 to open the search window.

In the following example, the system displays the initial screen of Transaction MM03 (Change Material). The cursor is in the **Material** field. Press F4 to open the search window. The search window now lets you search for the material based on several criteria.

Search Window for a Field

In this example, we want to find a specific slug but don't know the exact material description. You can use search patterns even if you know only a part of the search term. When working with search patterns, you define a pattern—that is, a character string—with which the required value can be identified in the SAP system. The pattern can contain both characters and digits and can be of any length. It can also contain various meta characters (such as + and *). The following table lists some examples of search patterns.

Search Pattern	Result
Slug 4711	Searches exactly for "Slug 4711".
Slug*	Outputs all hits that start with "slug".
ug	Outputs all hits that contain the "ug" character string, irrespective of the character strings before or after it.
+lug 4711	Outputs all hits that start with any character but then contain "lug 4711".

Examples of Search Patterns

12.2   The Help Menu

The **Help** menu in the menu bar provides additional support options and includes a wide range of information sources:

- Application help
- SAP library

- Glossary
- Release notes
- SAP Service Marketplace
- An option for creating support messages
- An option to customize the help (**Settings**)

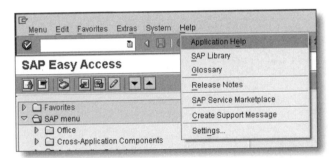

Options in the Help Menu

The following sections describe those options provided in the help menu.

Application Help

Application help offers the user context-sensitive help, or help that is executed based on the transaction the user is running. "Context-sensitive" means that the system doesn't display a general help but instead help topics that refer to the specific transaction or business process that is currently used.

SAP Library

The SAP library provides the entire documentation of the SAP system. Directly after logging on to the SAP system, you can use the menu bar to navigate to this documentation via the **Help ▶ SAP Library** path. Here you'll find instructions for operating the SAP system and for using individual components' functions. In the SAP library, you can navigate through a tree structure that is similar to the SAP Easy Access menu.

> **NOTE**
>
> **SAP Documentation—the SAP Help Portal**
>
> The SAP documentation is available on CD-ROM. Users with a web browser (such as Internet Explorer) also have free online access to the documentation via the URL *http://help.sap.com*.

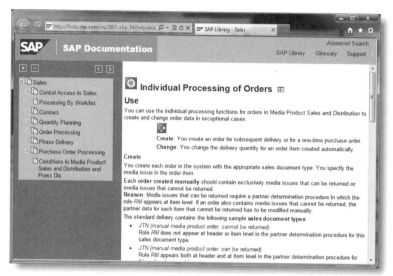

SAP Library

Glossary

The glossary lists and explains alphabetized technical concepts of the SAP world. You can access, search, and navigate the glossary via the **Help ▸ Glossary** path. Because the meaning and use of some concepts differs in various business departments, some keywords have multiple entries. The abbreviation of the respective SAP component is indicated in parentheses. You can navigate using the index and a full-text search.

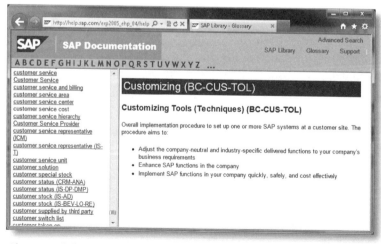

Glossary of the SAP Library

Release Notes

Release notes contain the release version of the used SAP system. Through release notes you can learn which updates have been installed and which functions have changed since the previous release.

To call the release notes, select **Help ▶ Release Notes** in the menu bar. The information is sorted by components.

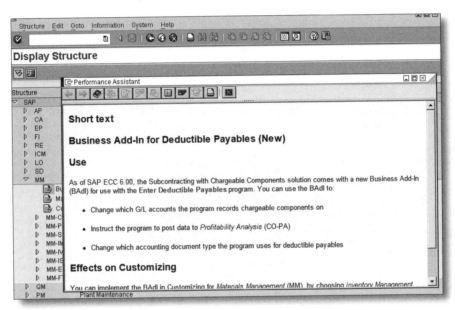

Release Notes

SAP Service Marketplace

The SAP Service Marketplace provides SAP customers, partners, and interested parties with additional information via an Internet portal. This includes:

- **SAP Support Portal**
  This portal supports all SAP Business Suite solutions (for example, customer messages and SAP notes, which require an account—that is, a user name and password).

- **SAP Help Portal**
  The SAP Help Portal provides web-based documentation on all SAP solutions in the SAP library. This offer is available to all Internet users free of charge at *http://help.sap.com/*.

■ **SAP Community Network**
The URL *http://www.sdn.sap.com* takes you to the SAP Community and SAP Developer Network, which is a social network for SAP experts and developers. The information is provided in English only and tends to be rather technical.

You can access the SAP Service Marketplace on the Internet via the URL *www.service.sap.com*. Though some areas can be accessed by anybody with an Internet connection, many of areas require a user name and password to enter. You can also navigate to the marketplace portal in the Internet via the **Help ▸ SAP Service Marketplace** menu item.

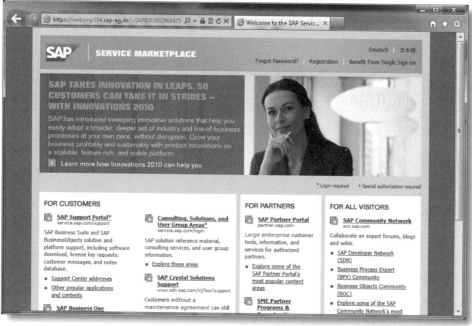

SAP Service Marketplace

Creating Support Messages

If an error occurs while you are using a transaction, you can create an error message using the **Help ▸ Create Support Message** path in the menu bar. The message is then forwarded directly to your business' support team (SAP Competence Center). The team will either solve the problem or forward it to someone else, and then provide feedback.

12.3   Customizing the Help

You can customize the help. The **Help ▶ Settings** path in the menu bar lets you choose how help windows are displayed.

You can view the predefined settings on the **F4 Help** tab in the **System Defaults** area, and adjust them in the **User-Specific Settings** and **Display** areas. You can command the system not to display the personal value list when you call the input help (**Do Not Display Pers. Value List Automatically** checkbox) and, if the search results in only one hit, whether this hit is directly displayed in the corresponding field and not in a hit list (**Only Return Value Directly if only one hit** checkbox). You can also specify how many hits a list of the input help is supposed to display. In the **Display** area, you can determine the display type of the hit list: If you select the **Control (Amodal)** radio button (the more recent display format) or **Dialog (modal)**, the hit list is displayed in the Performance Assistant or as a dialog box.

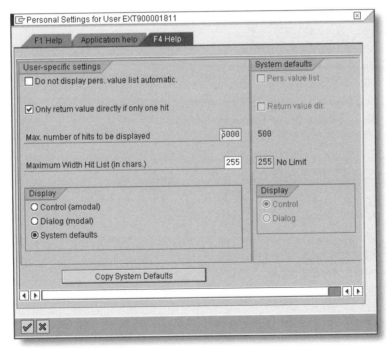

Help Settings—"F4 Help" Tab

On the **F1 Help** tab, you can choose whether the help is displayed as a search help control in the Performance Assistant or in a dialog box (modal window).

For this purpose, select the **in Performance Assistant** or **in Modal Window** radio button in the **Display** area. The result is shown in the following two figures.

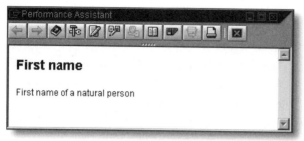

Help in the Performance Assistant (Control)

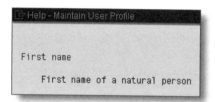

Help in a Model Window (Dialog Box)

The **Application help** tab lets you define whether you want to access the Internet help or the CD-ROM in the business network.

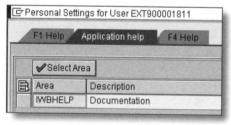

"Application Help" Tab

12.4 Try It!

Exercise 1

Start Transaction MM03 (Display Material) in the SAP Easy Access menu via the menu path: **Logistics ▶ Sales and Distribution ▶ Master Data ▶ Products ▶ Material ▶ Trading Goods**.

- If you want the system to display general information on the **Material** field, how do you proceed?

- Make use of the search window. Search for the `slug*` material description, and have the system display the material (select the **Basic Data 1** tab, and click the **Next** button). How many hits do you get?

- Position the cursor in the **Base Unit of Measure** field, and tell the system to display the list of possible base units of measure. How many base units of measure does the system display?

- What do you do to have the system display the help for the transaction you're currently working with?

Exercise 2

How can you effectively create a support message in a live environment?

Exercise 3

Which menu items do all SAP screens display?

Exercise 4

What is the SAP Service Marketplace?

Exercise 5

You are an SAP user and want work with the SAP system over the weekend. Unfortunately, you cannot access the business network. What options do you have for getting information on the system?

13   The Role and Authorization Concept

This chapter provides an overview of the roles and authorizations in SAP systems. An authorization concept in the SAP system protects functions and data against unauthorized access.

This chapter explains:

- What authorizations are
- The tasks of an authorization concept
- What a role concept looks like

13.1   Authorizations

In general, authorization gives you permission to do something. With regard to IT systems, *authorization* means that a specific user (or the corresponding user name in the system) is allowed to view (read) and change (write) specific data and use specific functions and transactions. So SAP authorizations control access to certain functions and data in the SAP system.

Every employee in a business has specific tasks assigned to his position. As the employee of a business in the SAP system, you receive the authorizations that are necessary for your tasks. If the authorizations are insufficient, then the tasks cannot be completed, but if the authorizations are unrestricted, then the user can access data that is outside his level of expertise. Consequently, authorizations should be as restrictive as possible; the users and the business are better protected when there are occasionally too few authorizations than if there are too many. In addition to user identities that correspond to specific employees, sometimes the implementation of certain programs requires authorization for technical users.

13

Authorizations in the SAP system restrict access to the following objects:

- Organizational units
- Transactions/programs
- Database tables

The assignment of authorizations is based on a business's authorization concept, which has both business and technical dimensions. The authorization concept defines how authorizations are assigned and checked in the SAP system. On the business side, it specifies a company's business processes and the necessary tasks associated with them.

The authorization concept must cover requirements that arise from various legal principles (for example, Generally Accepted Accounting Principles and data protection law).

> **INFO**
>
> **Separation of Duties**
>
> Certain tasks or functions should always be carried out by different people in order to avoid committing criminal offenses. For example, if the same employee can both maintain vendors in the SAP system and also trigger payments, then he could embezzle funds by creating fictitious vendors and paying fictitious invoices from which he benefits.

On the technical side, the authorization concept defines how authorizations are set up and checked.

These authorizations are controlled by authorization objects, which are defined in Customizing. An authorization object (for example, a transaction or a resource) consists of the individual authorization fields that define the authorizations in the SAP system.

You then assign the authorizations to users using something known as roles, which are discussed in the next section.

13.2   Roles

SAP uses a role-based authorization concept, which means that roles are assigned to employees. A role combines the authorizations that are assigned to users or groups of users to affect certain parts of a business process.

The following figure illustrates the essential objects of the authorization concept.

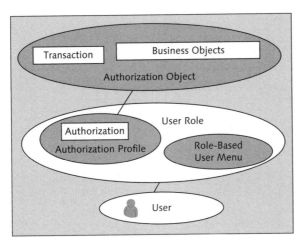

Overview of the Authorization Concept

Here is an example of the usage of the authorization concept: User "Lisa S." logs on to the SAP system using her user name and password. She works in Accounts Payable Accounting and is responsible for posting outgoing payments. After a successful logon, Lisa is assigned a user role, and has been authorized for the transactions and objects (organizational structures) for which she is responsible. The SAP Easy Access menu in which Lisa navigates is tailored to her user role and contains all transactions that she needs for her task area. These authorizations are combined in an authorization profile that is assigned to her role.

From the technical view, authorizations release access to objects in the SAP system. From the business view, roles define the process-oriented assignment of tasks.

A role is a package of executable transactions, reports, and other functions that are usually combined in a menu. When you assign a role in combination with an object (for example, an organizational unit) to a user, you determine that this person is authorized to perform the role-specific tasks for the respective object. It is important that the SAP administration has first created and enabled the roles, and that the business's organizational structure is maintained. Assigning and maintaining roles and authorizations is carried out by those people that have the corresponding authorization (the SAP administration).

13

The following table lists some examples of roles.

User	Role	Transaction	Authorizations
Karl B.	REPRUE	MIRO	Invoice verification
Lisa S.	BH_KREDITOREN	FB60	Posting invoices

Examples of Roles

If you want to know which roles a user has, you can have the system display his role assignment via Transaction SU01. Take the following steps:

1 Start the user maintenance by entering the Transaction SU01 in the command field. The system displays the initial screen of the user maintenance.

2 Enter his user name in the **User** field, and click ⟨⟩ (**Display**).

3 The **Groups** tab displays the **User** group that is assigned to the user (in this case, his logon name).

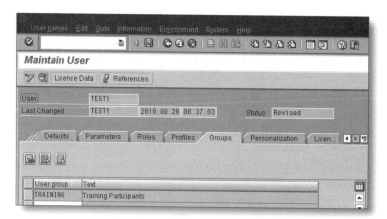

In this chapter you learned about the basic characteristics of the authorization concept. As a user, you have limited influence on the control of authorizations because they are maintained and monitored by the administration. However, knowing that roles and authorizations exist and how they function is critical to understanding why you cannot change or view certain transactions and data in the SAP system.

13.3   Try It!

Exercise 1

Describe the SAP role concept.

Exercise 2

Your colleague wants to change a customer master record. How would you explain to him why he can view but not change the master record?

13

The Most Critical SAP Components

14 Materials Management

Materials management is at the beginning of the supply chain. It ensures that the materials and services needed by the business are available at the right time and place, and procured from the best vendor at a reasonable price. This chapter provides an overview of the Materials Management component in SAP ERP (which we'll refer to as SAP MM).

In this chapter you will learn:

- The tasks of materials management

- Which organizational units are used in purchasing

- How to create material vendor master records and purchasing info records

- How to create a purchase order

- How to perform inventory management and invoice verification

- Which evaluations can be used in the standard version

14

14.1 Materials Management Task Areas

The goal of the purchasing department is to provide the business with the goods and services that its business processes require but that cannot be produced in-house. Additional strategic tasks fall into this area; purchasing in particular is increasingly significant, since it is an area in which high costs arise and thus major savings potential exists.

INFO

Purchasing or Procurement?

The concepts of *purchasing* and *procurement* are often used synonymously. If you were to differentiate between the two, procurement would refer to strategic purchasing that determines the procurement strategies, is responsible for vendor selection and evaluation, conducts market research, and negotiates long-term agreements. Operative purchasing is responsible for the actual purchase orders.

However, purchasing and procurement cannot be separated entirely because materials can also be procured internally. In this book, we will use the term purchasing for the sake of simplicity.

The next section gives an overview of the basic purchasing process (that is, the purchase order, goods receipt, and invoice verification) before discussing purchasing in the SAP system in more detail. Frequently, a purchase requisition triggers a corresponding purchase order.

INFO

Purchase Requisition

A user department issues a purchase requisition (PReq, for short) to notify purchasing of a material or service requirement it has. The requisition does not constitute a purchase order yet, since it only triggers the purchase order. Usually, the members of a user department deploy an online form, which is forwarded to purchasing. The PReq must be released by the cost center manager, depending on the costs and the relevant business guidelines.

At least three different departments are involved in this process: the purchasing department, the goods receiving department, and invoice verification, which, in some enterprises, is not performed by purchasing but by accounts payable accounting.

Basic Purchasing Process

You can further subdivide the purchasing process into the following phases:

1 Demand determination

Demand determination is the starting point. A user department can inform purchasing about demand for a material or enter a PReq (Transaction ME51N) in the system. This document is then transferred to the purchasing department. The demand determination can even be done by the SAP system in a process called automatic material requirements planning.

Automatic Material Requirements Planning

Automatic material requirements planning is responsible for punctual and accurate goods procurement. In this process, the focus is on optimal order scheduling, demand determination, and on-time requirements planning. The benefit is less capital commitment, shorter lead times, higher on-time delivery performance, and more flexibility in production.

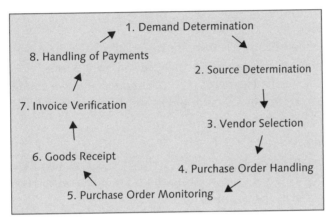

Advanced Purchasing Cycle

2   Source determination

It can make sense to take previous purchase orders into account when selecting a vendor (that is, a source). Before you decide on a new source, make sure that there are no suitable sources already available for the requirement. The source can be determined automatically in the SAP system.

3   Vendor selection

The vendor selection requires the user to obtain and compare different quotations from vendors, and choose the most favorable one.

4   Purchase order handling

The actual purchase order is handled in the next step, in which you determine the quantities, dates, and locations of the delivery, and transfer these to the vendor in a purchase order. A written purchase order gives legal weight to the framework conditions.

5   Purchase order monitoring

The purchase order can also be used for documentation within the business. Because several departments (the requesting department, purchas-

14

ing, and the goods receiving department) are involved in the process, the entire purchase order history can be reproduced.

6 **Goods receipt**

In this step, the person responsible refers to the purchase order as the preceding document. The quantity and quality of the goods are checked. Then the delivered goods are posted in specific stock types (for example, unrestricted-use stock or quality control). In accounting, the warehouse stock is increased.

7 **Invoice verification**

The last step of the purchasing cycle from the materials management perspective involves invoice verification. The invoice verification usually requires preceding documents like purchase order and material document from goods receipt. Again, the content, price, and figures are checked against the vendor invoice for accuracy.

8 **Handling of payments**

The handling of payments is responsible for clearing vendor invoices. However, this step is assigned to accounting and is no longer within the responsibility of materials management.

In SAP ERP, purchasing is implemented in the Materials Management component. SAP MM, in turn, consists of the following subcomponents:

- **Purchasing**
  The most extensive part of MM undertakes the tasks of stock determination, source determination, purchase order, and monitoring goods delivery (phases 1 to 5 in the process).

- **Inventory Management**
  This MM component deals with the quantity-based and value-based management of material stocks, the management of goods movements, and the implementation of inventory. These tasks are included in phase 6 of the process presented.

- **Invoice Verification**
  The MM component (phase 7) supports the completion of the purchasing process by checking the vendor invoice.

The three areas of the basic purchasing process are discussed in more detail in this chapter. Let's first take a look at the organizational structures that are relevant for materials management in the SAP system.

14.2   Organizational Structures

You can use organizational units to map an enterprise in the system. These units are defined in Customizing and are assigned to the corresponding tables; both client and company code are relevant for all SAP components.

- **Client**
  The client forms a unit that is closed in terms of commercial law and organization, or represents a corporate group or head office. Master data and tables are assigned to the client in the system. You must enter the three-digit numeric key of the client when you log on to the SAP system.

- **Company code**
  The company code is an organizational unit of external accounting (see Chapter 16, Financial Accounting) and maps a self-contained accounting in the SAP system. All commercial law-related events, including the business's profit and loss, are implemented at the company code level. The key of the company code is unique to a client.

- **Plant**
  The plant is a central organizational unit of logistics. Using a plant, you can map a business's production location, headquarters, central warehouse, or sales office. In the system, the plant is assigned to exactly one company code. The value-based inventory management of materials is done at the plant level.

- **Storage location**
  The quantity-based inventory management of different stock types is done at the storage location level. A storage location is assigned to a plant.

- **Purchasing organization**
  The purchasing organization is an organizational unit of purchasing. It is assigned to at most one company code, and always to the plant it procures for. For this reason, central purchasing is *not* assigned to a company code.

- **Purchasing group**
  A purchasing group combines a group of purchasers, and is not assigned to any other organizational units in the SAP system.

The following figure shows an example of a purchasing organizational structure.

14

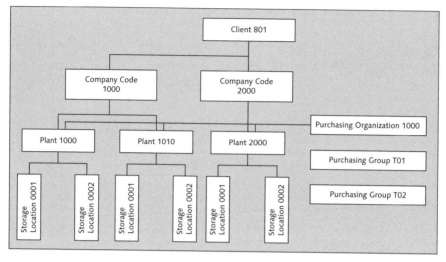

Example of an Organizational Structure in Central Purchasing (Purchasing Organization 1000)

14.3 Master Data

Master data is data that is stored in the system for a long time and is available to all authorized users and applications. The most important master data in SAP MM includes:

- Material master
- Vendor master
- Purchasing info records

The following section describes how to create this master data so that you can comprehend its relevance in the SAP system.

Material Master

A material master record contains various pieces of information arranged in different tabs (views). These are assigned to the user departments that work with the material master (such as purchasing or accounting). In production systems, authorization roles (see Chapter 13) control which users receive read or write access to which view, or whether this view is displayed to the users at all. The material master record is relevant not only for materials management, but also to the sales and quality management business processes. The following table lists examples of the role that the material master record plays for the areas indicated.

SAP Component	Usage
Any component	Material number, short description, weights, dimensions, and plant
MM	Material group, purchasing group, automatic purchase order, and goods receipt processing time
FI	Internal material evaluation (effect on financial statements), price control, and moving average price or standard price
SD	Procurement times
QM	Inspection settings and posting in inspection stock

Usage of Material Master Records in SAP ERP

> **INFO**
>
> **Material and Article**
>
> Instead of using the term *article*, SAP ERP uses *material*. In the industry business solution SAP for Retail, however, the common term *article* is used.

14

To create a material, proceed as follows:

1 Call Transaction MM01 via the command field or in the SAP Easy Access menu via the **Logistics ▸ Materials Management ▸ Material Master ▸ Create (General)** path.

2 In the initial screen of the transaction, enter the material (here, ZM-DEMO-01), industry sector (here, mechanical engineering), and material type (here, raw material) in the corresponding fields. Press the ↵ key.

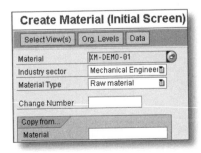

3 Select the tabs that are relevant for you in the view selection pane that opens. Choose the views **Basic Data 1**, **Purchasing**, and **Accounting 1**. To predefine this selection for the next time, click on the **Default Values** button. Press the ⏎ key.

4 The other views, such as **MRP** or **Quality Management**, are relevant if the system is supposed to plan the material automatically or procure it with quality assurance. In this example, you create the material so that external procurement (purchasing) is possible.

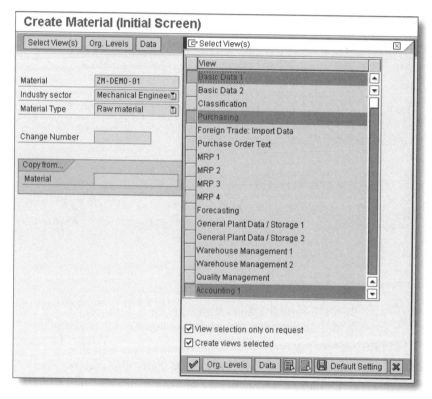

5 In the next step, specify the plant in which the new material is to be kept. For this example, enter 1000, and then press the ⏎ key.

6 In the next step, define the material name, base unit of measure, gross weight, and weight unit in the **Basic Data** 1 tab. If you want to reproduce this example in the SAP system, enter the following data:

– **Material**: Cooling element

– **Base Unit of Measure**: PC

– **Material group**: 00103

– **Gross Weight**: 0.5

– **Net Weight**: 0.3

– **Weight Unit**: KG

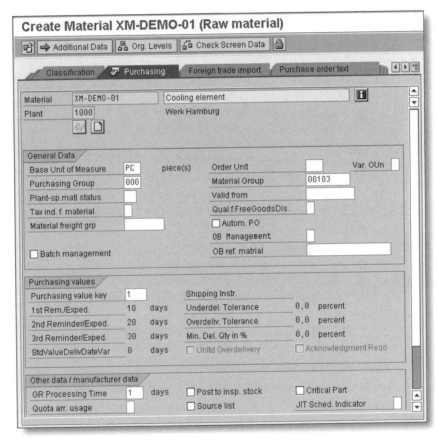

7 Click on the **Purchasing** tab. Enter the purchasing group, purchasing value key, and goods receipt processing time (known as the GR processing time). The following data is used for this example:

- Purchasing group: 000
- Purchasing value key: 1
- GR processing time: 1

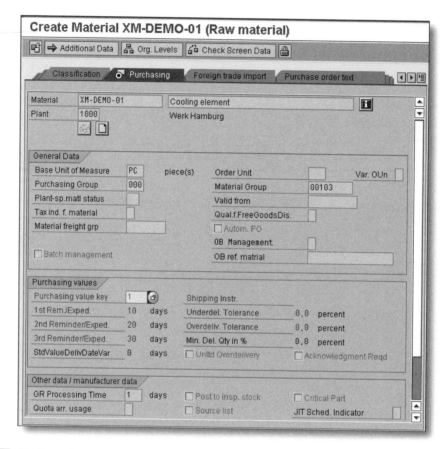

8 Click on the **Accounting 1** tab. Enter the valuation class, price control, and moving average price. Use the following data for this example:

- **Valuation class**: 3000 (relevant for controlling G/L accounts, which are updated in cases of goods movement)
- **Price Control**: V (moving average price for internal material valuation)
- **Moving Price**: 10 EUR

9 You have filled in all fields relevant for the material and can now save the new master record by clicking the **Save** button (🖫). The system displays a message informing you that the new material was created in the system: "Material ZM-DEMO-01 is created."

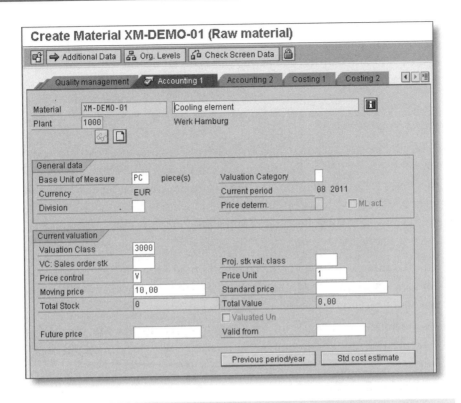

Create Material XM-DEMO-01 (Raw material)

⇒ Additional Data   Org. Levels   Check Screen Data

Quality management   Accounting 1   Accounting 2   Costing 1   Costing 2

Material   XM-DEMO-01   Cooling element

Plant   1000   Werk Hamburg

General data

Base Unit of Measure	PC piece(s)	Valuation Category
Currency	EUR	Current period 08 2011
Division	.	Price determ. ☐ ML act.

Current valuation

Valuation Class	3000	
VC: Sales order stk		Proj. stk val. class
Price control	V	Price Unit 1
Moving price	10,00	Standard price
Total Stock	0	Total Value 0,00
		☐ Valuated Un
Future price		Valid from

Previous period/year   Std cost estimate

INFO

Moving Average Price

The moving average price (MAP, for short) is used for inventory valuation for materials that were purchased at different prices. An average price is calculated from the moving average. An inventory management that uses the historic prices at which the materials were actually purchased would be unnecessarily complex.

14

Action	Moving Average Price
Creation of a master record	–
Purchasing: 10 pieces, 10 $ each	(10 pieces × $10) / 10 pieces total stock = **$10**
Purchasing: 10 pieces, 20 $ each	(10 pieces × $10) + (10 pieces × $20) / 20 pieces total stock = **$15**

Example of Calculating the Moving Average Price

More information is available in *Materials Management with SAP ERP: Functionality and Technical Configuration*, by Martin Murray (2011), which is published by SAP PRESS. After discussing the material master, let's move on to the vendor master.

Vendor Master

The vendor master record in the SAP system contains information on the business' vendors. Beside the name and address of the vendor, the vendor master record also includes information on currencies, payment terms, and contact persons. The information on vendors is used not only in SAP MM, but also in SAP FI. The following section shows how to create a vendor master record in the SAP system.

1 Start Transaction XK01 via the command field or in the SAP Easy Access menu path: **Logistics ▸ Materials Management ▸ Purchasing ▸ Master Data ▸ Vendor ▸ Central ▸ Create**.

2 In the initial screen, enter the vendor number, company code, purchasing organization, and the account group. Use the following data in this example:

- **Vendor:** ZK-DEMO-01
- **Company Code:** 1000
- **Purchasing organization:** 1000
- **Account Group:** ZTMM

3 Press the ⏎ key.

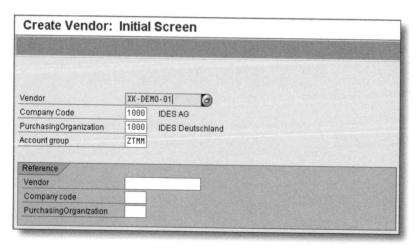

4 In the next screen, enter the title, name, address, and language. Use the following data for this example:

– **Name:** Mechanical Engineering Consulting

– **Search Term:** DEMO

– **Street, House Number:** West Park 4712

– **Postal Code, City:** 90449 Nuremberg

– **Country:** Germany

– **Region:** 09

– **Language:** English

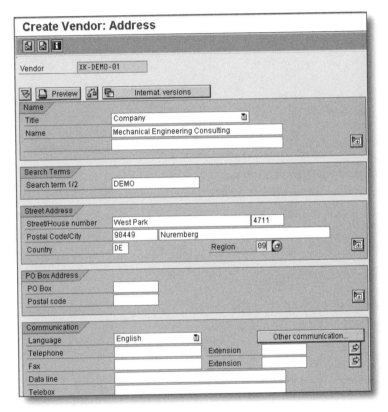

5 Select the button to navigate to the **Accounting Information Accounting** screen. Enter the following information:

– **Reconciliation account:** 160000

– **Data Screen:** Payment Transactions Accounting

– **Payment Terms:** 0002

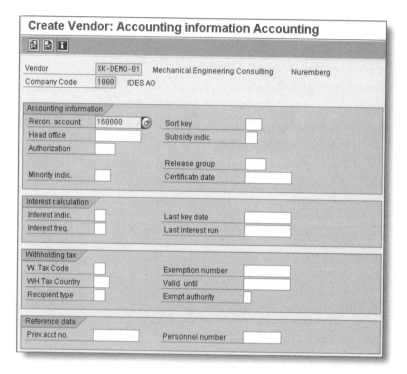

6 Navigate to the **Payment Transactions Accounting** screen via the 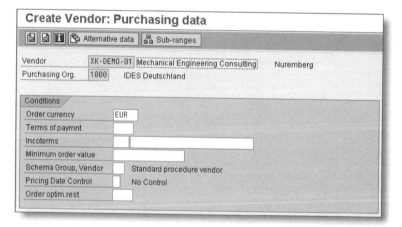 button. Enter the terms of payment here.

7 Save the vendor master record by clicking the **Save** button (🖫). The system displays a success message (here, "Vendor ZK-DEMO-01 was created
for company code 1000 and purchasing organization 1000").

The next section presents the third important master record in SAP MM: the purchasing information record.

Purchasing Information Record

The purchasing information record (or simply information record) connects a vendor master record and a material master record so you can procure a specific material from different vendors with different conditions.

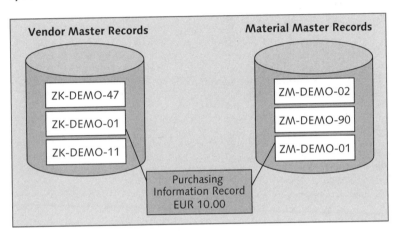

Purchasing Information Record

You can create an information record either manually or automatically in the SAP system. If you define a price in the information record, it will be proposed in the next purchase order. If the purchaser agrees on a new price with the vendor and changes it in the existing purchase order, the new price will be proposed in the next purchase order. The information record is an important source of information for purchasing.

So far, you've already defined a material and a vendor in the system. Now create an information record for this combination by doing the following:

1. An information record can be created via Transaction ME11. Start Transaction ME11 via the command field or in the SAP Easy Access menu via the **Logistics ▸ Materials Management ▸ Purchasing ▸ Master Data ▸ Info Record ▸ Create** path.

2. In the initial screen of the transaction, enter the vendor, material, and purchasing organization. Also enter the path here because different conditions may apply in another plant. Use the following data in this example:

- **Vendor:** ZK-DEMO-01
- **Material:** ZM-DEMO-01
- **Purchasing organization:** 1000
- **Plant:** 1000

3 Press the ⏎ key.

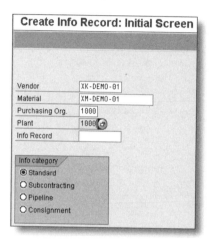

4 The system takes you to the general data from the initial screen. In this example, you don't have to enter any information in the general data. Click on **Purchasing Organization Data 1**.

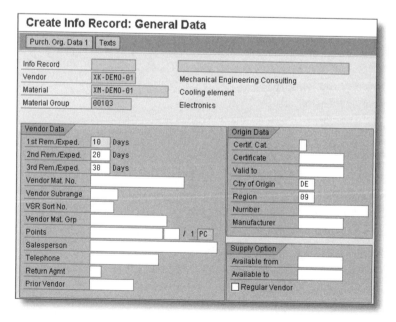

5 Specify the planned delivery time, purchasing group, standard quantity, and net price in the **Purchasing Organization Data** 1 screen. Enter the following data for this purpose:

- **Planned delivery time**: 1 day
- **Purchasing group**: 000
- **Standard Quantity**: 1 PC
- **Net Price**: 10.00 EUR

6 Click on the **Save** button (🖫) to save your entries.

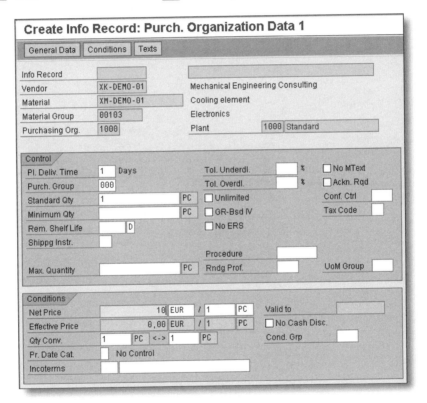

7 The system saves the information record and displays the following message: "Purchasing information record 5300006151 1000 1000 has been added."

With the master data, you've now formed the basis for the purchasing process, which you can reproduce in the next step using your own data.

14.4 Purchase Order

With a purchase order, you request a vendor to deliver a material or service based on the agreed conditions.

The purchasing process may differ depending on whether you want to purchase stock material or consumable material. Stock material is used to restock the business's inventory stock, whereas consumable material is used directly. Stock and consumable material are handled differently in the SAP system, as is indicated in the following table:

	Stock Material	Consumable Material
Input of material number	Mandatory	Optional
Account assignment group	–	Mandatory
Goods receipt	Mandatory	Optional
Posting	Material stock account	Consumption account
Update	Quantity and value in the material master, adjustment of the moving average price	No value update, update of quantity and consumption possible

Differences Between Stock and Consumable Material

This section uses an example to show how to order a stock material.

In the SAP system, you can find the transaction for the purchase order in the SAP Easy Access menu under **Logistics ▶ Materials Management ▶ Purchasing ▶ Purchase Order ▶ Create ▶ Vendor/Delivering Plant Known**. The transaction codes are ME21N (Create Purchase Order), ME22N (Change Purchase Order), and ME23N (Display Purchase Order). The transaction for creating a purchase order is subdivided into various areas (see the next figure).

You can create a purchase order with a reference to the purchase requisition (PReq, Transaction ME51N) or without a reference, like in this example.

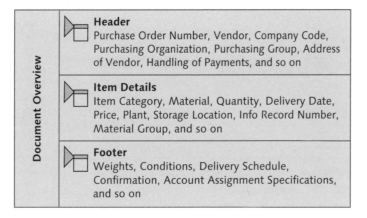

Purchase Order Structure

The following step-by-step example teaches you how you can order a stock material without creating a purchase requisition in advance. In this example, you use the master records you created at the beginning of this chapter. Proceed as follows:

1 Start Transaction ME21N in the command field or in the SAP Easy Access menu via the **Logistics ▸ Materials Management ▸ Purchasing ▸ Purchase Order ▸ Create ▸ Vendor/Delivering Plant Known** path.

2 You can show and hide the screen areas of the purchase order using the **Show/Hide Item** button or pressing Ctrl + F6 . Enter the vendor, material number, order quantity, plant, and storage location. To reproduce this example in the system, use the following data:

– **Vendor:** ZK-DEMO-01

– **Purchasing organization:** 1000

– **Purchasing group:** 000

– **Company Code:** 1000

– **Material:** ZM-DEMO-01

– **Order Quantity:** 100

– **Plant:** 1000

– **Storage location:** 0001

3 After you've pressed ↵ the system determines the net price for the material from the information record.

14

4 With the **Check** button ( ), you can check the purchase orders for completeness and plausibility. If the information is complete and conclusive, then the system displays a success message stating "No messages issued during check." Confirm by clicking on OK.

5 Then click the **Save** button to save your purchase order. A dialog window opens that contains a confirmation and a document number. In this example, it is "Standard PO 4500017149 has been created." Write down the document number for the upcoming steps. In the real business environment, you won't write down any document numbers, but in these exercises it is useful because you can easily refer to the unique document number in the next steps.

The vendor sends the goods (or services) based on the purchase order. The following section describes what happens next.

14.5   Inventory Management

After you've sent a purchase order, the ordered goods are delivered to the business and recorded in goods receipt in the SAP system. All tasks associated with goods movement are performed with the inventory management component (SAP MM-IM). SAP MM-IM has the following tasks:

- Manage material stocks (with regard to quantities and values)
- Plan and record goods movements
- Run inventories

The following are the different types of goods movements:

- **Goods receipt**
  In goods receipt, you post the delivery of goods that you've ordered. Goods receipt increases the warehouse stock, which is also relevant for accounting purposes because the value of materials in the stock (that is, the stock value) increases.

- **Goods issue**
  Goods issue occurs if goods are delivered to a customer or another department (for instance, to production). Goods issue reduces the warehouse stock.

- **Stock transfer**
  In case of stock transfer, goods are moved to another storage location within the business, either within a plant or between two different plants.

- **Transfer posting**
  A transfer posting is the system recording of a goods movement; its effects on internal accounts are similar to physical goods movement.

With the movement type, you control which of these goods movements is used. The stock type indicates the material's usability; you need this piece of information to determine the available stock in materials requirements planning, for the withdrawal of goods, and to implement the inventory. The following three stock types can be found at one storage location:

14

- Unrestricted use stock
- Quality inspection stock (for when the quality of goods is being checked)
- Blocked stock

In addition, special stocks at the vendor or at the customer can be unrestricted-use stock or quality inspection stock. The individual stock types can be reposted via a goods movement.

This chapter focuses on both goods receipt and stock transfer.

When you post a goods receipt, you usually refer to a preceding purchase order (the preceding document). Since the entire process was mapped uniformly in the SAP system, you can copy data from the preceding document and thus reduce the entry effort and avoid possible input errors. Proceed as follows:

1 Start Transaction MIGO by entering the transaction code in the command field or selecting the SAP Easy Access menu path: **Logistics ▶ Materials Management ▶ Inventory Management ▶ Goods Movement ▶ MIGO – Goods Movement.**

2 Check that the selection A01 **Goods Receipt** R01 **Purchase order** is set. When you enter the preceding purchase order (PO) number (here, "R01 Purchase Order") and press the ⏎ key, then the SAP system will propose the material and the quantity from the purchase order.

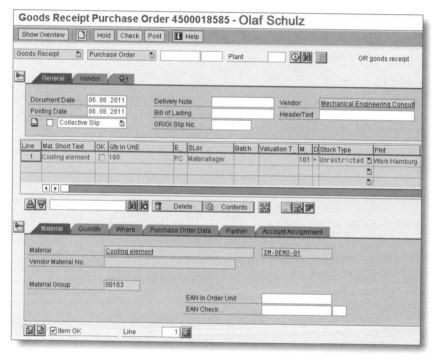

3 If the quantity and material that was delivered corresponds to the figures stated in the purchase order, then every item must be marked with OK. Then you can post the goods receipt by clicking the **Post** or **Save** button (🖫). The system displays the material document number (here, the message is "Material document 5000011937 has been posted").

Once the goods receipt has been confirmed and completed in the system, the system will create a material document and an accounting document.

Stock or material transfer postings can be done within a plant or across plants within the corporate group. The material is physically moved—transferred—to another location. The goods movement is posted in the SAP system, which increases or decreases the stock value.

In the example in the following figure, 30 of the 100 cooling elements in stock are transferred and posted to another storage location.

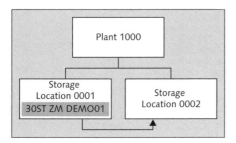

Stock Transfer in the Same Plant

Take the following steps:

1 Call Transaction MIGO. Set the transaction to **Transfer Posting Other** and enter the appropriate field values in the **Transfer Posting** tab. Then post the material document by clicking on the **Save** button ( ).

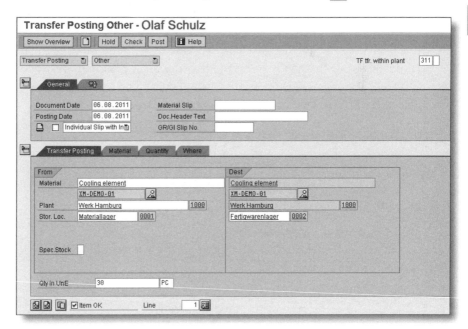

2 You can check the transfer posting's result using Transaction MMBE. When you enter the material and the plant in the initial screen of the transaction, the stock overview (basic list) is displayed. In this example, 70 pieces of the material ZM-DEMO-01 are still located at storage location 0001; 30 pieces are available at storage location 0002.

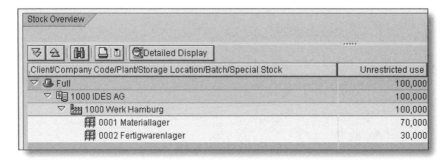

After you've created the purchase order and posted the goods receipt, you can run the invoice verification in the next step.

14.6   Invoice Verification

In the invoice verification component (SAP MM-IV), you compare the conditions of the purchase order with the invoice you received from the vendor with an eye for content, price, and figures. The SAP system determines possible deviations, which must then be coordinated with the vendor. The material document of the goods receipt tells you which quantities were actually delivered. The following conditions must be met to be able to perform ideal invoice verification:

- A purchase order is created in the SAP system.
- Goods receipt is posted in the SAP system.
- The vendor's invoice is available.

The SAP system has three types of invoice verification:

- **PO-based invoice verification**
  In this case, all items of the preceding purchase order are settled. A goods receipt is not necessary.
- **GR-based invoice verification**
  Here, every goods receipt is settled separately.

- **Invoice verification without purchase order reference**
  No preceding document exists in this process, so after invoice verification, a post is made directly to a material account, fixed asset account, or G/L account. Consider, for example, a purchase order by telephone, which doesn't directly enter a purchase order into the SAP system without additional steps.

Let's use a short example to understand invoice verification. The data from the previous purchase order example is used here.

Do the following:

1 Start Transaction MIRO by entering it in the command field or selecting the **Logistics ▶ Materials Management ▶ Logistics Invoice Verification ▶ Document Entry ▶ Enter Invoice** path in the SAP Easy Access menu.

2 Enter the following information in the invoice verification:

  – **Invoice Date**: invoice document (current date)

  – **Amount**: gross amount of invoice

  – **Tax Code**: 1I (input tax 10 %)

  – **Purchase Order Number**: document number

3 Press the ↵ key and make sure that the indicator 1I input tax 10 % is set here.

14

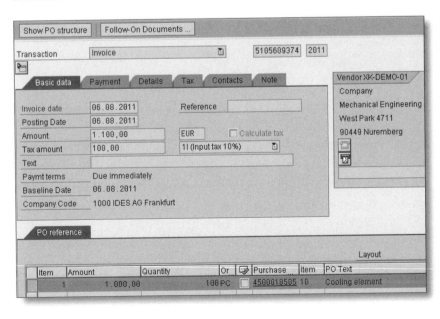

4 If you get a balance of 0.00 EUR, no deviations were found, and you can post the invoice by clicking the **Save** button ( ). The message "Document No. 5105608698 has been added" is displayed in this example.

Invoice verification results in two documents: logistics invoice document and accounting document (see the next two figures).

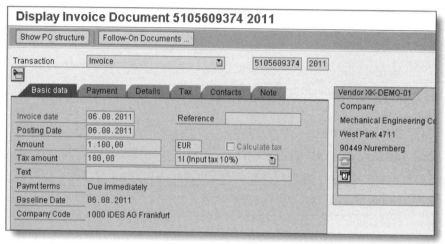

Invoice Document

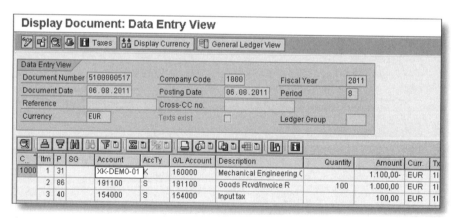

Accounting Document

Invoice verification in SAP MM is closely integrated with the adjacent components, SAP FI and SAP CO. It forwards the information required to settle the invoice amount and to post to SAP FI and SAP CO.

Sometimes goods are delivered for which no invoice exists yet or, inversely, the goods have not been delivered yet when the invoices are received. In this case, a goods receipt/invoice receipt clearing account (GR/IR account) is used. Once the missing goods or invoice are received, the GR/IR account is credited. The corresponding items are not cleared.

Let's discuss an example to clarify this:

- **A. Initial situation**
  The opening balance of the material stock account ❶ is $1,000.

- **B. Goods receipt for purchase order**
  Goods are ordered for another $1,000, and goods receipt occurs. The material stock account ❷ and the GR/IR account ❷ are posted to.

- **C. Invoice receipt (invoice verification)**
  Once the invoice has been entered, the GR/IR account is cleared, and the vendor account receives the posts until it, too, is cleared after the outgoing payments of accounts payable accounting are made.

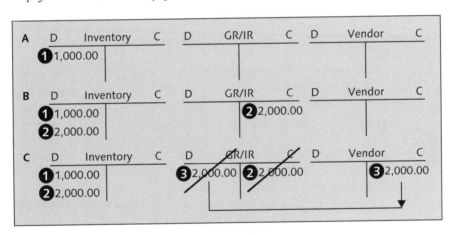

Account Movements for Goods Receipt and Invoice Receipt

The invoice of the vendor is entered in the SAP system. It does not have any deviations from the purchase order, and the correct materials were delivered in the correct quantity. The GR/IR account ❸ is cleared, and the vendor account ❷ is posted to. The vendor account is cleared when the invoice is paid.

14.7   Evaluations

The standard version of the system analyzes the logistics area in several ways to evaluate the data basis and use this information to derive future decision-making bases. Evaluation options are available in the SAP Easy Access menu under Information systems ▶ Logistics ▶ Purchasing.

The table shows some more examples for standard reports in MM.

Transaction	Evaluation
ME2L	Purchase orders by vendor
ME80	General evaluations
MC$0	Purchasing group purchase values
MC$G	Purchase values

Examples of Standard Reports in Materials Management

> **TIP**
>
> **Additional Information**
>
> Detailed information on MM is available in the book, *Materials Management with SAP ERP: Functionality and Technical Configuration*, by Martin Murray (2011), which is published by SAP PRESS.

15   Sales and Distribution

Sales and distribution is the link between a business and its customers. It is responsible for creating quotations, entering sales orders, and invoicing the delivered goods or services. In the SAP system, the sales tasks are supported by the Sales and Distribution component (which, moving forward, we'll refer to as SAP SD).

This chapter discusses:

- Critical tasks of sales
- How to enter and process sales orders
- Specific invoicing concerns
- The procedure of availability check
- Complaints processing
- Sales and distribution evaluation options

15.1   Sales and Distribution Task Areas

This chapter describes all sales and distribution processes, from customer inquiry or quotation, to entry of sales order, to invoicing. In the business world, many companies distribute these tasks among various user departments and thus SAP users. For example, customer accounting monitors the handling of payments.

Several steps must happen before the customers receive the desired goods or a service is rendered).

15

1. Customer Inquiry/Quotation (Optional)

9. Payment   2. Sales Order

8. Invoicing   3. Availability Check

7. Goods Issue   4 Delivery

6. Picking ← 5. Transport

The Sales Cycle

1 Customer inquiry and quotation

In the pre-sales phase (which is optional), customer inquiries and quotations are entered. For example, a customer inquires whether specific goods are in stock or how much they cost. The quotation presents a legally binding readiness to deliver goods or render a service to the customer on the established conditions. The data stored in the inquiry and quotation form the basis for subsequent documents in the SAP system.

2 Sales order

The sales order forms the starting point of the sales process. For example, a customer calls and orders goods or a service, and the sales representative enters the sales order into the SAP system. This can be either a one-time purchase order or a long-term agreement. In this case, special conditions can be stipulated and defined in the SAP system condition master records.

3 Availability check

During order entry, the sales representative checks whether the inquired materials are available for the requested delivery date. After the sales order has been saved in the SAP system—and if the material is indeed available in the required quantity at the desired point in time—then a delivery can be created. If the material is not available at that time, the system suggests a new delivery date. The delivery can be made in partial deliveries or as a full delivery at a later point in time.

> **INFO**
>
> **Standard Orders**
>
> An order type is made up of control parameters that guide further processing in the system, such as which fields must be completed by the order taker. The default order type in the SAP system is the standard (sales) order.

4 Delivery

Next, the delivery to the customer is triggered.

5 Transport order

The transport order that is now created in the SAP system involves the transport of goods to picking, not the transport of goods to the customer.

6 Picking

Here the goods are packaged and the shipping documents are added.

7 Goods issue

Once the goods issue has been posted in the SAP system, the goods are sent to the customer.

8 Invoicing

Next the delivery is invoiced and the customer account is debited.

9 Payment

The incoming payments are monitored in financial accounting. The debited customer account is cleared.

Customers send complaints if they receive incorrect or defective goods, or if the invoice is incorrect. Complaint processing in the SAP system offers a solution for these complaints: the customer can return the goods and receive a replacement or a credit memo.

In addition, the output or subsequent processing of documents in the SAP system is mapped via message control and documents (orders, invoices, etc.). Transactions use specific interfaces to make this easier.

Prices are calculated through the pricing and condition technique, which takes specific conditions into consideration.

SAP SD consists of functions that support the employees in sales processes. This chapter focuses on sales order processing, availability check, and complaints processing. The following sections show how sales are mapped in the SAP system with organizational units.

15

15.2 Organizational Structures

In the SAP system, the sales department of a business is mapped with organizational units. In addition to units used only in sales, the company code and plant organizational units are also relevant in this department. The plant is the delivering plant in sales with SAP—that is, from where the customers are provided with products. Beyond these, the following are some organizational units that are maintained and used in sales:

- **Sales area**
  The sales area is responsible for selling materials to the customers. It is assigned to a company code.

- **Sales organization**
  All sales documents are assigned to the sales organization. One or more sales organizations can be assigned to a sales area.

- **Distribution channel**
  The distribution channel is the way materials and services reach the customers. Typical distribution channels are wholesale trade (B2B, or *business to business*), retail trade (B2C, or *business to customer*), mail order, or direct sales.

- **Division**
  Similar products are combined in a division—that is, a grouping of materials and services that are distributed by the business—which organizes the responsibilities for these products within the business. Cross-division examples of similar products include sales, pumps, and motorcycles.

- **Storage location**
  Materials are managed on a quantity basis (not on a value basis) at the storage location level. One or more storage locations are assigned to a plant.

- **Shipping point**
  The shipping point handles shipping. They may be physically detached from the business (for example, loading ramps or airports). The shipping point can be determined automatically during order entry.

The next section discusses the master data in sales.

15.3   Master Data

Up-to-date and accurate information about the customers, goods (materials), and sales conditions is crucial for effective execution of sales processes. Important master data in SAP SD include:

- Customer master data
- Material master data
- Condition master records

You need to know the master data to understand the activities in the sales process. The following section describes how to create customer, material, and condition master records using the required fields.

Creating Customer Master Records

A company's customers are managed in a customer master, where all information relevant for sales is maintained. Customer master records are created in sales and then made available to the entire SAP system, which helps to avoid redundancies and data inconsistencies. Consequently, the users in accounting also work with the customer master data. However, different departments work with different views (or tabs). The customer master record has various levels on which the relevant data is defined. There is a general level that applies to the entire client, and also views for accounting and sales; these are each subdivided into the following data areas:

- General data (data at the client level), such as addresses and communications links
- Accounting data (data at the company code level), such as bank details
- Sales data (data at sales area level), such as delivery locations

Let's walk through an example to practice creating a customer master record.

1 To call the transaction that creates a customer master record (Transaction XD01), enter the transaction code in the command field or select the **Logistics ▸ Sales and Distribution ▸ Master Data ▸ Business Partner ▸ Customer ▸ Create ▸ Complete** path in the SAP Easy Access menu.

2 In the initial screen, enter the account group, customer (customer number), company code, sales organization, distribution channel, and division:

- **Account Group:** ZK01
- **Customer:** zzcust01

15

- **Company Code**: 1000 IDES AG
- **Sales organization**: 1000 Germany Frankfurt
- **Distribution channel**: 12 Reseller
- **Division**: 00 Cross-Division

3 To exit the initial screen, press the ⏎ key. The system takes you to the **Create Customer: General Data** view.

4 You can now enter the remaining data in the respective tabs. By clicking the **Company Code Data** and **Sales Area Data** buttons, you navigate to the corresponding tabs.

5 You maintain the customer's address and other details in the **Address** tab for the general data. Use the following data for this example:

- **Title**: Company
- **Name**: Special Machinery Inc. (or any other name)
- **Search term 1/2**: ZXCUST01
- **Street, House Number**: Mainstreet 1 (or any other address)
- **Postal Code, City**: 91056 Erlangen
- **Country**: DE
- **Region**: 09 Bavaria
- **Transportation zone**: 90000 Region South

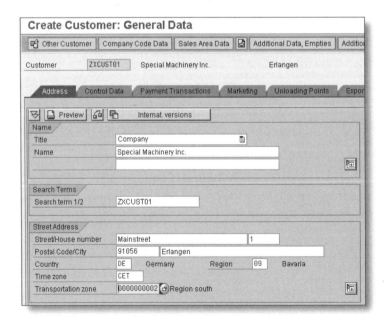

6 For this example, enter **Tax ID** DE47110815 in the **Control Parameters** tab.

7 For the company code data (available via the correspondent button), enter **Reconciliation Account** 140000 in the **Account Management** tab (see Chapter 16, Financial Accounting, for a description of the reconciliation account's function).

8 For the sales area data (available via the correspondent button), enter the **Customer Group** 02 in the **Sales** tab.

9 Enter the following sample data in the **Shipment** tab:

- **Shipping Condition:** 10 immediately
- **Delivering Plant:** 1000 Hamburg

10 You maintain the data required for issuing an invoice in the **Invoice** tab. Use the following data in this example:

- **Incoterms:** CFR
- **Terms of Payment:** ZB01 payable immediately without deduction
- **Tax Classification:** 1 subject to tax

11 Finally, save the customer master record with the **Save** button 🔘 (key combination [Ctrl]+[S]).

Remember to save the customer master record after you've filled all relevant fields.

Creating a Material Master Record

You require a material that the purchasing department procures (see Chapter 14, Materials Management) and that is then resold to the customer.

> **NOTE**
> **Procedure for Creating Material Master Records**
> Chapter 14 provides a detailed description of material master record creation.

For this purpose, create the following material in your system by starting Transaction MMH1 via the command field or in the SAP Easy Access menu via the **Logistics ▸ Sales and Distribution ▸ Master Data ▸ Products ▸ Material ▸ Trading Goods ▸ Create** path.

The following table contains the data that you need in order to reproduce this example.

Material number	zzmat01
Industry sector	Mechanical engineering
Material	Finished product
Required views	Basic Data 1, Sales: Sales Organization Data 1, Sales: Plant Data, Purchasing, Purchase Order Text, Accounting 1
Plant	1000
Sales organization	1000
Distribution channel	12
"Basic Data 1" View	
Material	Control panel
Base unit of quantity	Piece
Material group	Electronics/hardware
Gross weight	1 kg
Net weight	0.5 kg
"Sales Organization 1" View	
Base unit of quantity	Piece
Delivering plant	1000
Material group	002
Tax data	1 Full tax
"Sales General Plant" View	
Transportation group	0001 Pallets
Loading group	0003 Manual
"Sales Text" View	
Purchase order text	Control panel block of 10; splashproof

Sample Data for the Material Master Record

"Purchasing" View	
Purchasing group	000
Base unit of quantity	PC
Material group	002
Purchasing value key	1
"Accounting 1" View	
Valuation class	3000
Price control:	V
Moving average price	100.00 EUR

Sample Data for the Material Master Record (Cont.)

Material Master Record

Because the master record has been recently created and no material has been procured yet, the stock is 0. The basic procurement process has already been described in Chapter 14, Materials Management. Now use Transaction ME21N to order 1,000 pieces of the material (zzmat01) from vendor 1000, and implement the goods receipt (Transaction MIGO).

Creating Condition Master Records

A condition master record is created in the SAP system if a business relationship has existed with a customer for a long time. Once you define the agreed conditions in the condition master record, they will be proposed when you enter a purchase order in the future. This section uses an example to describe how to create a condition master record for a customer and the material.

In this example, you define a price of €200 per piece in the system. This means that if customer zzcust01 orders material zzmat01, the purchase order will automatically propose a price of €200 during the order entry.

1 To create the condition record, start Transaction VK11 via the command field or the SAP Easy Access menu path: Logistics ▸ Sales and Distribution ▸ Master Record ▸ Conditions ▸ Select Using Condition Type ▸ Create. Select Condition Type PR00 Price in the initial screen.

2 A condition type maps a specific criterion for pricing in the system. Surcharges, discounts, and prices that arise during the business process are assigned to the condition types.

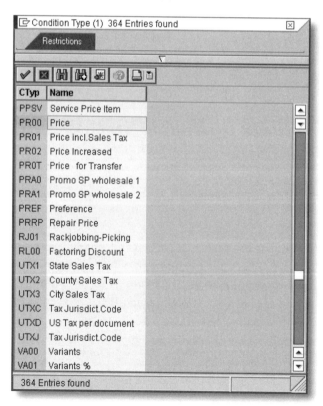

3 Confirm the key combination **Customer/Material with Release Status,** and then define condition PR00. A key combination determines the type of combination with which the condition master record is created.

4 You then maintain the conditions in the next screen: If customer zzcust01 orders material zzmat01, a price of €200 is proposed during the order entry. The addition "with release status" indicates that material master records that are used here are released and not locked.

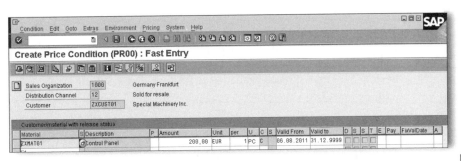

5 Save the defined condition via the **Save** button 🖫 (key combination `Ctrl`+`S`).

Now that you know the most important organizational structures and master data, the following sections focus on central sales processes.

15.4   Sales Order Processing

Master data forms the basis for sales work. Now bring your attention to the processes that occur in daily sales work that include the creation of a sales order, delivery, and invoice.

The following section discusses the actual sales process and the most important steps of sales order, delivery, and invoice. The pre-sales process often includes the customer inquiry and the quotation (Transactions VA11 and VA21). After a customer agrees to a quotation, you will reference this document when you create the standard order.

Basic Sales Process

Entering Sales Orders

This section gives you an example to show how you can enter a sales (standard) order in the SAP system. A customer calls and wants to order 10 pieces of material zzmat01. For this, the condition master record will propose the condition €200 per piece. Proceed as follows:

1. To enter the standard order, start Transaction VA01 via the command field or via the **Logistics ▶ Sales and Distribution ▶ Sales ▶ Order ▶ Create** path in the SAP Easy Access menu.

2. In the initial screen, specify order type OR (standard order), sales organization 1000, distribution channel 12, and division 00. Press the ⏎ key or choose the **Continue** button ✅ to open the screen that creates the purchase order.

3 In the standard order screen, enter the sold-to party and any purchase order number in the header, for instance DEMO[current date]. For the requested delivery date, enter the current date plus ten days. Specify the material number and the order quantity (10 pieces) of the items. Press ⏎ to transfer the €200 per piece condition from the condition record to the standard order.

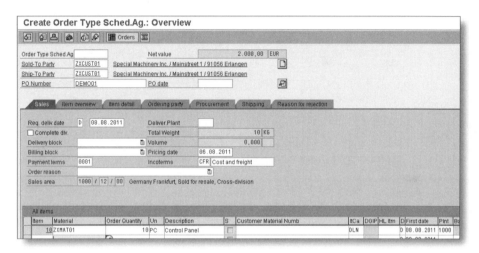

4 Once you've entered the order, save it by clicking the **Save** button 🖫 (key combination Ctrl + S).

The order entry is now complete. The SAP system provides internal documents for the next steps in the process.

Creating Deliveries

In the next step, you create a delivery in the SAP system.

1 Call Transaction VL01N via the command field or via the SAP Easy Access menu path: Logistics ▸ Sales and Distribution ▸ Shipping and Transportation ▸ Outbound Delivery ▸ Create ▸ Single Document ▸ With Reference to Sales Order.

2 For this example, enter 1000 in the **Shipping Point** field as the date that is ten days in the future in the **Selection Date** field (in this case, 01.09.2011), and the document number of the sales order.

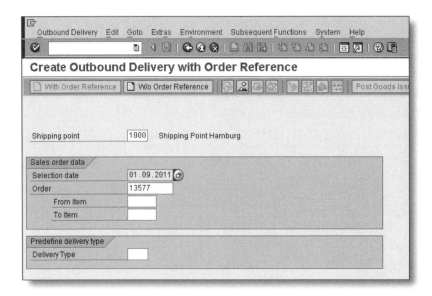

3 Save your delivery in the subsequent screen **(Create Outbound Delivery)**. Do not post a goods issue yet because the delivery has not been created in the SAP system yet.

4 Write down the document number of the delivery. To post the goods issue, start Transaction VL02N via the command field or use the SAP Easy Access menu path: **Logistics ▸ Sales and Distribution ▸ Shipping and Transportation ▸ Outbound Delivery ▸ Change ▸ Single Document.**

5 The system proposes the delivery's document number. Click on **Post Goods Issue**.

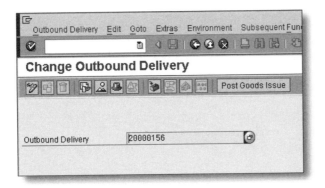

The stock of the material is reduced accordingly. You can check the stock using Transaction MMBE.

Invoicing

After the goods have been delivered, you can invoice the delivery to the customer. This step is mapped in the SAP system as follows:

1 Call Transaction VF01 by entering the transaction code in the command field or via the **Logistics ▶ Sales and Distribution ▶ Billing ▶ Billing Document ▶ Create** path in the SAP Easy Access menu. The SAP system automatically proposes the document number of the preceding delivery.

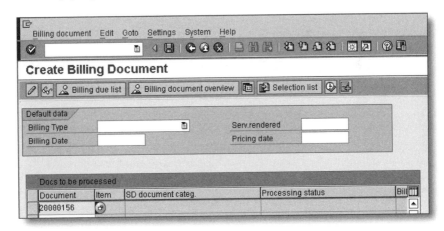

2 Save the invoice via the **Save** button 💾 (key combination Ctrl + S).

View the print preview of the invoice using Transaction VF03 by taking the following steps.

1 Select **Billing Document ▶ Output** in the menu bar, or enter Transaction VF03 in the command field.

2 Select the message and click on the **Show Invoice** button ⬛ to generate the print preview.

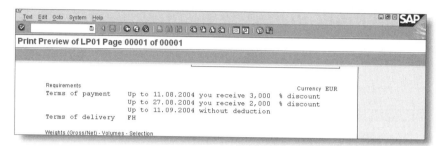

3 The customer account, which is determined based on the unique customer number the SAP system, is thus debited (see Chapter 16, Financial Accounting). You can output the invoice with Transaction VF31 or via the **Logistics ▶ Sales and Operation ▶ Billing ▶ Output** menu path.

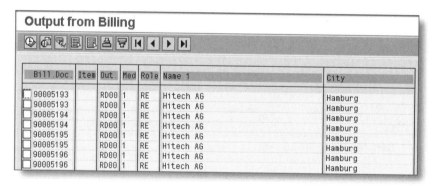

The basic procurement process is complete with the invoice. As you saw in the section about sales and distribution task areas, the SAP system lets you do an availability check. The next section gives you more information on this topic.

15.5   Availability Check

Customers care about the price, quality, and availability of goods on the requested delivery date. Remember that during sales order creation you can check in the SAP system whether the required material is available on the requested date and can thus be delivered on time. For the availability check, SAP SD is closely integrated with the materials management and production planning and control components of SAP so that a delivery date can be confirmed for the customer.

Since the availability check in the SAP system occurs at the plant and storage location level, it is crucial that the storage location be specified in the sales order. You can set various availability check methods in the SAP system (for example, considering the available warehouse stock and planned receipts and issues, using product allocations for individual customers or regions, or using forecasting).

If the availability check is positive, it is confirmed with a sales order. If it is negative, the desired goods are manufactured (for in-house production) or ordered (for external procurement).

Take the following steps to check for availability on the SAP system: Transaction VA01 (Create Sales Order) includes the **Availability Check** button at the bottom of the screen. To familiarize yourself with the function, create a new sales order with the master records you've already created. Do not save it yet, but select the item. Click on to run an availability check.

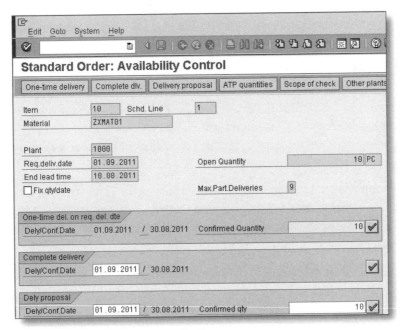

Implementing the Availability Check

The figure shows that the desired quantity can be confirmed for the delivery date. A scheduling agreement delivery schedule arises if, for example, the customer orders 400 pieces and requires 200 pieces in ten days and the other 200 pieces in two months. You can check these scheduling agreement delivery schedules against the availability check (for example, whether the delivery can be made on time for the desired point in time).

15.6   Complaint Processing (Returns)

If customers receive incorrect or defective goods, or if the invoice is incorrect, they send a complaint. Several methods of responding to these complaints are available to you in complaint processing:

- **Customer returns the goods (returns)**
  The customer returns the ordered goods or parts thereof and receives, depending on the agreement, either a substitute delivery or a refund of the entire or partial invoice amount.

- **Customer does not return the goods**
  It is possible to refund the paid amount to the customer or replace the goods without their return. For example, if the invoice amount was too high, a credit memo is created based on the complaint. A debit memo is created if the amount invoiced was too low.

This section addresses the complaint processing with returns. For this purpose, you must create returns in the SAP system. If the returned goods reach the warehouse, you must post the goods receipt with reference to the returns you've previously created. After the returns check, you can refund the corresponding amount to the customer by creating a credit memo request or a subsequent delivery that is free of charge.

You create complaints or returns in the SAP system with Transaction VA01 (menu path **Logistics ▶ Sales and Distribution ▶ Sales ▶ Order ▶ Create**). In this example, one piece of the material that you've sold (zzcust01) was damaged during transport, so the customer receives a credit memo.

Procurement Process with Returns

In the initial screen of the transaction, first select order type RE for returns. Then reference the preceding sales order.

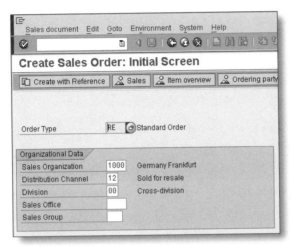

Initial Screen: Create Returns (Transaction VA01) with Order Type RE

The next figure shows how to create returns.

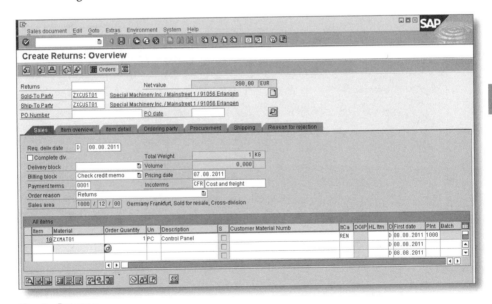

Create Returns

15.7   Evaluations

The SAP system offers a wide range of standard reports, also found in the SAP SD sales information system (**Logistics ▸ Sales and Distribution ▸ Sales Information System ▸ Standard Analyses**).

If you need an overview of order quantities and sales volumes, you can use the customer analysis (Transaction MCTA). Enter the required selection criteria in the initial screen.

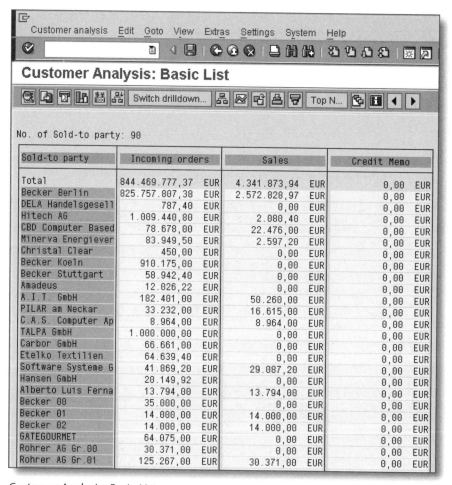

Customer Analysis: Basic List

Transaction	Evaluation
MCTA	Standard analysis, evaluation by customer
MCTC	Standard analysis, evaluation by material
MCTE	Standard analysis, evaluation by sales office

Examples of Evaluations in Sales

Additional Information

Refer to the book *Sales and Distribution—Practical Guide* by Matt Chudy and Luis Castedo SAP PRESS 2011 to obtain more information on the sales process in the SAP system.

15

16   Financial Accounting

Financial Accounting is the veteran of the SAP system, so to speak, because accounting software was the first product that SAP developed in the 1970s. This chapter provides an introduction to financial accounting with SAP, which we'll refer to as SAP FI throughout.

This chapter discusses:

- The primary tasks of financial accounting
- G/L accounting functions
- Managing open payables and open receivables
- Which reports are available in financial accounting in the SAP system

16.1   Financial Accounting Tasks

Accounting gathers all information about a business's financial status and services. Its task is to document historical values and use them to derive statements on the company's status at a specific point in time (usually, year-end closing). The core task of SAP's accounting component therefore is to transparently and comprehensibly map all business transactions for accounting purposes based on documents in the IT system. A business transaction involves every transaction relevant to business that can be quantified (such as payments and goods movements). In this context, three basic questions need to be asked:

- How much capital does the business have at a specific point in time?
- Has the enterprise gained profits or suffered losses in the course of a fiscal year?
- Is the enterprise solvent?

16

It is the task of financial accounting to answer these questions. Financial accounting is also known as external accounting because it presents the business's financial status to the outside world. The results are made available to the authorities, creditors, and outside creditors like stockholders, banks, and other investors. Controlling, or managerial accounting, is discussed in Chapter 17.

External accounting is bound to commercial and tax laws and regulations. The tasks of financial accounting include the provision and disclosure of information about capital, financials, and profits, which are used as the basis of taxation. This information is presented in the financial statement as well as the profit and loss statement. The financial statement communicates how much capital a business has and provides information about its existing resources by comparing capital (assets) and debts (liabilities) in account form. The profit and loss statement gathers a list of all expenses and profits in the course of a fiscal year.

All accounting data is entered according to the document principle. Readers should be able to get a complete representation of the information, even on an individual document level. A business' accounts must be kept in such a way that third parties can get an overview of its financial situation (transparency).

> **INFO**
>
> **The Document Principle**
>
> Since documents are the link between business transaction and posting, there must be a document for every posting because only then can each posting be checked for accuracy. Documents include receipts, incoming and outgoing invoices, checks, bank statements, and other items. Because of their important role, documents' structure is defined strictly. Every document is identified by a unique document number in the SAP system and has a document header (which contains the type of business transaction), the date of the document and posting, posting period, reference, currency, and descriptive text.

Financial accounting is closely integrated with the remaining components of the SAP system. This is because all transactions that are relevant for accounting and come from logistics and human resources management (see also Chapter 18) are posted in financial accounting in real time, and sometimes forwarded to controlling.

Financial accounting is responsible for opening accounts at the beginning of the fiscal year, keeping postings current during the year, and preparing the year-end closing. The maintenance of current postings demands the most space and time.

Double-Entry Accounting

The system of double-entry accounting is usually deployed in the private sector. Double-entry accounting has a long history, as it was invented by Luca Pacioli, an Italian Franciscan monk, at the end of the 15th century. The concept "double" refers to the fact that every business transaction (posting record) is entered twice, once as a debit and once as a credit, to ensure accuracy.

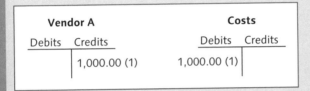

Sample Posting in Duble-Entry Accounting

In accounting, accounts in T form (in which debits are entered on the left side and credits on the right side) are used to keep presentations clear and uncluttered.

In addition to that, all postings are shown in the financial statements and the profit and loss statement.

16

Accounts are the central unit in accounting. An account consists of two columns (one for debits and one for credits), and an account number. The general ledger and various subledgers (which represent the business transactions in a more differentiated approach) are kept in double-entry accounting. The general ledger consists of all accounts to which business transactions are posted and that are listed in a chart of accounts. Postings in the subledgers (for example, accounts receivable accounting for customers and accounts payable accounting for vendors) automatically generate a corresponding posting in the general ledger in the SAP system.

The customer in subledger accounting is linked with the receivables account in general ledger accounting through the reconciliation account, which you enter in the master record of the customer.

For every complex posting in the SAP system, you must enter the following information at the minimum: document date, posting date, document type, posting key, the account number, and amounts.

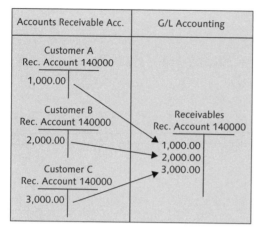

Connection Between Subledger and General Ledger Accounting

SAP FI's most important functions refer to the following areas:

- **General ledger accounting**
  This records all business transactions relevant for accounting on G/L accounts (accounts in the chart of accounts).

- **Accounts payable accounting**
  This area posts all business transactions that refer to vendors and gets its most of its data from purchasing (see Chapter 14, Materials Management).

- **Accounts receivable accounting**
  This records all business transactions that refer to customers, and receives most of its information from sales and distribution (see Chapter 15, Sales and Distribution).

- **Asset accounting**
  This records all business transactions that refer to the business's assets. In this context, its assets include all complex fixed assets that are permanently available for value creation (for example, buildings, machines, or securities). In terms of accounting, the evaluation (asset values, depreciations) is particularly interesting.

- **Bank accounting**
  This records and manages business transactions that involve banks or the business's payment transactions.

The following sections discuss accounts receivable accounting and accounts payable accounting. Asset and bank accounting is not further discussed in this book. First, however, let's discuss the foundations that must be laid before users can work with SAP in financial accounting.

16.2 Organizational Structures in Financial Accounting

You are already familiar with organizational structures from the previous chapters and particularly in Chapter 4, Organizational Structures and Master Data. Before you can work with SAP, you must first make some basic settings in Customizing and map the business structures in the SAP system. From the financial accounting perspective, the following organizational structures are particularly important. Here again, the client is paramount.

- **Company code**
  The company code is the smallest unit for which complete accounting is possible in the SAP system. Among other things, a chart of accounts and a currency is assigned to the company code, which creates its own financial statement.

- **Business area**
  The business area describes a defined activity area within the enterprise, but definition and usage aren't mandatory in the SAP system. Example of business areas are:
  - 5000: Energy production
  - 6000: Transport engineering
  - 7000: Medical engineering

  Deploying business areas can help you create evaluations more easily; a business area serves internal purposes because it gets an overview of business-relevant data. This way, you can evaluate results or financial statements separately according to business areas.

- **Chart of accounts**
  The accounts in the general ledger are structured according to a chart of accounts that represents a directory of all general ledger accounts. The following information must be available for each account:
  - Account number
  - Description
  - G/L account type (profit and loss account or balance sheet account)

16

It is mandatory that a chart of accounts (which can be used by several company codes) be assigned to every company code.

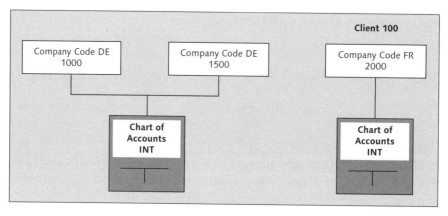

Organizational Structures in Financial Accounting

You can map several company codes in a client, even if you use different charts of accounts and must comply with different national regulations.

Now that you know the most important organizational units in financial accounting, let's discuss general ledger accounting.

16.3   General Ledger Accounting

General ledger accounting is the central instance of financial accounting because it forms the basis for statutory reporting (financial statement and profit and loss statement). The financial accounting general ledger component is responsible for general ledger accounting in the SAP system, which is based on G/L accounts. The G/L accounts, in turn, must be specified in the chart of accounts and also created together with the relevant master data so that postings can be made to these accounts. The primary cost element in Controlling derives from the G/L account (see Chapter 17).

> **NOTE**
>
> **Transfer from Subledgers**
>
> In SAP FI, data is available in real time. If a posting is made in a subledger (for example, in the vendor account), a corresponding posting is also automatically made in the general ledger. This is known as automatic entry.

The general ledger and the subledgers are linked by a reconciliation account. This is a special header account of G/L accounting that guarantees the automatic entry of all items of the subledgers in G/L accounting. You need at least one reconciliation account for customers and one reconciliation account for vendors.

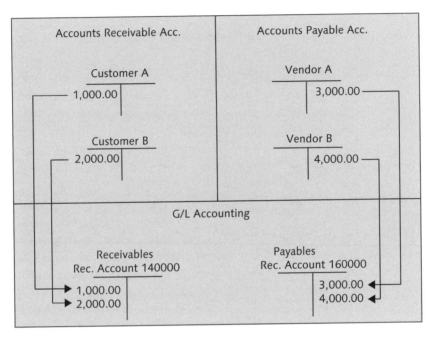

Reconciliation Account Function

You enter the number of the reconciliation account in the master record or the customer/vendor to link the subledgers (accounts receivable accounting and accounts payable accounting) with G/L accounting.

The following are the essential roles of G/L accounting:

- It forms the basis for the financial statement.
- It is used for account management and guarantees a full proof of all business transactions.
- It forms the basis for the profit and loss statement.

The financial statement is a compact list and evaluation of all assets of a business. An opening financial statement is created when an enterprise is founded, and a closing financial statement is made at the end of each fiscal year. Throughout the fiscal year, all business transactions are posted in general ledger accounts that are merged for the closing financial statement at the end of the fiscal year.

A profit and loss statement is created based on information from the general ledger and published at the end of the fiscal year. It compares expenses and gains to indicate the operating income.

Why Financial Statement and Profit and Loss Statement?

"When you post every transaction in the profit and loss statement and the financial statement at the same time, you can determine at any time which resources are available (financial statement) and which path you've already completed (profit and loss statement). You could compare this with a car: If you travel from Munich to Hamburg, you will only feel comfortable when you know how much gas is left (financial statement) and what distance you've already covered (profit and loss statement). Of course you would also reach your destination if you only had a mileage indicator and you stopped every 100 miles to check with a probe how much gas is left in the tank. This corresponds to an accounting where the expenses and gains are permanently posted and a review is made once at the end of the year. Modern cars, however, have a mileage indicator and a gas gauge that provide the correct values simultaneously and in real time. This also applies to modern accounting; both the financial statement and profit and loss statement are updated at the same time." (Translated from Brück, *Praxishandbuch SAP-Controlling*, 2009, page 29.)

In the SAP system, you can automatically call the structure of either statement for each or several company codes *if* you've assigned G/L accounts to the individual, bottom-line financial statement and profit and loss statement items in Customizing. The standard version of SAP provides the classic financial statement and profit and loss statement structures. Populate these with the G/L accounts from your chart of accounts. Let's assume your financial statement items are structured like in the following figure.

Assets	Liabilities
I (In)tangible Assets II Current Assets	I Stockholder's Equity II Special Items with Reserves III Liabilities

Items in the Financial Statement Structure

In this case, you must assign the corresponding accounts to the individual items (for instance, intangible, financial, and current assets) in Customizing. Then you can call the financial statement for your company code via Transaction S_PL0_86000028.

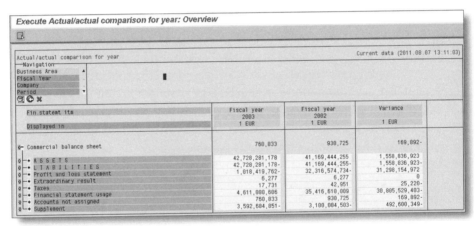

Financial Statement for a Company Code

You can implement the foreign currency valuation and advance return for tax on sales/purchases in G/L accounting within the scope of closing operations. This always requires that the relevant settings be made in Customizing, though their description would surpass the scope of this book. Additionally, the SAP system gives you a comprehensive information system on G/L accounts, balances, and line items in general ledger accounting, which is briefly discussed in the last section of this chapter.

After this presentation of the most important functions and options in G/L accounting, the next section discusses accounts payable accounting.

16

16.4   Accounts Payable Accounting

Accounts payable accounting does two things: it deals with business transactions that concern vendors, and manages the business's payables. These tasks are primarily associated with the administration and posting of the following business transactions:

- Invoices
- Credit memos
- Outgoing payments

The corresponding SAP component is FI-AP, and is closely interlinked with purchasing (Materials Management, see Chapter 14). For accounting, the invoice verification component (in which you can post incoming invoices) is of particular interest. Outgoing payments are made based on the posted invoice.

Accounts that are kept in accounts payable accounting (and accounts receivable accounting) are known as subledger accounts. The subledger accounts of accounts payable accounting are referred to as vendor accounts. The prerequisites for these are the vendor master records in the vendor account, which you create via Transaction FK01 or the SAP Easy Access menu under **Accounting ▶ Financial Accounting ▶ Accounts Payable ▶ Master Records ▶ Create**. You can change the account via Transaction FK02.

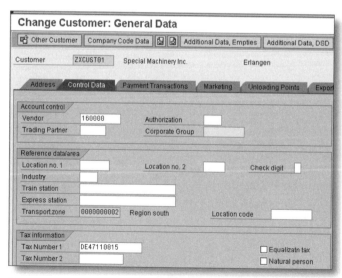

Transaction FD02 "Change Vendor"

There you enter various data: address, tax information, payment transaction data, terms of payment, and so on.

One-Time Accounts

What happens if you post an invoice only once, and a payment must be made to the vendor? In this case, you create and post to a one-time account as a collective account for various one-time vendors.

The following sections guide you through the complete procurement process—from purchase order to outgoing payment—in the SAP system from the accounting perspective. The next figure provides an overview of the process.

1   Initially, you create a purchase order in the system in SAP MM.

2   Goods receipt is posted for the purchase order in SAP MM.

3   This is followed by invoice verification in SAP MM.

4   The vendor's balances are displayed in FI-AP.

5   Next, the outgoing payment is posted in FI-AP, and a transfer document is sent to the bank.

6   Finally, the new balance and the account transactions of the vendor are displayed in FI-AP.

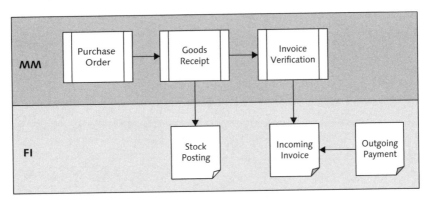

Procurement Process Extended By Outgoing Payment

To understand the following example, familiarize yourself with the basic purchasing process from Chapter 14, Materials Management. This example shows what this process looks like in the SAP system from the accounting perspective.

1 First, the purchase order is created in SAP MM; it is not mapped in accounts payable accounting.

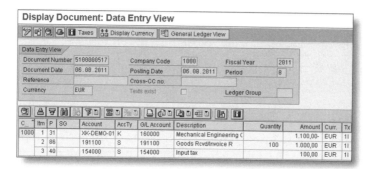

2 The goods receipt is posted in materials management with reference to the purchase order. This document is mapped in G/L accounting. SAP MM automatically generates a posting to the material stock account and to the goods receipt/invoice receipt account (GR/IR account) as the offsetting entry.

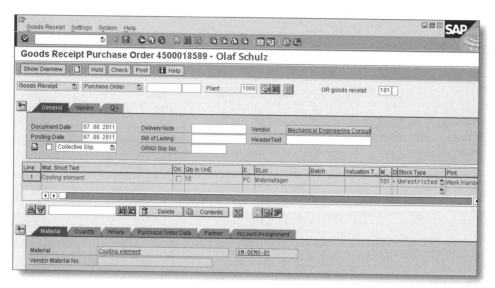

3 In the next step, you perform invoice verification (posting of the incoming invoice) with reference to the purchase order in materials management. An SAP FI document is automatically created on the vendor account and on the GR/IR account as the offsetting entry.

4 Next, have the system display the balances of the vendor. Call Transaction FK10N via the command field or the SAP Easy Access menu path:

Accounting ▸ Financial Accounting ▸ Accounts Payable ▸ Account ▸ Display Balances. Maintain the following data for the example in the initial screen:

- **Vendor**: ZXCUST01
- **Company Code**: 1000
- **Fiscal Year**: 2011

5 Then click on 🔾 (**Execute**).

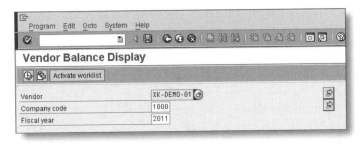

6 The system shows the vendor's balance display, which presents the liability account. The open amount from invoice verification is displayed on the credit side.

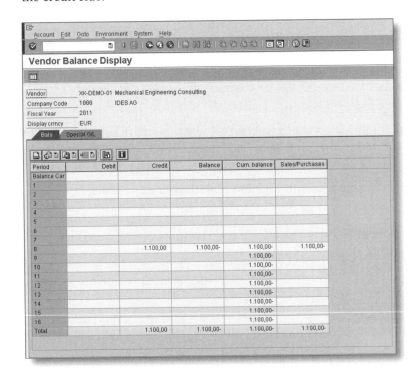

16

7 If you select on row in the table and click on 🔳 (**Call Line Item List**), the system takes you to the vendor line item display.

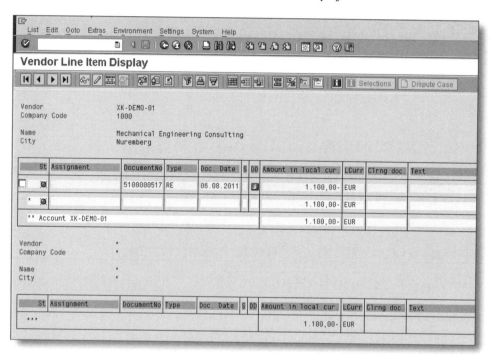

8 Finally, the outgoing payment is posted. Call Transaction F-53 via the command field or select **Accounting ▶ Financial Accounting ▶ Accounts Payable ▶ Document Entry ▶ Outgoing Payment ▶ Post** in the SAP Easy Access menu.

9 Enter the data for the example in Transaction **Post Outgoing Payments**. Enter the current date in the **document Date** field (for example, 07.08.2011). The same date is used in the **Posting Date** field.

10 Maintain the following entries in the **Bank Data** screen area:

- **Account**: 113130

- **Amount**: 1100.00 EUR

- **Value date**: Current date

11 Enter XK-DEMO-1 in the **Account** field in the **Open item selection** area. Press ⏎ after you've entered the data.

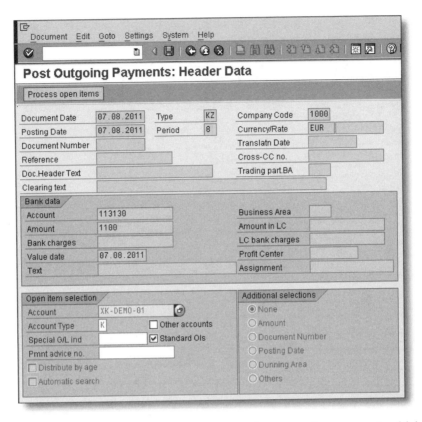

12 In the **Vendor Balance Display** screen, the entered amount should be identical to the assigned amount. Post the outgoing payment by clicking the **Save** button 🖫 .

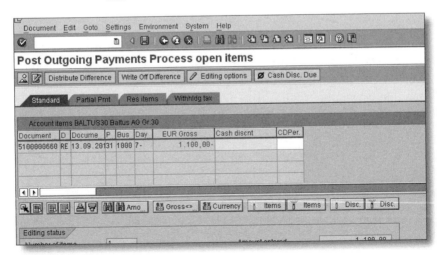

13 Let the system display the vendor's balances once again. The account is now cleared.

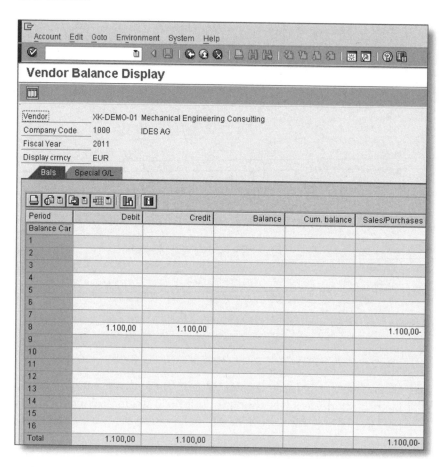

Consider the following example: You receive a vendor invoice, but you have not created a purchase order in the SAP system. According to this, no preceding documents exist, and this incoming invoice is directly posted in accounts payable accounting (and not as invoice verification in materials management).

1 Start Transaction FB60, or navigate via the SAP Easy Access menu to **Accounting ▶ Financial Accounting ▶ Accounts Payable ▶ Document Entry.**

2 Enter the following data in **Enter Vendor Invoice:**

- Transaction: Invoice
- Vendor: BALTUS00
- Invoice Date: Today's date
- Posting Date: Today's date
- Amount: 110.00 EUR
- Tax Amount: 10.00 EUR
- Tax Code: 1I (Input tax 10 %)
- G/L account: 890000
- Amount in Document Currency: 100.00 EUR
- Cost center: 4100

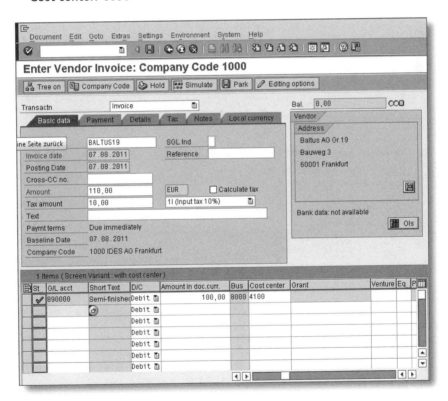

3 Once you've entered the values, click on the **Simulate** button. The system displays the following document overview.

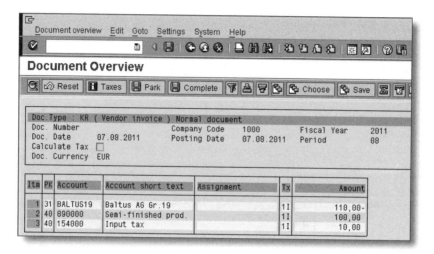

4 Now call the balance display of the vendor. Notice that the vendor account is not cleared.

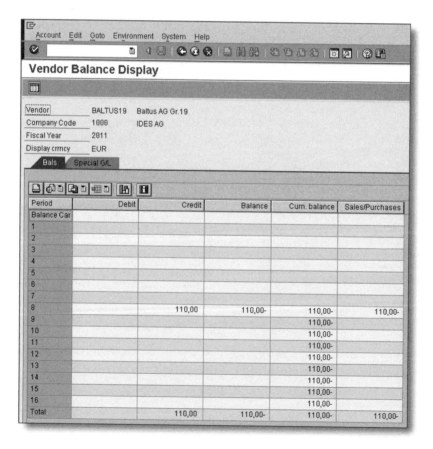

5 Call Transaction F-53 (Post Outgoing Payments) or go to the menu path: **Accounting ▶ Financial Accounting ▶ Accounts Payable ▶ Document Entry ▶ Outgoing Payment**. Here, enter the following values:

- **Document date**: Today's date

- **Posting Date**: Today's date

- **Invoice Date**: Today's date

6 Populate the following fields in the **Bank Data** area:

- **Account**: 113100

- **Amount**: 110.00 EUR

- **Tax Code**: 1I (Input tax 10 %)

- **Value date**: Today's date

7 Enter BALTUS19 in the **Account** field in the **Open item selection** area. Then press the ⏎ key.

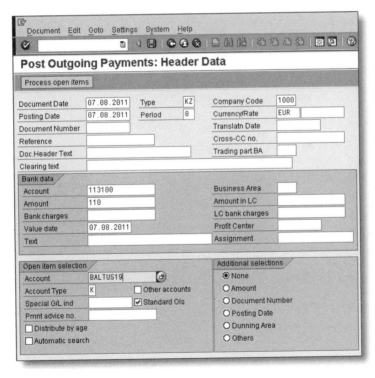

8 The entered amount should be identical to the assigned amount (a balance of 0.00 EUR). Post the outgoing payment by clicking on the **Save** button 🖫.

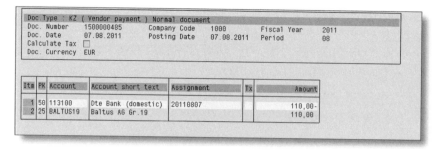

9 Have the system show the balance display for the vendor.

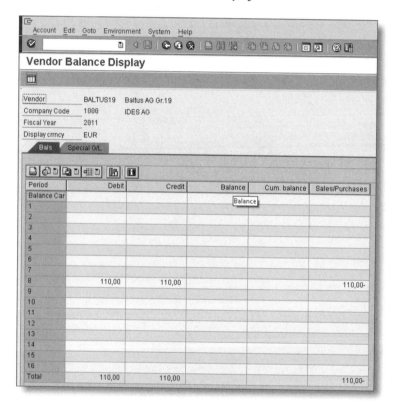

In the following example, the system displays the balances of a vendor to obtain an overview of the balances.

1 Call the Transaction Vendor Balance Display from the SAP Easy Access menu path: Accounting ▸ Financial Accounting ▸ Accounts Payable ▸ Information System ▸ Reports for Accounts Payable Accounting ▸ Vendor Balances ▸ Vendor Business. Alternatively, you can enter Transaction S_ALR_87012093 in the command field.

2 In the initial screen of the transaction, enter BALTUS19 in the **Vendor** field and 2011 under **Fiscal Year**. Then click on ⊕ (Execute).

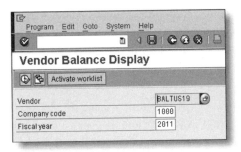

3 The system displays all balances for the vendor you've specified in the initial screen.

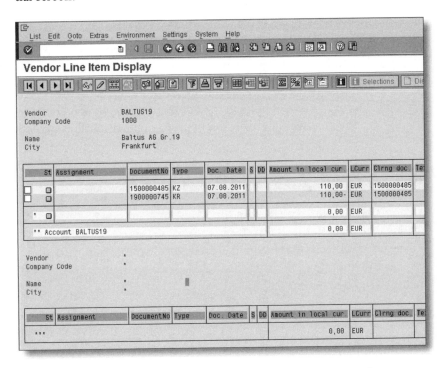

This section provided a brief overview of how to post an invoice from materials management to accounts payable accounting. You've also learned how to enter an invoice manually in accounts payable accounting and how to implement a manual payment. You can also post credit memos, which are analogous to the invoices. In addition to the standard documents, you can create transfer posting documents or cancel all documents in case of an error.

Automatic Payment Program

It is important to mention the automatic payment program, through which you can handle the payment transactions with customers and vendors. As the result, the SAP system creates a file including payment data that you send to the bank for processing, or prints a check that you can send to your vendor.

You can automatically print the balance confirmations from the SAP system and start specific adjustment postings for the closing operations both in accounts receivable accounting and in accounts payable accounting. Adjustment postings include transfer postings of receivables and payables based on remaining terms (for example, if the remaining term is less than one year, one to five years, etc.). These functions are not discussed in more detail due to their complexity.

Like in G/L accounting, you are provided with a comprehensive information system on vendor master data, balances, and line items (see the upcoming section about evaluations).

You now have an overview of the functions and options in accounts payable accounting. The next section finally discusses accounts receivable accounting.

16.5 Accounts Receivable Accounting

Accounts receivable accounting in the SAP system deals with business transactions that concern the enterprise's customers. These primarily involve the management of receivables from the customer. Invoices that were posted in sales and distribution are forwarded to financial accounting. Customers are managed in both SAP SD and FI-AR.

The following are the day-to-day activities in accounts receivable accounting:

- Management of customer master records (payment targets, delivery blocks, dunning levels, etc.)
- Receivables management
- Monitoring and recording incoming payments
- Closing operations and dunnings

The sales process (also known as order-to-cash) is connected to accounting in the following way:

1 The order is created in sales in SAP SD and sent to the customer.

2 If the goods must be delivered (that is, if it doesn't involve a service), a delivery document is created in SAP SD.

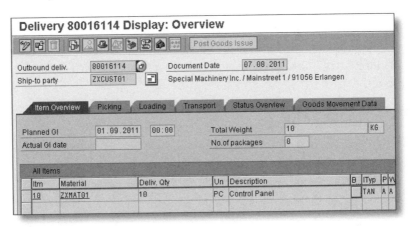

3 If the goods are available and the credit standing check of the customer is positive (the customer is solvent), the goods are delivered (goods issue) in SAP MM.

4 The invoice is issued and sent to the customer, and the receivable is posted in accounts receivable accounting in SAP SD and SAP FI.

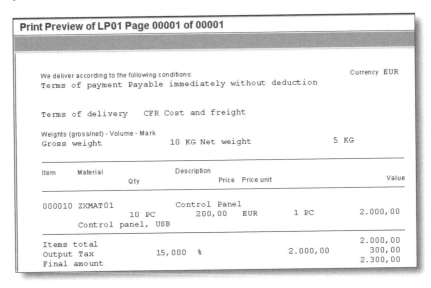

16

5 If the customer does not pay as agreed upon in the terms of payment, the dunning process is started in SAP FI.

6 From an accounting standpoint, if the money is debited to the business's account, the incoming payment is posted in SAP FI.

The business transactions in accounts receivable accounting are registered in the customer account. You create a customer account via Transaction FD01 or the menu path: **Accounting ▸ Financial Accounting ▸ Accounts Receivable ▸ Master Records ▸ Create**. Like for the vendor accounts, various data is entered here: address, tax information, payment transaction data, terms of payment, and so on.

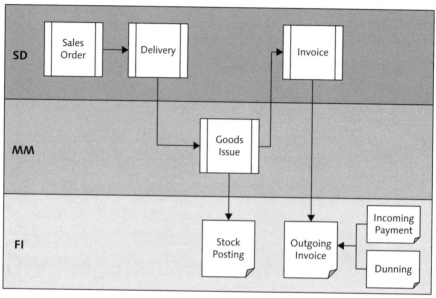

Sales Process with Incoming Payment and Dunning

The following example shows how to display a customer's open items and post incoming payments. You have received a standard order of customer T-S50A12 for ten pieces of T-AS112 and 20 pieces of T-AS212, and now you want to implement commissioning, goods issue, and invoice (see Chapter 15). Do the following:

1 Call Transaction FBL5N via the command field or start it via the SAP Easy Access menu path: **Accounting ▸ Financial Accounting ▸ Accounts Receivable ▸ Account ▸ Display/Change Items**.

2 In the transaction's initial screen, **Customer Line Item Display**, enter ZXCUST01 in the **Customer Account** field and select **Company Code** 1000. Then click on 🔄 (Execute).

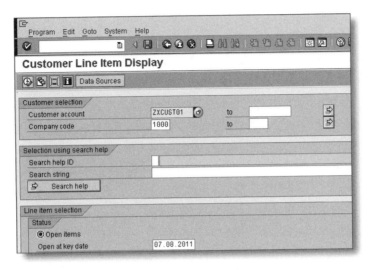

3 The system displays the customer's open items. Special Machinery, Inc. still owes €2,300.00.

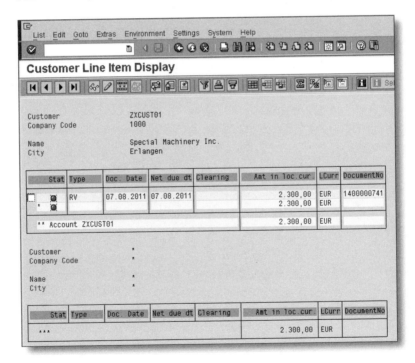

4 After the customer has paid, call Transaction F-28 to post the incoming payment via the command field or via the SAP Easy Access menu path: **Accounting ▸ Financial Accounting ▸ Accounts Receivable ▸ Document**

Entry ▸ Incoming Payments. Alternatively, enter Transaction F-28 directly via the command field.

5 In the initial screen of Transaction F-28, enter the current date in the **Document Date** and **Posting Date** fields.

6 Populate the following fields in the **Bank Data** area:

– **Account:** 113100 (the G/L account in the chart of accounts for the bank account)

– **Amount:** €1338.60 (this amount deviates from the amount in the line item list because the customer receives a cash discount of 3%)

– **value date:** Current date

7 Enter ZXCUST01 in the **Account** field in the **Open item selection** area.

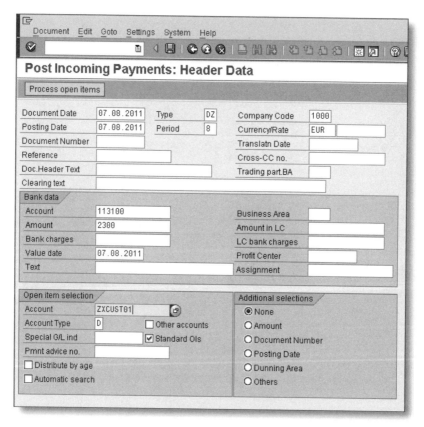

8 After you've pressed the ↵ key, the system takes you to the processing of open items. Post the customer's incoming payment by clicking on 🖫

(Save). Check the result by having the system display the customer's open items one more time.

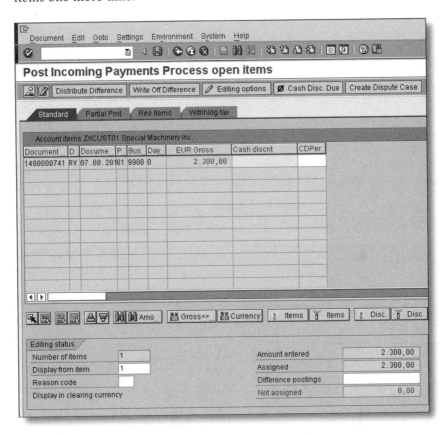

This section presented the most important daily postings in accounts receivable accounting.

16

In accounts receivable accounting, you can also print balance confirmations and dunnings during closing operations, and start automatic transfer postings after the remaining terms. Like in other subcomponents of accounting, a comprehensive information system on customer master data, balances, and line items is available.

16.6 Evaluations

This chapter concludes with the representation of some standard reports for financial accounting. You can find the SAP FI standard reports in the information system in the SAP Easy Access menu under **Information Systems ▸ Accounting ▸ Financial Accounting**.

An example shows how to evaluate how much turnover was achieved with the sales orders of the last fiscal year.

1 Start Transaction S_ALR_87012186 via the command field or choose the **Information Systems ▸ Accounting ▸ Financial Accounting ▸ Accounts Payable ▸ Reports for Accounts Payable Accounting ▸ Vendor Balances S_ALR_87012186 Customer Sales** path in the SAP Easy Access menu.

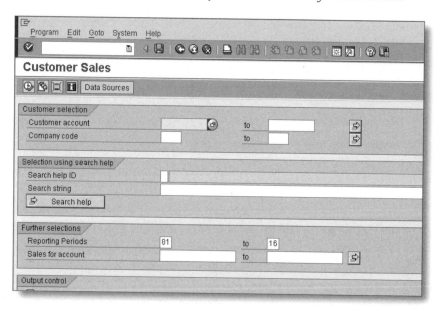

2 Enter the following field values:

- **Company Code:** 1000

- **Fiscal Year:** 2010

- **Reporting Periods:** 01 to 12

3   Then start the report using the [F8] function key or clicking on ⊕ (**Execute**).

4   The report is displayed.

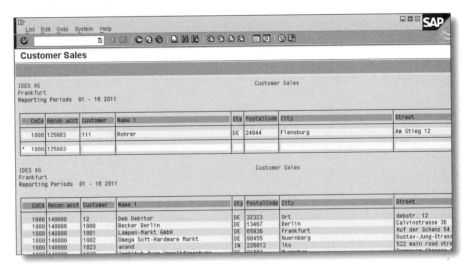

The table lists some examples for reports in SAP FI.

Transaction	Function
S_PL0_86000030	G/L accounts balances (new)
F.08	Balances list
S_ALR_87012093	Vendor sales
F.01	Financial statement
S_ALR_87012186	Customer sales
S_ALR_87012172	Customer balances

Examples of Standard Reports in Financial Accounting

From this chapter you learned about the tasks and functions associated with external accounting. Chapter 17 describes managerial accounting, known as Controlling.

Additional Information

Get more information about SAP FI from *SAP ERP Financials: Configuration and Design* by Naeem Arif and Sheikh Tauseef (SAP PRESS 2011).

17 Controlling

Chapter 16, Financial Accounting, provided a brief overview of the accounting tasks through which business transactions are posted according to legal regulations. Controlling lays the foundations for strategic and operational corporate decisions. These decision-making processes require deep insights into corporate figures (mainly costs and revenues) from all areas of the enterprise. As its name implies, the task of controlling is to control the enterprise rather than to monitor it.

This chapter describes:

- The tasks of controlling
- The organizational units that are used in controlling
- How overhead costs and product costs are settled
- How the profitability analysis works
- Which controlling reports exist in SAP

17.1 Task Areas in Controlling

To implement corporate governance and make strategic decisions, the business's management requires information from all areas of the organization (such as sales and distribution, production, purchasing, etc.). The figures from financial accounting do not provide sufficient information for this purpose, because information that is required from managerial accounting (another name for controlling) has to be more detailed than in external accounting. Financial accounting is closely integrated with controlling since it is the source of much of the latter's data. Nevertheless, financial accounting cannot answer the following questions, as controlling can:

- How can costs be assigned to individual departments and products in the business?

- How can revenue/profit and costs be assigned to customers and products?
- Which revenues/profits and costs will be incurred in the future?

Information in controlling is usually monitored with the help of key performance indicators. Key performance indicators (KPIs) are prepared in compressed (aggregated) form and reflect the success or failure of an enterprise. KPIs are determined from figures that exist in the SAP system and are provided by the individual user departments.

Key Performance Indicators

Key performance indicators are critical to controlling. They provide information about a business situation in a quantifiable and aggregated form, help keep the business objective transparent, and to ensure that the standard of success is measurable. The following are examples of key performance indicators from various areas of the business:

- *Sales volume per customer*: What is the average sales volume per customer?

- *Absence ratio*: What percentage of the planned working time is lost due to employee absences?

- *Storage duration*: How long are the goods or raw materials (and thus capital) stored in the warehouse on average?

- *Service level*: How many sales orders were delivered on the requested delivery date minus all returns?

- *Total Cost of Ownership (TCO)*: What are the costs for operating a device or facility (for example, an IT system like SAP) in a specific period?

Key performance indicators can be either absolute (the number of employees, for example) or relative (price per piece, for example).

Controlling can be divided into two areas: operational and strategic controlling.

In operational controlling, costs and revenues are collected and variances against the predefined plan are calculated and analyzed. One example of the question answered by operational controlling might be: Why did the production costs for a product increase?

The main tasks of operational controlling include:

- Ensuring cost transparency
- Identifying and taking countermeasures against bottlenecks
- Monitoring the ratio of costs and revenues

The core task of strategic controlling is to identify opportunities and risks for a business. In this context, the data lays the foundation for early warning systems in enterprises. If variances between actual and planned costs are identified, effective countermeasures and actions can be taken in the future.

The main tasks of strategic controlling include:

- Planning all business factors
- Ensuring the existence of the enterprise in the long term
- Implementing strategic plans in operational processes

The costs that a business incurs can be examined from various perspectives:

- What costs have been incurred? This question is answered in cost-element accounting by linking the cost elements with the accounts.
- Where have the costs been incurred? Cost center accounting deals with this question by associating the costs with cost centers (departments).
- Why (for which products) have the costs been incurred? This is answered in cost object accounting by associating the costs with work orders, sales orders, or projects.
- Which results are achieved per product, customer, or sales order, for example?

These questions are critical for profitability analysis where costs and revenues are associated with individual market segments.

The following sections describe these concepts in greater detail.

When you examine costs, you are either assessing records from past transactions or projected (future) transactions. Costs from the actual consumption of goods and services are called actual costs, whereas costs of the future are planned costs. You additionally differentiate between full costs and variable costs. In full absorption costing, all costs—including the fixed costs (overhead costs)—from a specific period are allocated to the corresponding cost objects, which gives rise to the term fully loaded cost; in variable costing, in contrast, only the "decision-relevant" costs (strictly speaking, the variable part) are allocated.

17

EXAMPLE

Planned/Actual Costs

The following example illustrates how planned and actual costs are determined. You've planned your costs per cost element; the actual values are set based on those in financial accounting and compared to the planned values, and then possible variances are analyzed.

Cost Element	Planned (in US$)	Actual (in US$)	Planned/Actual Comparison (in US$)
Energy Costs	10,000	12,000	2,000
Rental Costs	20,000	21,000	1,000
Telephone Costs	3,000	2,500	– 500

You might also want to make similar planned/actual comparisons for different windows of time (for example, a fiscal quarter or a year).

EXAMPLE

Absorption and Variable Costing

What's the difference between variable costing and absorption costing? To answer this question, let's assume you manufacture two products and generate sales volumes in US$ per product.

Variable costing (contribution margin accounting) only takes the variable costs, such as material consumption, into account. These costs depend on the production quantity in the sense that the material input will vary with the volume of goods produced. The following table provides an example that illustrates variable costing.

	Product 1	Product 2	Total
Sales Volume	10,000	16,000	26,000
Variable Costs	6,000	11,000	17,000
Variable Costing	4,000	5,000	9,000

Absorption costing takes both the fixed costs and the variable costs into account. Fixed costs are incurred regardless of the production quantity (for example, heating costs for a warehouse).

	Product 1	Product 2	Total
Sales Volume	10,000	16,000	26,000
Variable Costs	6,000	11,000	17,000
Variable Costing	4,000	5,000	9,000
Fixed Costs	2,000	4,000	5,000
Profit	2,000	1,000	4,000

The profit can be determined only after you have considered all costs (both fixed and variable).

In the SAP system, the controlling component answers questions concerning costs and revenues in enterprises. The following are the most important sub-components in SAP CO:

- **Overhead Cost Controlling**
  Overhead costs are costs that cannot be directly allocated to products or services. This component mainly manages cost centers and internal orders. In the SAP system, Overhead Cost Controlling is especially closely integrated with SAP FI. This means that any overhead costs recorded in financial accounting are mapped in the SAP system to the cost elements and cost centers.

- **Product Cost Controlling**
  This area deals with product costing. Consequently, Product Cost Controlling retrieves a lot of data from production planning (SAP PP) and purchasing (SAP MM). Cost object accounting is used to record the product costs in the SAP system, capturing the material usage and work performed per product.

- **Profitability Analysis**
  This area matches revenues from sales and distribution with costs from overhead cost and product cost accounting, so it receives critical data from sales and distribution (SAP SD). This interaction provides information on the profitability or on the contribution margin.

These three main areas of controlling are introduced in this chapter. As in the previous chapters, however, let's first take a look at the structures on which the Controlling component of SAP ERP, which we'll refer to as SAP CO, is based.

17

17.2   Organizational Structures

You've already got to know organizational structures in the previous chapters (particularly in Chapter 4, Organizational Structures and Master Data). This section discusses the organizational units that are relevant for controlling. Though client and company code also play a role in controlling, they are not explained again.

- **Controlling area**
  The controlling area is a self-contained unit; it is at this level that cost accounting (controlling) is implemented. One or more company codes can be assigned to a controlling area. In turn, one or more controlling areas can be assigned to an operating concern.

- **Operating concern**
  The operating concern is a part of the business that is used to structure the sales market. It provides a complete view of the business's operating profits.

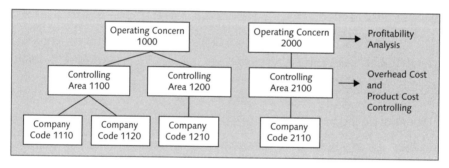

Organizational Units in Controlling

In controlling, further organizational units play a role but are maintained in other SAP components: plant and storage location (SAP MM), company code (SAP FI), and sales area (SAP SD).

The following sections discuss the critical areas of controlling. We start with overhead cost controlling, which also covers the largest part of this chapter, because overhead costs represent a large part (often the majority) of the costs that are incurred in an enterprise.

17.3 Overhead Cost Controlling

In contrast to direct costs, overhead costs are those costs that cannot be directly assigned to products or services (such as rental costs, wages and salaries, general energy costs). This distinction may sound simple, but overhead cost accounting is very demanding because the correct entry, analysis, and settlement of overhead costs is very complex. The Overhead Management component (CO-OM) enables you to plan, control, and monitor overhead costs for corresponding cost centers.

Before this section illustrates how overhead cost controlling works in the SAP system, it first explains the most important concepts from this area:

- True and designated overhead costs
- Cost centers
- Activity types
- Internal orders
- Primary and secondary cost elements

It is important to distinguish between direct and indirect overhead costs. True overhead costs cannot be directly assigned to an account assignment object, such as a cost center. Examples include salaries, energy costs, or facility costs. Designated overhead costs can be assigned to an account assignment object, but this process involves a disproportional amount of effort. Theoretically, you can record them as direct costs and allocate them to an individual product. However, this procedure can be relatively time-consuming, so overhead costs are often distributed to the cost centers using a percentage-based allocation. Depending on the type of overhead costs, the basis for this distribution can be the number of employees, the space requirements of the department, the number of computers in the department, and so on.

The most important areas of overhead cost controlling are cost center accounting and internal orders.

A cost center is a business-specific account assignment object to which expenses are posted. Cost center accounting lets you implement precise cost planning and allocation in the SAP system so you can track the costs back to their origin.

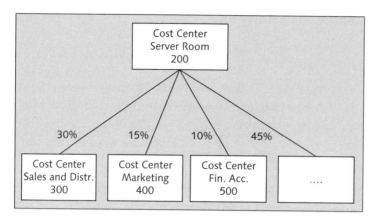

Example of Cost Distribution to Cost Centers by Percentage

Cost centers help assign costs within the business. In most cases, cost centers are set up to correspond to the functional areas in the business, such as sales and distribution, marketing, human resources, IT, and financials. Accordingly, in the SAP system a cost center is assigned to a department or production plant. In very small businesses, however, departments often encompass multiple cost centers in order to ensure transparent cost records and cost accounting. The reason for the assignment is to ensure that the actual costs in the cost centers do not exceed the planned costs or budget costs.

Cost centers belong to central master data in SAP CO. In the SAP system, you can create cost centers via the Transaction KS01 or the SAP Easy Access menu path: **Accounting ▸ Controlling ▸ Cost Center Accounting ▸ Master Data ▸ Cost Center ▸ Individual Processing ▸ Create**. Here, you can enter key data, such as the person responsible for the cost center, controlling area, business area, and so on. Cost centers can be linked hierarchically (that is, a cost center group for a department can contain several cost centers). In this case, however, you can make a posting only to the cost centers at the lowest level.

EXAMPLE

Cost Centers in the IT Department

The cost centers for the IT department could be subdivided into cost centers for hardware, software, support, or consulting.

- K100   IT
- K1001   IT—Hardware
- K1002   IT—Software

- K1003   IT—Support

- K1004   IT—Consulting

Cost center K100 is used for reporting purposes only; individual postings are made to cost centers K1001-K1004.

In the SAP system, you can create and maintain cost center groups via the menu path: **Accounting ▶ Controlling ▶ Cost Center Accounting ▶ Master Data ▶ Cost Center Group ▶ Create/Change/Display.**

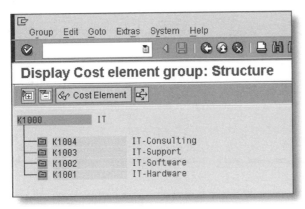

Cost Center Group in the SAP System

Activity types are used for comprehensive cost center management. An activity type assigns performed activities to cost centers; they are then valuated using prices (output price).

EXAMPLE

Activity Types

Let's assume a cutting machine is mapped by a cost center. To perform an activity with the cutting machine, you need both the machine and an employee to operate it. This example involves machine activities and person activities. If you map these activities in time units, the two activity types are defined as machine time and person time, in which certain activities are performed simultaneously at the cutting machine in a specific period.

A critical process within cost center accounting is variance analysis, which compares actual and planned costs.

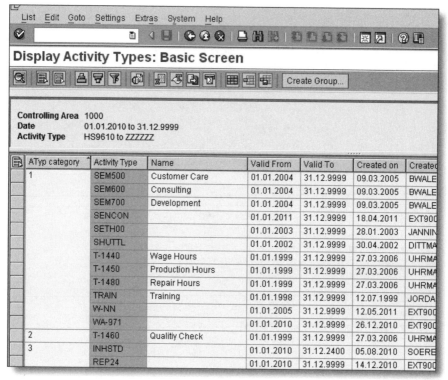

Activity Types in the SAP System (Transaction KL13)

Internal orders provide an additional option for determining actual costs. They are monitored to provide a permanent comparison of actual costs and revenues with planned costs and revenues. As you can with cost centers, you can compare the actual costs of an internal order with its planned costs. However, internal orders for internal projects (like an SAP implementation) provide more transparency because the costs are listed for individual tasks and not for the entire cost center. Internal orders are activated for a certain period, such as for the duration of the project; once the project has been completed, they are locked. Cost centers, by comparison, have a longer lifecycle, though they, too, can change their assignments or managers over time.

In the SAP system, you can create an internal order via Transaction KO01 or the menu path: **Accounting ▸ Controlling ▸ Internal Orders ▸ Master Data ▸ Special Functions ▸ Order ▸ Create.**

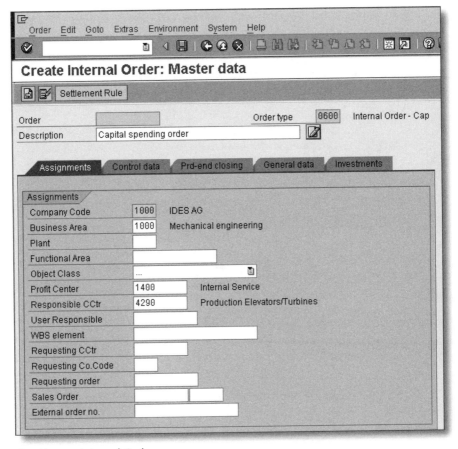

Creating an Internal Order

In controlling, all postings are recorded using cost elements in the controlling area. Cost elements are G/L accounts (see Chapter 16, Financial Accounting), which are relevant for SAP CO. The following are examples of cost elements:

- Material costs
- Personnel costs
- Service costs
- Costing-based costs (depreciations, interests, etc.)
- Taxes and fees

If you have defined a G/L account as a cost element in SAP CO, you have to check that the costs for the cost element are assigned to an SAP CO account assignment for every posting. Usually the account assignment is a cost center or internal order. If you don't enter an SAP CO account assignment (initiating object), you can't complete the posting and the system issues an error message.

EXAMPLE

Cost Elements

If you post a vendor invoice of $100 travel expenses in G/L account 474240, the SAP CO component automatically implements a parallel posting of the same amount for cost element 474240. This must be associated with a cost center or order.

Vendor (Payables)—FI 100 Euro	G/L Account 474240—FI 100 Euro

Cost Element 47420—CO 100 Euro	CO Account Assignment Cost Center 300

Example of a Parallel Posting of Cost Elements in Controlling

This way you can separate the costs from G/L accounting at a later stage.

Cost elements are divided into primary and secondary cost elements. Primary costs are directly transferred to controlling as actual costs if the primary cost element has been defined as a G/L account in the chart of accounts. Secondary cost elements, by comparison, are only used for cost management within controlling and are not mapped in financial accounting. That is, no G/L accounts are created for secondary cost elements in the chart of accounts. Secondary cost elements are assigned to a different number range from the one used for primary cost elements. This way, you can quickly determine in controlling which posting was recorded as a primary posting (invoice entry) and which posting was made as the result of cost allocation.

EXAMPLE

Primary and Secondary Cost Elements

A business has a cafeteria that incurs costs. However, the cafeteria does not provide services for itself but instead for two departments—administration and production. So at the end of the month, the cafeteria costs are charged to the respective departments by creating a transfer posting. The transfer posting is made using the secondary cost element.

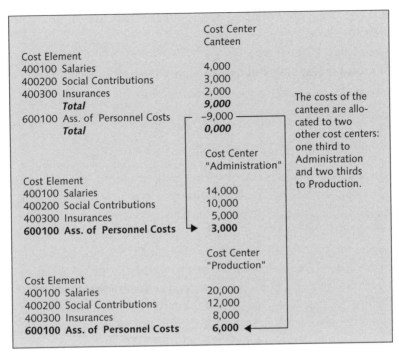

Cost Assessment Using Secondary Cost Elements

17.4   Product Cost Controlling

It is critical for every business that sells a product to have the product costs under control. If the production or procurement costs increase, the profitability can be directly and seriously affected. Consequently, the SAP component for product cost controlling provides options for calculating and recording product and service costs. This product costing component is also referred to as CO-PC, and focuses on the following tasks:

- Product costing
- Inventory valuation
- Simultaneous costing
- Variance calculation

Product cost controlling is based on the use of a standard cost estimate that sets the standard price for internally produced materials based on the BOM (Bill of Material) and routing. CO-PC is closely integrated with SAP PP, in which you create the bills of material and routings. These are then used to calculate costs in CO-PC.

The Production Planning and Control Component
SAP PP handles the planning and control processes for the manufacture of goods (production processes).

Here, you distinguish between material costs and activity costs.

Material costs include all goods that are purchased, produced, or sold in the business (for example, raw materials, intermediate products, finished products, trading goods, supplies, assemblies, packaging material, and even services). Material prices are used to determine the costs of materials. They are calculated using the consumption quantity (from the BOM) and the material price (from the material master). The relevant information is stored in the material master in the SAP system (see Chapter 14, Materials Management). The material master is created in the SAP MM component and contains information about all materials that a company procures, produces, stores, or sells.

Activity costs are charged when a direct activity allocation takes place within overhead cost controlling and uses activity types that are valuated with a price. The individual production steps are listed in the routing or recipe.

Bill of Material and Routing
The bill of material lists the quantities and materials that are required to produce something. A BOM for a book in DIN A5 format with 16 pages can include the following:

- 8 pages A4
- 1 cover
- 2 clips

The routing defines which steps are necessary to produce a product. For our book, the following steps are necessary:

- Printing
- Cutting
- Folding
- Stapling
- Binding

Product costing is used to determine the standard price that will be used to valuate the inventory of the respective material. A product cost estimate is usually performed for products manufactured in-house, and sets the standard price while purchased materials are valuated with a moving average price.

> **Moving Average Price**
>
> The moving average price (short: MAP) is used for the valuation of items that have been purchased at different prices over time. With each goods movement case, the system automatically adjusts the material prices in order to include the price variances caused by the goods movements and invoices. You can find an example for the determination of a MAP in Chapter 14, Materials Management.

In cost object accounting, the costs are planned for every production order on the basis of the BOM of the material to be manufactured and the routing. This cost is then used for simultaneous costing. Because the exact costs for the production of a product can only be determined retroactively using the material ledger, simultaneous costing is used in the interim to determine the financial effects of price reductions and additional expenses. Any variances between actual costs and planned costs (such as price changes for purchased materials or the additional consumption of materials) can be analyzed in detail in order to detect the cause of the difference.

The following is an example of product cost controlling in the SAP system: Product costing with quantity structure is normally carried out per material. A quantity structure is a detailed representation of all material components (from the BOM) and services that are required to manufacture a product. Costing without quantity structure excludes BOMs and routings, and is usually used if the quantity structure data from production planning is incomplete or unavailable. If you use a quantity structure, the system implements the costing automatically. For this reason, BOMs and routings need to be available in the SAP system.

In the SAP system, do the following: Start Transaction CK11N, or navigate in the SAP Easy Access menu. Create a material cost estimate with quantity structure in the application menu via **Controlling ▸ Product Cost Controlling ▸ Product Cost Planning ▸ Material Costing ▸ Cost Estimate with Quantity Structure ▸ Create.**

In the initial material cost estimate screen, enter the plant in which the material will be manufactured, the material number, and the costing variant. Then click on ⊕ (**Execute**). In the **Selection** area, you enter the plant (here, 1000), the material number (here, T-F210), and the costing variant (here, PPC1) in the respective fields. The **Output** area is **Cost Component View** 1 in the example.

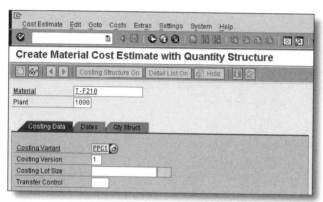

Create Material Cost Estimate with Quantity Structure—Costing Data

The screen in the SAP system displays the material's components to the left. To the right, you can view the costing for the selected material.

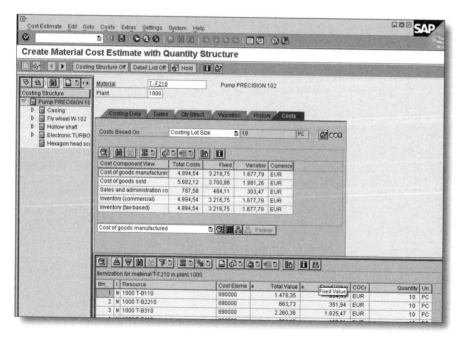

After this overview of product cost accounting, the next section focuses on the profitability analysis.

17.5   Profitability Analysis

One of the key reasons to implement controlling is to understand profitability. Here, the focus is on with which product or customer the highest profit is made. Profitability analysis (CO-PA) answers this question.

It is used, for example, for variable costing (contribution margin accounting) or absorption costing in combination with specific criteria such as customer, product, or region. Businesses incur costs for wages, salaries, energy, materials, and so on. Selling the manufactured goods leads to revenues. At its simplest, the difference between revenues and costs is the profit. The contribution margin is the difference between the earned revenues and the variable costs, and thus refers to the amount that is available to cover fixed costs. In full absorption costing, in turn, all costs are allocated to cost objects. That is the business perspective.

In addition, it can be important to know the difference between costs and revenue per product, customer, market segment, and so on. To determine this, you have to integrate data from other SAP components. Because this data is mainly sales-related, the central information is provided by SAP SD. In the Customizing of Profitability Analysis, you define which information from SAP SD you want to copy as a characteristic to CO-PA (for example, division, article, customer, or material group) and which numeric values you want to transfer from SAP SD to CO-PA (for example, sales quantity or gross revenue).

INFO

Characteristics and Value Fields

The data structure in CO-PA consists of characteristics and value fields that let you structure, select, and sort your data in Profitability Analysis. You can copy the characteristics from SAP SD or directly from the article or customer master. For example:

- Division (SAP SD)
- Product (SAP SD sales order)
- Customer (SAP SD sales order)
- Material group (article master)

> Alternatively, you can derive your characteristics from an existing characteristic. For example, you can derive the continent from the country of the customer and thus sort your evaluations by country and continent.
>
> Value fields represent values or quantities, for example:
>
> ▪ Sales quantity (SAP SD sales order)
>
> ▪ Gross revenue (SAP SD conditions)

The advantage of the data structure in Profitability Analysis is its flexibility. Since there is no defined structure, you can develop the structure according to your specific requirements. You decide whether you want to have the bill-to-party or ship-to-party as a characteristic in addition to the customer, or whether you need discounts from the SAP SD conditions in addition to the level of detail already being transferred from CO-PC to cover the product costs.

	Sales Revenues
./.	Variable Costs
=	Contribution Margin I
./.	Product-Related Fixed Costs
=	Contribution Margin II
./.	Product Group-Related Fixed Costs
=	Contribution Margin III
./.	Fixed Area Costs
=	Contribution Margin IV
./.	Fixed Enterprise Costs
=	**Operating Profit**

Example of Profitability Analysis

The operating profit for a product is calculated using the sales revenue minus all variable and fixed costs. The individual contribution margins are calculated as subtotals. To give you an overview of how you can call your CO-PA data, the following example displays a profitability report for the individual divisions.

Call Transaction KE30 via the command field, or navigate via the SAP Easy Access menu path: Accounting ▸ Controlling ▸ Profitability Analysis ▸ Information System ▸ Execute Report.

If the system prompts you to, set the operating concern before the system takes you to the initial screen. Then, continue with the ↵ key or ✔ button (**Accept**). The operating concern in this example is IDEA (IDES global).

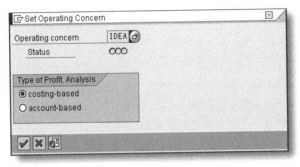

Setting the Operating Concern

In the next screen, you have to select the profitability report that you want to view. Select the report, and continue with the ↵ key or **Next** button. The profitability report in this example is SAP01-001.

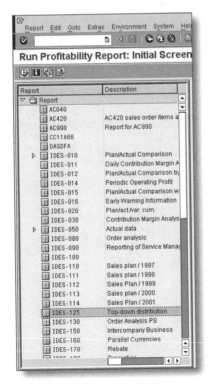

Selecting the Report

In the initial screen of the transaction, enter the fiscal year, period, and version. To see the example shown, make sure that the graphical report output is selected. Click the **Execute** button ( ), or press the F8 functional key. In the **Report Selections** area, make the following specifications: **Fiscal Year** 2002, **From Period** 001.2002 and **To Period** 012.2002, **Version** 100. The version is used to differentiate the various costing variants for one material. Under **Output Type**, you can select the graphical report output.

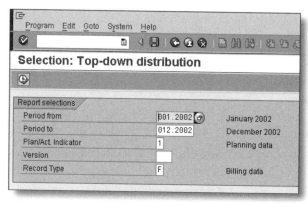

Selection for the Profitability Report

The next screen displays the profitability report for the individual divisions.

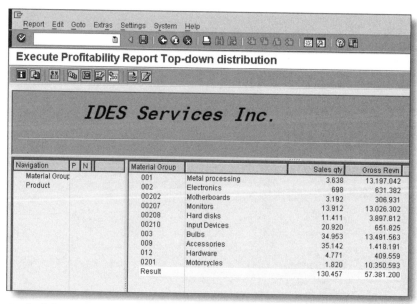

Profitability Report

In the lower part of the screen, you can now see your sales quantity and gross revenues (value fields) as planned and actual data, absolute variances, and variances in percentages as the total. By double-clicking on this navigation area, you get detailed information about division, article, customer, or material group characteristics. Evaluations

Now you know some of the tasks and transactions of SAP CO. Especially in controlling, evaluation of the various data from a business's various departments is critical for making decisions and planning processes. The SAP system also provides a range of standard reports for SAP CO (for example, planned/actual comparisons, line item reports, and business unit analyses).

This section provides an overview of some evaluations that are available in the SAP system. The following report, for example, provides information on planned and actual costs of a sales order: **Logistics ▶ Production ▶ Shop Floor Control ▶ Information System ▶ Controlling Reports ▶ Product Cost by Sales Order ▶ Detailed Reports ▶ For Sales-Order Cost Estimate and Order BOM Cost Estimate.**

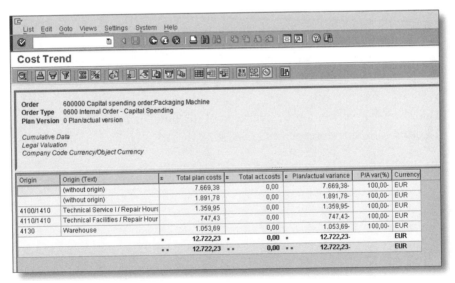

Analyzing a Sales Order—Transaction KKBC_ORD

The following table lists some standard reports for controlling in SAP ERP 6.0.

Transaction	Evaluation
KKBC_ORD	Analysis of sales orders
KE30	Profitability analysis
S_ALR_87010779	Comparison between current and previous year
S_ALR_87012082	Vendor balances
S_ALR_87012173	Open customer items
S_ALR_87012186	Customer sales

Sample Reports in Controlling

Because complex report requirements are common in controlling, reporting tools that can be used to create individual evaluations are more important here than in other areas of the enterprise. This includes the Report Painter and Drilldown Reporting tools that were introduced in Chapter 8, Creating Evaluations and Reports.

Additional Information

If you want to access additional information on CO, refer to *Controlling with SAP—Practical Guide* by Janet Salmon (SAP PRESS 2012).

This chapter gave you a brief overview of the functions of SAP CO. Chapter 18 deals with human resources in SAP ERP HCM.

18 Human Resources

"Employees are the key asset of any enterprise" is a common business adage that speaks to the importance of effectively cultivating and managing an employee base. The significance of employees in an enterprise is also reflected in the name of SAP's latest component for human resources, SAP ERP HCM (Human Capital Management). In earlier SAP releases, the component had been called SAP HR (Human Resources), but was renamed with the release of mySAP ERP 2004.

This chapter describes:

- The business' structural organization and how to manage it
- Searching for new employees
- Maintaining HR master data
- Training employees
- The functions for recording working times
- Implementing payroll for salaries and wages

18.1 Tasks in SAP Human Resources

The tasks of SAP ERP HCM encompass much more than just managing a business's employees. In fact, the tasks of the HR department are versatile: For example, if a new position supposed needs to be filled, the position—which was created first in the organizational structure through organizational management—must be advertised. Recruitment helps you manage applicant data and thus search for and select the appropriate candidate for the job. Once an appropriate applicant is hired, important HR master data (address, date of birth, marital status, and so on) needs to be entered into the system. This data that is managed in Personnel Administration is mandatory for nearly all HR processes.

Perhaps a new colleague recently started working for your company. The payroll department is now responsible for transferring the salary to the employee's account and for making the payroll results available to financial accounting and controlling. (Due to deviations in regulations on taxes and social security contributions, payroll is highly country-specific.) Time management is closely tied payroll. Here, employee's working times, vacation days, and sick days are recorded and evaluated. The management of business trips also falls into the realm of the HR department. For this purpose, you can use SAP Travel Management.

An additional task of the HR department is personnel development. Because employees have to develop their skills in order to master changing business requirements, "employee lifelong learning" ceases to be a meaningless buzzword and becomes a business necessity. Trainings are planned, implemented, and processed with Training and Event Management.

The smooth execution of HR business processes saves time and money because employees in this department should deal with administrative tasks as infrequently as necessary.

The following are the central elements of SAP ERP HCM that support businesses in meeting these requirements:

- **Personnel Administration**
  You use Personnel Administration to enter and edit employee-related data. The SAP system checks the data for plausibility, and the processing history of the data remains transparent in the system. The information on each employee is stored in infotypes that structure the data, facilitate its entry, and enable time-based data storage. The infotypes for a process are combined in personnel actions.

- **Recruitment**
  Recruitment is everything that falls between creating applicant data and filling vacant positions. The SAP system supports the management of applicants as well as the selection process and communication with applicants.

- **Talent Management**
  This SAP subcomponent supports enterprises in training employees. You can implement continuing education and trainings both to motivate employees and to respond to organizational and structural changes in the business.

- **Payroll**
  Payroll ensures that the remuneration for performed work is determined and paid to an employee; it includes the preparation, settlement, and

transfer of the remuneration, and takes tax specifications and social security contributions into consideration. That is why payroll is highly country-specific.

- **Time Management**
  With Time Management, you can manage time accounts and provide information to payroll. This subcomponent lets you enter time data and integrates with time recording tools.

- **Organizational Management**
  This subcomponent enables you to map the business structure (for example, the department hierarchy) and the reporting structure in a structural organization. You can use it to implement Talent Management and to recruit efficiently.

- **Training and Event Management**
  This SAP subcomponent helps you plan, implement, postprocess, and settle events. You can maintain the information that is required for the event (rooms, materials, etc.), determine the requirements for the event, schedule dates, manage participants, and allocate costs.

- **Travel Management**
  Use this to enter and allocate employees' travel costs.

Due to its versatile usage areas, SAP ERP HCM is closely connected to other SAP components. This is specifically discussed in later sections of this chapter.

The following sections give you a detailed overview of the essential HR tasks with SAP with emphasis on organizational management, recruitment, personnel administration, time management, and payroll. The first section deals with a component in which numerous prerequisites are met and structures are defined: Organizational Management. In this context, it also briefly explains the organizational structures in SAP ERP HCM.

18.2 Organizational Management

In the organizational management component in HCM, you maintain data that maps the business structure or structural organization. This data is used, for example, to create organization charts, job descriptions, job indexes, and evaluations. Organizational Management is also useful when you want to develop an authorization concept (see Chapter 13, The Role and Authorization Concept), but isn't required by all businesses that deploy SAP ERP HCM.

Organizational structures map the business' structural organization in the SAP system from the human resources perspective. The structural organization reflects the task-related (that is, functional) organizational structures of the company, such as positions, which are filled by employees and linked to each other. You can also define further links (for example, to tasks or jobs).

The various structural organizations are known as plan versions in the SAP system. These let you reproduce different scenarios (for example, a reorganization of the company) with different plans.

The organizational structure is made up of the individual organizational units so that the hierarchies of the existing business structure are transferred to the SAP system. In contrast to the logistics or accounting organizational structures, the HCM organizational structures are not defined in Customizing but in Organizational Management.

Organizational Management also lets you integrate organizational units that are created in other SAP components, such as cost centers. A cost center is an internal account assignment object in the business and is usually sorted by functional areas. Cost centers are maintained in Financial Accounting and assigned to the organizational units in Organizational Management.

The following objects or organizational units play a central role in Organizational Management:

- **Organizational units**
  Organizational units describe the business' structural organization according to business, regional and responsibility aspects.

- **Jobs**
  Jobs classify tasks in the business. Accordingly, the respective task areas and employee requirements are assigned to jobs. Jobs have general descriptions, such as *Head of Financial Accounting* or *Agent for Accounts Payable Accounting*.

- **Positions**
  Positions are concrete jobs in a business that are filled by employees. The company defines the respective numbers of positions. So a job is kind of a template for the position.

- **Persons**
  Persons are objects that fill positions. Examples could be:
  - J. Doe fills the *System Administrator* position.
  - H. Smith fills the *Personnel Consultant* position.

- **Infotypes**

  An infotype is a summary of a data record's fields (HR master record). In SAP, you enter master data using infotypes. More information on infotypes can be found later in this section.

The following figure shows a typical business structure. Sales and distribution and financial accounting report directly to management. Sales and distribution is subdivided into enterprise customers and private customers. Financial accounting is subdivided into accounts payable accounting and accounts receivable accounting.

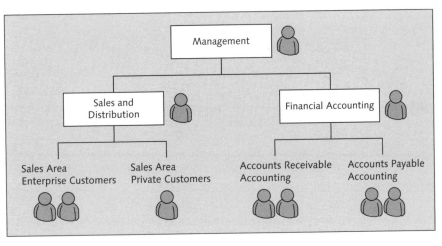

Example of an Enterprise Structure

To create an organizational unit (for example, a position) in HCM, take the following steps:

1 In the SAP Easy Access menu, select **Human Resources ▸ Organizational Management ▸ Organizational Plan ▸ Organization and Staffing** (Transaction PPOCE).

2 The initial screen for creating a root organizational unit opens. Define the validity period and confirm it with ↵.

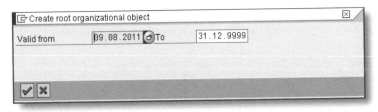

18

3 Double-click on the organizational unit you want to create in the left
screen area to select it, and then create it by clicking on the **Create** button
(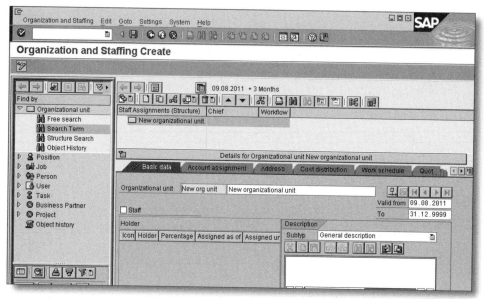).

Create Organization and Staffing (Transaction PPOCE)

After this overview of the organizational structures in SAP ERP HCM, the
next section deals with recruitment.

18.3   Recruitment

It is very important for businesses to meet changing requirements in terms of
employees, especially as the enterprise grows. For applicants, too, a potential
employer is very attractive if its human resources department responds
quickly and professionally to their job applications. The SAP component for
recruitment helps you determine workforce requirements, advertise open
positions, manage applicant information, and select the appropriate applicants.

Usually, the process of searching for a new employee is as follows:

1. The workforce requirements are determined and defined.

2. A job is advertised inside or outside the business.

3. Applicant data is entered into the system and evaluated.

4. The applicants are contacted, and interviews are carried out for the selection process.

5. An employment contract is generated once an applicant is hired.

6. Finally, the applicant data is entered in the HR master.

Recruitment Process Steps

In the SAP system, you can create a requirements profile for the job you want to fill. In this profile, you can select the qualifications that you will look for in applicants (Transaction PBAP).

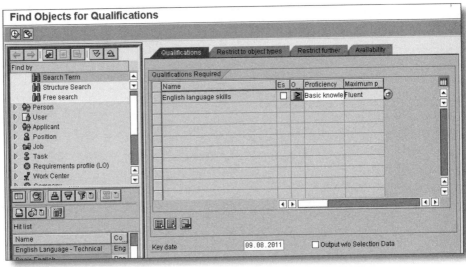

Searching for Applicants with Defined Qualifications—Transaction PBAP

Information about applications can either be entered by HR department employees or by applicants themselves via a job-seekers' portal.

Applicant Portals

More and more businesses provide specific portals for online applications on their websites. Another common option is using commercial job
exchanges. In both cases, the applicant himself enters his data, which is
transferred to the SAP system and processed there. Not all businesses
that deploy HCM use this option, but it does mean that employees from
the HR department don't have to enter the applicant data manually into
the system.

You can call the applicant data via Transaction PB20 or through the SAP Easy
Access menu path: **Human Resources ▸ Personnel Management ▸ Recruitment
▸ Appl.master data.**

The infotypes that are maintained in the applicant master record are selected
with a green checkmark ✔ . To view an infotype, select the line and click 🔍
(Display).

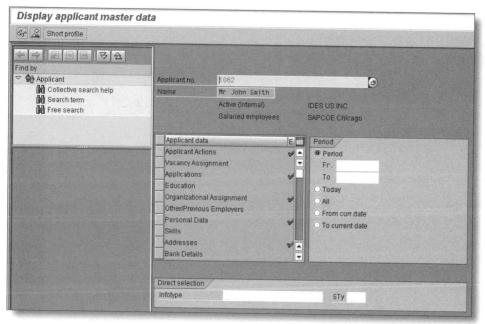

Applicant Master Record

The short profile provides a summary of the applicant profile. Click on the
Short Profile button to display the applicant's short profile.

In addition to helping users select the best applicants, HCM aids in corresponding with them during the recruitment process. This correspondence includes the generation of acknowledgments of receipts, invitations for interviews, and letters of rejection. If an applicant is hired, his data is transferred to HR master record and maintained in Personnel Administration.

The next section discusses the SAP ERP HCM Personnel Administration component.

```
Display Text:


        Mr John Smith
        5 Westbrook Center
        Oakbrook  60164

        Telephone: 7089473400

        Date of Birth:   1949.12.02
        Gender:          Male
        Nationality:     American
        Letter language: English

        Actions:
          Action: Further application,
                  valid from 1996.02.13
          Status: In process

        Application(Activities):
          on 1996.02.12 , Advertisment 00000015 from 1996.01.01
                          in Employee Kiosk
            - Receipt scheduled on 1996.02.13 , at 00.00 Uhr.
            - Receipt finished on 1996.02.12 , at 17.06 Uhr.
          Vacancy: Controller (US)
          Building/Room number: 330 / HR210
            - Interview inv. finished on 1996.02.12 , at 17.06 Uhr.
            - Hiring scheduled on 1996.02.12 , at 00.00 Uhr.
          Vacancy: Controller (US)
            - Transfer data scheduled on 1996.02.14 , at 00.00 Uhr.
          Vacancy: Controller (US)
          on 1996.02.13 , Advertisment 00000111 from 1996.01.10
                          in New York Times
            - Receipt scheduled on 1996.03.13 , at 00.00 Uhr.
```

Short Profile of the Applicant

18.4   Personnel Administration

The personnel administration area covers all business activities that are carried out within the scope of employee management, including the creation, maintenance, and assignment of HR master data. Maintaining quality HR master data is critical to performing personnel activities effectively.

Good Master Data Maintenance

HR department employees are responsible for keeping the master data complete, up-to-date, and correct. Changes should always be implemented immediately. In addition, in SAP ERP HCM it is very important to not delete historical data but keep it in the SAP system.

Examples of central master data in personnel administration include the personnel number by which you uniquely identify an employee and the employment status that indicates whether an individual is currently employed by the business.

Human Resources and Data Protection

Master data in HCM is highly sensitive personal data that must be treated with due diligence by the business and responsible employees. Violating the legal requirements that regulate data protection can lead to legal consequences for the business and the involved HR department employee.

Of course, this does not only apply to the information stored in HCM, but also to general personal data. In the SAP system, a role concept ensures that only authorized employees can access the data and transactions. Chapter 13 provides more information on roles and authorizations.

The management of employee data is based on predefined processes called personnel actions. The HR data maintenance processes include each employee's employment (or reentry), organizational change (when employees change departments), or leave (for example, due to termination or retirement).

Employee data is stored in infotypes, which play a central role for your work with HCM. A personnel action consists of the infotypes for which you have to enter data during the personnel action. For example, if a new employee is hired, you subsequently process all fields that are necessary for this personnel action.

Infotypes consequently refer to a logically related area of data. The following table lists the infotypes that must be maintained for the *Employment* personnel action in personnel administration.

Infotype	Name
0000	Actions
0003	Payroll Status
0001	Organizational Assignment
0002	Personal Data
0006	Addresses
0007	Planned Working Time
0008	Basic Pay
0009	Bank Details
0012	Tax Data
0013	Social Security Data
0020	Pensions
0016	Integral Parts of the Contract
0019	Monitoring of Tasks
2006	Absence Quotas

Infotypes for the "Employment" Personnel Action

All of this master data needs to be entered when a new employee is hired. To call personnel actions, enter Transaction PA40 in the command field or select **Human Resources ▶ Personnel Management ▶ Administration ▶ HR Master Data** from the SAP Easy Access menu. The system displays the initial screen for personnel actions. Enter the entry date, along with the hired employee's personnel number. Then select the **Employment** action type and click **Execute**. Processing the **Leave** action type (when an employee leaves the business) is similar.

Proceed with the infotypes that are necessary for each action and which were already listed in the table. Maintain the respective fields for each infotype. After entering all data, click **Save**. The SAP system then prompts the next infotype that needs to be maintained for the action's completion.

A lot of the infotypes already contain default values. In addition, the SAP system checks the plausibility of the entries and questions anything unlikely.

18

Every infotype has a time constraint that defines whether it can contain several records. There are four types of time constraints:

- **Time constraint 0**
  One infotype record exists and does not change throughout the entire period of validity of the HR master.

- **Time constraint 1**
  One valid infotype record must exist.

- **Time constraint 2**
  Either no or exactly one valid infotype record exists.

- **Time constraint 3**
  Either no or multiple valid infotype records exist in parallel.

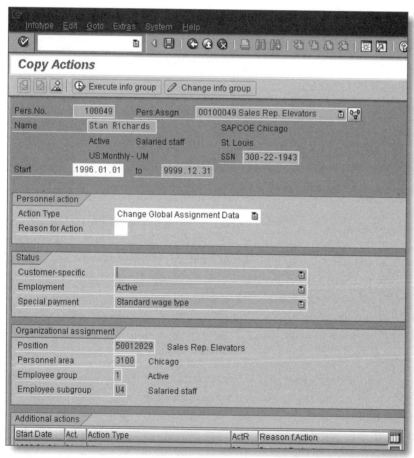

"Leave" Personnel Action

Time Constraint

Let's take Infotype 0021 (Family/related person) as an example of the different time constraint types:

- *Time constraint 0*: The employee must always have the same spouse.

- *Time constraint 1*: The employee must always be married, but not necessarily to the same spouse.

- *Time constraint 2*: The employee can have a spouse but doesn't have to (the realistic scenario).

- *Time constraint 3*: The employee can have no, one, or several spouses.

(Source: *Praxishandbuch SAP-Personalwirtschaft* by Junold et al., 2011)

If you want to have the system display an infotype for your work, you can call the infotype by entering the number, for example, in Transaction PA20 (Display HR Master). In the SAP Easy Access menu, the path is: **Human Resources ▶ Personnel Management ▶ Administration ▶ HR Master Data.** You can determine and view the HR master record by entering the personnel number. If you don't know someone's personnel number, you can search for the master record in the SAP system using search criteria. Call the search window with the **Input Help** button. In the **Personnel Number** field, enter the personnel number, and press the key. Alternatively, use the search window of the input help to find the person.

Enter the required infotype number into the **Infotype** field, and then click (**Display**).

Calling an Infotype

The following figure shows the HR master record for personnel number 70089, a fictitious employee named John Smith.

18

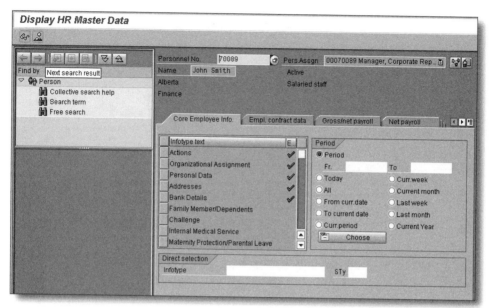

Example of a HR Master Record

The next section discusses Personnel Planning and Development.

18.5 Talent Management

Qualified and motivated employees contribute to the success of every enterprise. The personnel development area in HCM, today known as Talent Management, enables strategic HR work in order to train and motivate employees. In combination with Training and Event Management, Talent Management provides options for planning and implementing measures to further educate and train employees. The requirement for personnel development can be derived from the job description and the employee's existing qualifications.

Employees' qualifications are managed in a qualification catalog that lists the skills and knowledge that are necessary for each job in the enterprise. This catalog helps the HR department manage the required qualifications of employees (and applicants) and compare them with the requirements of the individual tasks. The following figure shows a section from the qualification catalog.

```
1.1 MS Office
1.2 Event Organization
1.3 Office General
2.1 Internal Accounting
2.2 External Accounting
2.3 Knowledge Taxes
3.1 Translation simultaneous Spanish
3.2 Spanish written
4.1 Knowledge C++
4.2 Knowledge ABAP
4.3 Knowledge Java
5.1 Project Management
```

Section from the Qualification Catalog

In HCM, you store the qualifications that are required for a specific job in requirements profiles. The qualifications of individual employees are also stored in profiles. In addition to qualifications, you also assign interests, dislikes, assessments, and so on to the employee. These qualifications do not only include specific certifications or language skills but also soft skills, such as leadership qualities and organizational skills. You can compare the requirements profile with the employee's qualification profile and derive measures for further training based on deviations.

EXAMPLE

Measures for Further Training

The employee Jane Doe is supposed to become the assistant to the Head of Production in the next fiscal year. The job description for this position says that HCM knowledge is a requirement for management tasks. Currently, the employee only has knowledge of SAP SCM, so Jane Doe will attend further training sessions. Ann external SAP trainer will support the employee for three days during her first days with HCM.

18.6   Time Management

On one hand, Time Management is used to enter attendance times, including the duration and length of attendance times and breaks, information on working times outside the usual workplace (such as business trips), and activities performed during the time recorded. On the other hand, it is also used to maintain deviations from the original work schedule, such as overtime,

18

extra shifts, reduced hours, or reintegration. You can also document absences (for example, sick days and leave days) in the system.

You can only evaluate this information if the planned working times of an employee are specified in a work schedule. It documents the agreed number of hours per week and which days the employee doesn't work (for example, public holidays). Like in the other HCM components, the time data is stored in infotypes.

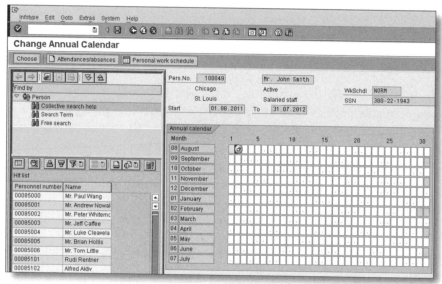

Annual Calendar (Working Days) of an Employee

The time recording process can be automated in the time recording system by HR employee deemed responsible for the task, or by the employee himself. The time can be recorded using both positive recording and negative recording. (Combinations of all of these are also possible.) With positive recording, the times when the employee arrives and leaves are recorded, usually via time-recording terminals (for example, time cards). In negative recording, defined working times are presumed and only the deviations are documented.

EXAMPLE

Integration with Other HCM Components

An employee requests leave for a week in August during which he is registered for a training session on the new IT system. The SAP system sends a message that indicates the time conflict to the HR department.

The following could be considered deviations from the planned working schedule:

- Extra shifts
- Reintegration after illness
- Parental leave

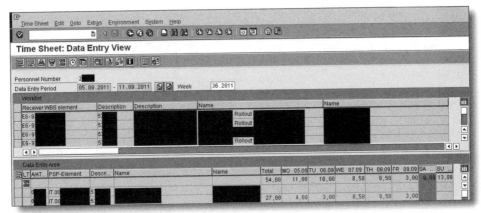

Time Management data is a critical source of information for Payroll, which is described in the next section.

CATS

SAP provides a user-friendly time recording tool for employees called CATS (Cross-Application Time Sheet). It lets you record working times that can be assigned to a WBS element and a cost center. (WBS stands for Work Breakdown Structure and refers to the model that hierarchically maps the activities that need to be carried out in a project.)

CATS is an Employee Self-Service application that is made available to the employees as a web application in an Internet browser (and not in SAP GUI).

18

18.7 Payroll

Payroll calculates the remuneration for employees. It consists of the preparation, settlement, transfer, social security contributions, and transport of the data to Financial Accounting (SAP FI). Payroll processes are very country-specific because they take into consideration numerous legal requirements that govern taxes and social security contributions. If the business has subsidiaries abroad, it is possible that you need to take into account both your own country's special requirements and those of foreign countries. SAP ERP HCM considers the legal requirements from more than 50 countries.

> **INFO**
>
> **Retroactive Accounting**
>
> The section about Personnel Administration already taught you that HCM always also stores historical data. Because this also applies to information from Payroll, settlements from the past can be corrected. If relevant infotypes are changed retroactively, the system automatically triggers retroactive accounting. To document the changed settlement results, the SAP system creates a history.

The Payroll component is closely integrated with SAP FI. The remunerations are paid to the employee via DME (Data Medium Exchange) from HCM, and then the totals from Payroll are posted in SAP FI. The data from Time Management and Personnel Administration is processed for settlement, and finally the results are transferred to SAP FI and SAP CO.

The settlement process occurs as follows:

1. The settlement is prepared once the relevant data is maintained in HCM. This includes information on taxes and social security as well as variable salary components, such as paid extra shifts, end-of-year bonus, and so on.

2. Next payroll is implemented. The gross and net amounts of the remuneration are determined. The net amount is derived from legal deductions (taxes, pension insurance, unemployment insurance, health insurance) and optional deductions, such as retirement plans. Before the settlement can start, it must be released.

3. After the results were checked and if no corrections were necessary, the amount is paid to the employees and the corresponding remuneration statement is created.

4. Social security contributions, taxes, and so on are calculated and transferred to the respective tax offices and social security carriers at defined intervals (usually monthly).

5. At this time, you can carry out various evaluations as required.

6. Finally, the results from the settlement are posted in SAP FI; to which cost centers the costs are allocated is recorded in SAP CO.

Before you start the actual settlement process, you can simulate a settlement to check if the master data has been maintained correctly.

The following example illustrates the payroll process for an employee. The settlement simulation creates the payroll for any period. Start the settlement simulation via Transaction PC00_M99_CALC_SIMU or via the SAP Easy Access menu path: **Human Resources ▶ Payroll ▶ International ▶ Payroll**.

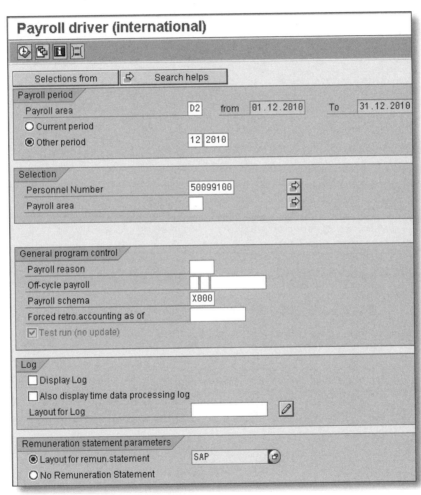

Selection Screen for the Payroll Simulation

The system displays the settlement, as shown for the example in the following figure. Notice that the result shown here is not very realistic because the net amount is the same as the gross amount.

```
Payroll run for      R September 2004
Training Caliber A Bicycle Company       Date  12.08.2011  Page   1

Your administrator is
                                   Personnel no...   50099100
                                   Date of birth..  05.05.1955
                                   Entry..........  01.01.2003
                                   Cost center....
                                   Department.....

        Ms.
        Catherine Camino                   Leave Account
        52 Sap Street
        19111 SAPberg                      Entitlement.....       0,00
                                           Remainder........      0,00



      Paymts/Deduct           Dy/Hrs      Euro        Month   Annual totals

      Monthly salary                               3.000,00

      GROSS TAX/GROSS SI ─────────────────────────────────────────────────
      Total gross amount                           3.000,00     27.000,00

      STATUTORY DEDUCTIONS ───────────────────────────────────────────────

      Statutory net                                3.000,00

      PERSONAL PAYMENTS / DEDUCTIONS ─────────────────────────────────────
      Recalc.diff.to last payr.                    3.000,00-
```

Sample Payroll

18.8   Standard Reporting

The standard version of the information system in Human Resources already provides you with numerous different reports and evaluations. You can find them via the SAP Easy Access menu path: **Human Resources ▸ Information System ▸ Reports**.

Transaction	Function
S_AHR_61015509	Applicants by Names
S_AHR_61015512	Applications
S_AHR_61015513	Applicant Statistics

Examples of Evaluations in HR

Transaction	Function
S_PH9_46000223	Entered and Left
S_PH9_46000221	Birthday List
S_AHR_61016354	Telephone Directory

Examples of Evaluations in HR (Cont.)

> **TIP**
>
> **Additional Information**
> For additional information on SAP ERP HCM, refer to *Discover SAP ERP HCM* by Greg Newman (SAP PRESS 2009).

This chapter introduced you to human resources in SAP ERP HCM. Chapter 19 combines the information from the last five chapters in a case study, which you can reproduce in the SAP IDES system.

18

19   Case Study

This chapter helps you reinforce your knowledge and deploy it with a real-life case study. As an exercise, you implement a case study by carrying out various tasks and processes in the system.

During the course of this case study, you will:

- Create a material master record
- Create a vendor master record
- Create a purchasing info record
- Create a purchase order
- Receive goods
- Verify an invoice
- Display open items
- Post an outgoing payment
- Create a customer master
- Add customer data to the material master record
- Create a condition
- Enter a sales order
- Deliver and issue goods
- Create an invoice
- Post an incoming payment
- Create a sales evaluation (profitability report)
- Create an employee telephone book

Our case study consists of a list of tasks that you or your team need to process.

You can use limitless resources to aid you during this case study; in fact, use all means that are available to you if they are available to you in "real life."

Cooperating with colleagues and sharing your experiences with them will also solidify your understanding of these concepts.

To implement the complete case study, you require an IDES system. SAP provides IDES as a test environment to its customers.

Documentation

Document your work. In "real life," you may have to present your progress to a project team. Good documentation also makes repeating individual steps at a later stage much easier.

Carry out these tasks in the sequence they are presented because the individual process steps are based on each other. Tasks that have the *optional* addition aren't relevant for subsequent processes, so you don't have to perform them.

Remember: Always implement the case study in a training environment and never in a live SAP system! If you're unsure, ask your SAP administrator, supervisor, or trainer.

Good luck!

19.1 The Sample Business

You're an employee in a business called Sportbikes International, which produces and sells road bikes and mountain bikes. These bikes are distributed to resellers and directly to end customers. The company is headquartered in Germany but has plans to start subsidiaries in Great Britain and the U.S. in the medium term. Currently, 200 employees work for the business. The bikes are manufactured in-house but also procured from a supplier and resold. Sportbikes International recently decided to implement SAP in order to support logistics and financial accounting. It plans to use the following components: SAP FI, SAP CO, SAP SD, SAP MM, and SAP ERP HCM.

You, as an experienced user, are a member in the project team for the SAP implementation, and you are provided with work packages with various tasks for testing functions and processes in the system.

19.2   The Enterprise Structure

In this case study, you work in the existing IDES enterprise structure (that is, in the SAP training environment), so you don't have to make specific Customizing settings.

First, get to know the business' structure and its presentation in the SAP system. The following table lists relevant information on the business structure:

Client	(Your client)
Company Code	1000
Plant	1000 Hamburg
Storage Location	0001
Storage Location	0002
Purchasing Organization	1000
Purchasing Group	000

Organizational Units for the Case Study

Check that you have the necessary authorizations and logon information.

In the next table, enter your logon information:

Logon Name	
Password	

Logon Information

Complete the following tasks associated with the business structure:

1. Outline the enterprise structure in an organization chart.
2. To how many company codes can a plant be assigned?
3. Which information is mandatory for logging on to an SAP system?
4. Can the key of a plant (for example, 1000) be assigned several times in a client if the plant is located in another company code?
5. What's the purpose of storage locations?

19.3   Creating Material Master Records

Your company sells two kinds of bikes: road bikes and mountain bikes. For these products, which are called materials in the SAP system, you require the respective material master records, which you must first create.

Complete the following tasks associated with material master records:

Create the material master records for the two bikes in the SAP system using the data listed in the following table. Use the transaction in the SAP Easy Access menu under **General Create**. Make sure that you select the correct organizational units and views.

	Road Bike	**Mountain Bike**
Material Number	ZM-BIKE-10	ZM-BIKE-20
Industry	Mechanical engineering	Mechanical engineering
Material Type	Finished good	Finished good
Required Views	Basic Data1 Purchasing Purchase order text Accounting1 Plant data/Warehouse1	Basic Data1 Purchasing Purchase order text Accounting1 Plant data/Warehouse1
Organizational Units	Plant 1000 Storage location 0001 Purchasing org. 1000	Plant 1000 Storage location 0001 Purchasing org. 1000
Material Short Text	Roadbike Speed XL	Mountainbike Alpine XL
Base Unit of Measure	Piece	Piece
Gross Weight	25	25
Net Weight	13	13
Weight Unit	kg	kg

Material Master Data Sheet: Sample Data for Materials

	Road Bike	Mountain Bike
Material Group	0202 (alternatively: Z00)	0202 (alternatively: Z00)
Purchasing Group	000	000
Purchase Order Text	Roadbike Speed XL, RH 56, aluminum	Mountainbike Alpine XL, RH 54, steel
Valuation Class	7920 (alternatively: 3000)	7920 (alternatively: 3000)
Price Control	MAP	MAP
Moving Average Price	400	300

Material Master Data Sheet: Sample Data for Materials (Cont.)

1 Add the transaction code for creating material master data to your favorites. How do you proceed?

2 How do you test the functioning of the material master records?

3 What are "views" used for in material master records?

4 What is the "moving average price?"

5 Determine the moving average price for the following scenario:

- Opening stock: 10 pieces, price per piece €400.00
- Purchase: 20 pieces, price per piece €300.00

6 Can you also procure material ZM-BIKE-10 for another plant (for example, 1200)?

19.4   Creating Vendor Master Records

Your business purchases materials from several vendors. This time create master records for the vendors. The following table contains the required field content for two vendors.

Complete the following tasks associated with vendor master records:

1 Create the two vendor master records for vendor A and vendor B in the system using the data in the table. Use the transaction in the SAP Easy Access menu under **Central**.

	Vendor A	Vendor B
Vendor Number	ZK-A-10	ZK-B-10
Name and Address	Any name and address	Any name and address
Organizational Units	Company code 1000 Purchasing org. 1000	Company code 1000 Purchasing org. 1000
Account Group	ZTMM	ZTMM
Search Term	ZK-A-10	ZK-B-10
Country	Germany	Germany
Language	German	German
Reconciliation Account	160000	160000
Purchase Order Currency	EUR	EUR
Terms of Payment Purchase	0002	0002

Vendor Master Data Sheet: Sample Data for Vendors

2 Test the two vendor master records by creating (but not saving) a purchase order.

3 Add the transaction to your favorites.

19.5   Creating Purchasing Info Records

The purchasing department notifies you that prices for the road and mountain bikes have already been negotiated with the vendors. Enter these conditions into the system using purchasing info records.

Complete the following tasks associated with purchasing info records:

1 Create the corresponding info records in the system. Use the agreed upon conditions from the following table.

	Vendor A	Vendor B
Material for Plant 1000	ZK-A-10	ZK-B-10
Road Bike **ZM-BIKE-10**	€400.00/1 PC	€410.00/1 PC
Mountain Bike **ZM-BIKE-20**	€320.00/1 PC	€300.00/1 PC
Planned Delivery Time	1 day	1 day
Purchasing Group	000	000
Standard Quantity	1 piece	1 piece
Validity	Unlimited (12/31/9999)	Unlimited (12/31/9999)

Sample Data for Purchasing Info Records

2 After creating the info records, check them using Transaction ME1L or via the SAP Easy Access menu path: **Logistics ▶ Materials Management ▶ Purchasing ▶ RRF/Quotation ▶ Request for Quotation ▶ Reporting ▶ Purchasing Information System ▶ Environment ▶ Master Data ▶ Info Record**.

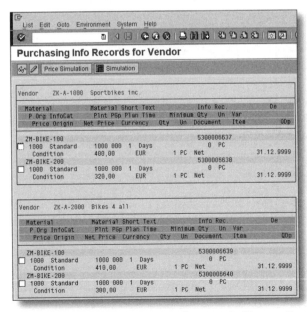

List Display of the Purchasing Info Records (Transaction ME1L)

Transaction ME1L lets you view all info records of vendors that are stored in the SAP system.

19.6   Creating a Purchase Order

With this task, you start the procurement process. In the subprocess of the example, you procure finished bikes (the finished goods) from the vendors.

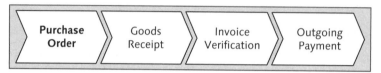

First Step in the Procurement Process: Purchase Order

Ten ZM-BIKE-10 road bikes are required for a trade show. Your task is to procure them from vendor ZK-A-10.

Complete the following tasks associated with the purchase order:

1 Create the purchase order in the SAP system. Check it for accuracy before you save it.

Use the data from the following table for the purchase order:

Vendor	ZK-A-10
Purchasing Group	000
Purchasing Organization	1000
Company Code	1000
Material	ZM-BIKE-10
Quantity	10
Plant	1000 Hamburg
Storage Location	0001

Sample Data for the Purchase Order

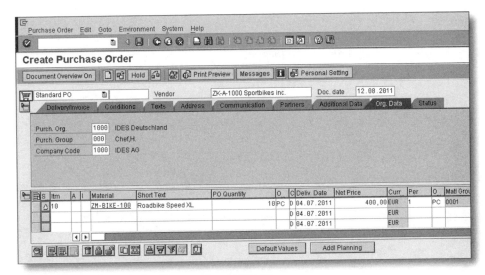

Creating a Purchase Order (Transaction ME21N)

2 Which price does the system propose?

3 Write down the document number.

4 What is the stock quantity of material ZM-BIKE-10 in the Hamburg plant? You can check the material stock using Transaction MMBE or via the SAP Easy Access menu path: Logistics ▸ Materials Management ▸ Material Master ▸ Others ▸ Stock Overview.

19.7 Receiving Goods

You now receive the goods for the previously made purchase order. Assume that the purchase order you created in the previous section has been implemented and that the goods have been delivered accordingly.

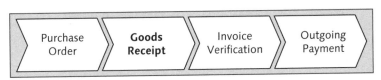

Second Step in the Procurement Process: Goods Receipt

Complete the following tasks associated with goods receipt:

1 Post the goods receipt of the ordered road bikes. Refer to the purchase order number from the previous step. Select **OK** for the item, and store the road bikes in storage location 0001.

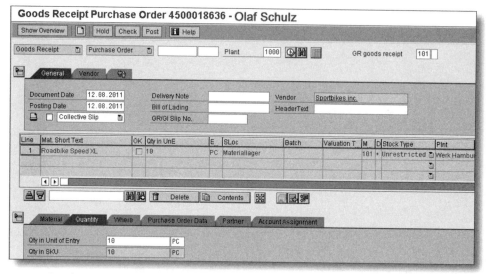

Line	Mat. Short Text	OK	Qty in UnE	E	SLoc	Batch	Valuation T	M	D	Stock Type	Plnt
1	Roadbike Speed XL	☐	10	PC	Materiallager			101	+	Unrestricted	Werk Hambur

Goods Receipt (Transaction MIGO)

2 Write down the number of the material document.

3 Check the stock quantity of material ZM-BIKE-10 in the Hamburg plant. What is the stock quantity now?

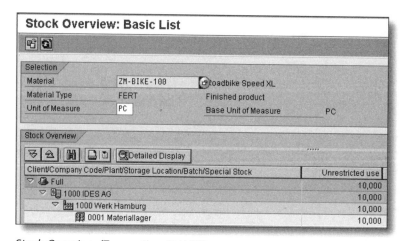

Stock Overview (Transaction MMBE)

19.8   Verifying an Invoice

After the goods have been delivered, the vendor sends the invoice. You now have to verify the invoice in order to initiate its payment. Verify the invoice for the previously made purchase order and for the received goods.

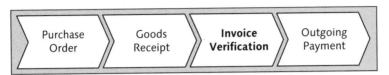

Third Step in the Procurement Process: Invoice Verification

Vendor ZK-A-10 provides the invoice for the ordered and stored road bikes.

Complete the following tasks associated with invoice verification:

1 Verify the invoice. Refer to the document number of the purchase order that you've already created.

2 The invoice contains the information that is listed in next table.

Vendor	ZK-A-10
Date	Today
Net Amount	4,000.00 EUR
Tax Rate	1I (Input tax 10 %)
Gross Amount	4,400.00 EUR

Sample Data for the Invoice Verification

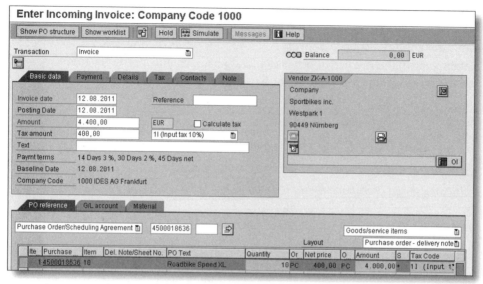

Invoice Verification (Transaction MIRO)

3 How does the transaction indicate whether the goods receipt has been carried out after the purchase order?

19.9   Displaying Open Items (Optional)

Before you post the incoming payment, you want to get an overview of the open items (that is, of outstanding payments to the vendor). For this part of the exercise, use the following sample data.

Have the system display the open items for vendor ZK-A-10. Use the data from the following table for the example:

Vendor	ZK-A-10
Company Code	1000
Fiscal Year	Current year

Sample Data for Selecting the Open Items

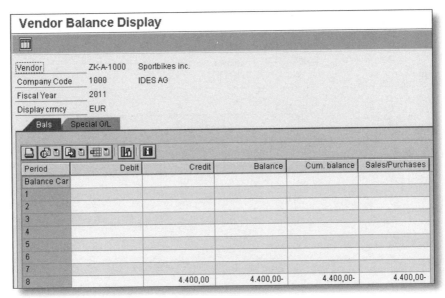

G/L Account Balance Display (Open Items) (Transaction FK10N)

19.10 Posting Outgoing Payments

The purchasing process is now completed, and it's time to pay the invoice. This task is performed in financial accounting. For this process, refer to the previous documents that exist in the system and were generated in the previous procurement steps.

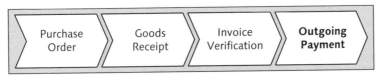

Fourth Step in the Procurement Process: Outgoing Payments

Complete the following tasks associated with outgoing payments:

1 Post the outgoing payments using the data from the next table:

Document Date	Today
Posting Date	Today

Sample Data for Outgoing Payments

"Bank Data" Area	
Account	113130
Amount	€4,400.00
Value Date:	Today
"Open Item Selection" Area	
Account	ZK-A-10
Discount	None

Sample Data for Outgoing Payments (Cont.)

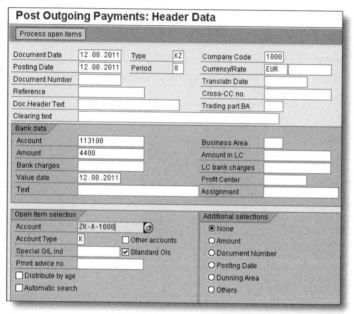

Posting Outgoing Payments (Transaction F-53)

2 Again, check the open items of the vendor using the data from the table.

Vendor	ZK-A-10
Company Code	1000
Fiscal Year	Current year

Sample Data for Selecting the Open Items

19.11 Creating a Customer Master

Your business sells the bikes to end customers and resellers. For the sales and distribution process, create the necessary customer master records in the SAP system.

Complete the following tasks associated with the customer master record:

1 Create the customer master record using the data from the table.

Account Group	ZK10 sold-to-party group 10
Customer	ZD-A-10
Sales Organization	1000
Distribution Channel	12 reseller
Division	00 cross-division
General Data, Address	
Name and Address	Any name and address
Country	DE
Region	State
Transport Zone	Depends on ZIP
General Data, Tax Data	
Tax Number 1	DE47110815
Company Code Data	
Reconciliation Account	140000
Terms of Payment	Immediately without discount
Sales Area Data	
Shipping Condition	Immediately
Delivering Plant	Hamburg
Tax Classification	Subject to tax

Sample Data for the Customer Master Record

2 Test the customer master record that you created. How could you do this?

19.12   Add Sales Data to the Material Master Record

The Sales and Distribution: SalesOrgDatA1 and Sales and Distribution: General/Plant Data views are supposed to be added to the existing material master records. Currently, the existing materials can be procured but not sold. Though you don't have to create the material master records again, you do have to add the sales data to the existing master records.

Complete the following tasks associated with adding sales data to material master records:

First, select the transaction for adding a material. In the Material Number field, enter preexisting material number. Then, additionally select the Sales and Distribution: SalesOrgDatA1 and Sales and Distribution: General/Plant Data views. Enter the required sales data and save the master record. Carry out these steps for both master records.

Add the data from the following table to the master records:

	Road Bike	Mountain Bike
Material Number	ZM-BIKE-10	ZM-BIKE-20
Plant	1000	1000
Sales Organization	1000	1000
Distribution Channel	End customer sales	End customer sales
"Sales and Distribution: SalesOrgDat1" View		
Base Unit of Measure	Piece	Piece
Delivering Plant	Hamburg	Hamburg
Material Group	0202	0202
Tax Data	Full tax	Full tax
"Sales and Distribution: General/Plant Data" View		
Transport Group	0001 Pallets	0001 Pallets
Loading Group	0003 Manual	0003 Manual

Material Master Data Sheet: Sample Data for Adding Sales Data to the Material Master Record

19.13 Creating Conditions

Define conditions in the system for sales organization 1000 and distribution channel 12. When a customer orders goods within the organizational units, the system prompts the conditions that you defined.

Carry out the following tasks regarding the conditions:

Create the conditions for the case study in the SAP system using the data from the table.

Condition Type	PRO0
Sales Organization	1000
Distribution Channel	12
Material	ZM-BIKE-10
Amount	€800.00/1 piece

Sample Data for Conditions

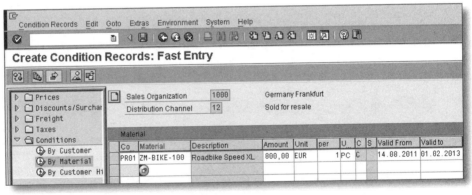

Conditions in the SAP System (Transaction VK31)

19

19.14 Creating a Standard Order

In this case, the actual sales process starts with the sales (standard) order. Again, use the data that has been created for this case study.

One of your customers now orders mountain bikes via telephone.

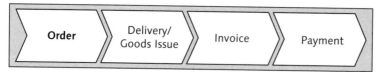

First Step in the Sales Process: Order

Complete the following tasks associated with the sales order:

1 Enter the standard order in the system using the data from the table.

Order Type	TA
Sold-To-Party	ZD-A-10
Purchase Order Number	Any
Requested Delivery Date	2 weeks from today
Material	ZM-BIKE-10
Order Quantity	1 piece
Incoterms	Ex works
Terms of Payment	Cash without discount

Sample Data for the Standard Order

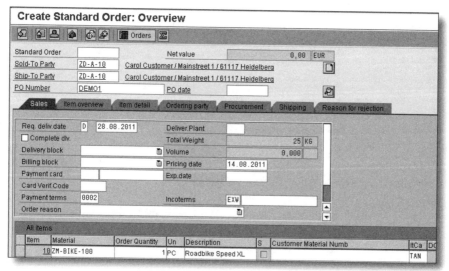

Standard Order (Transaction VA01)

2 Save the standard order, and write down the document number.

19.15   Delivering and Issuing Goods

Create the delivery, referring to the sales order that you created in the previous section. Then post the goods issue and deliver the goods to the customer according to that standard order.

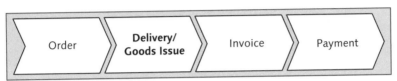

Second Step in the Sales Process: Delivery and Goods Issue

Complete the following tasks associated with goods issue:

1 Create the delivery for the previous sales (standard) order, and write down the document number.

Shipping Point	Hamburg
Selection Date	2 weeks from today
Order Number	

Sample Data for the Delivery

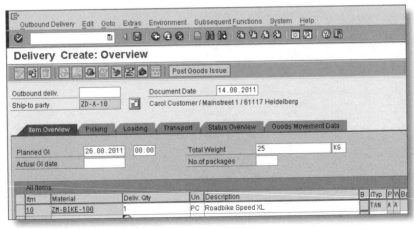

Delivery (Transaction VL01N)

2 Post the goods issue.

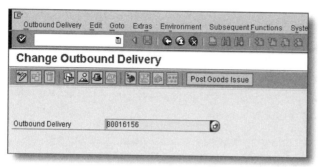

Goods Issue (Transaction VL02)

19.16 Creating an Invoice

Now invoice the delivered bikes to the customer.

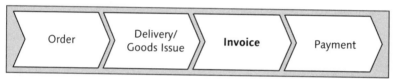

Third Step in the Sales Process: Invoice

Invoice the sales order, and write down the document number.

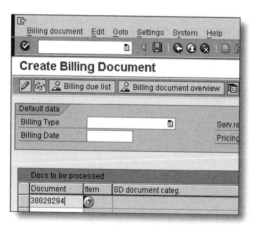

Creating an Invoice (Transaction VF01)

After invoicing your delivery, you can post the incoming payment.

19.17 Posting Incoming Payments

The customer has transferred the complete invoice amount, which corresponds to the already performed sales order, and you can post the incoming payment.

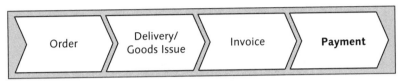

Fourth Step in the Sales Process: Incoming Payments

Complete the following tasks associated with incoming payment:

1 Post the incoming payment of the customer using the data from the following table:

Document Date	Today
Bank Data	
Account	113100
Amount	€920.00
Selection of Open Items	
Account	ZD-A-10

Sample Data for Incoming Payments

19

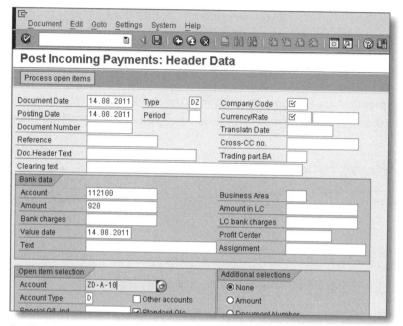

Posting Incoming Payments (Transaction F-28)

2   What is the stock quantity of material ZM-BIKE-10?

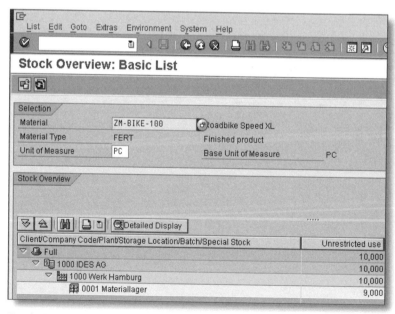

Stock Overview (Transaction MMBE)

19.18 Creating a Profitability Report (Optional)

Controlling will evaluate the Sportbikes International material group sales. You can do this using a profitability report.

Complete the following tasks associated with the profitability report:

1 Have the system display the profitability report from controlling (**Accounting ▸ Controlling ▸ Profitability Analysis ▸ Information System ▸ Execute Report**) using Transaction KE30, and determine the result for material group 0202 bikes.

Transaction	KE30
Operating Concern	IDES global
Profitability Report	SAP01-001
Fiscal Year	Current year
From Period	1
To Period	12
Version	100

Sample Data for Profitability Report

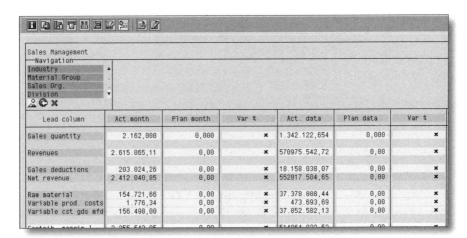

Profitability Report (Transaction S_AHR_61016354)

2 What is the result in the material group?

19.19   Creating a Telephone Directory (Optional)

Not all of Sportbikes International's employees have access to SAP. You have been asked to create a telephone directory that will be available to all employees via the Intranet. Create the directory using the employee data found in the SAP system.

Have the system display a telephone directory, and export it to Microsoft Excel. Use Transaction S_AHR_61016354.

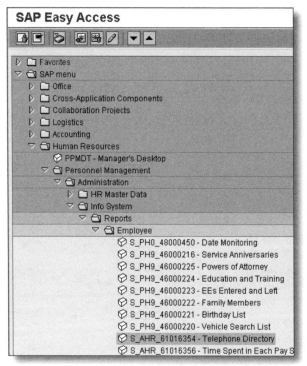

Telephone Directory (Transaction S_AHR_61016354)

Congratulations! You have successfully implemented numerous processes in the SAP system. If you had any difficulty performing the tasks, you can find solution notes for the exercises on the SAP PRESS website at *www.sap-press.com/H3213*. Enter the access code that is printed on the first page of this book.

Part IV

Appendix

A   Abbreviations

Abbreviation	Long Form	Explanation
ABAP	Advanced Business Application Programming	SAP programming language; see Chapter 3
AP	Accounts Payable (FI-AP)	Accounts payable accounting; see Chapter 16
AR	Accounts Receivable (FI-AR)	Accounts receivable accounting; see Chapter 16
PReq	Purchase Order Requisition	See Chapter 14
BI	Business Intelligence	See Chapter 3
CATS	Cross-Application Time Sheet	See Chapter 18
CO	Controlling	Controlling component from SAP ERP; see Chapter 17
CRM	Customer Relationship Management	Customer relationship management; see Chapter 3
EC	Enterprise Controlling	Enterprise controlling
EDI	Electronic Data Interchange	Electronic data exchange, see Chapter 9
ERP	Enterprise Resource Planning	See Chapter 3
ESS	Employee Self-Service	See Chapter 18
FI	Financial Accounting	Financial accounting; see Chapter 16
FSCM	Financial Supply Chain Management	See Chapter 3

Abbreviation	Long Form	Explanation
GL	General Ledger (FI-GL)	General ledger accounting; see Chapter 16
GUI	Graphical User Interface	User interface; see Chapter 5
P&L	Profit and Loss Statement	See Chapter 16
HCM	Human Capital Management	Human resources; see Chapter 18
HR	Human Resources	Human resources
IDES	Internet Demonstration and Education System	See introduction
IMG	Implementation Guide	Implementation guide; see Chapter 2
IS	Industry Solution	Industry solution; see Chapter 3
IV	Invoice Verification (MM-IV)	Invoice verification; see Chapter 14
LO	Logistics	Logistics (general); see Chapter 3
MDM	Master Data Management	Master data management; see Chapter 3
MM	Materials Management	Materials management; see Chapter 14
OM	Overhead Management (CO-OM)	Overhead cost controlling; see Chapter 17
PA	Profitability Analysis (CO-PA)	Profitability analysis; see Chapter 17
PA	Personnel Administration (HCM-PA)	Personnel administration; see Chapter 18
PLM	Product Lifecycle Management	Product lifecycle management; see Chapter 3

Abbreviation	Long Form	Explanation
PM	Plant Maintenance	Plant maintenance; see Chapter 3
PP	Production Planning	Production planning and control; see Chapter 3
PT	Personnel Time Planning (HCM-PT)	Time management; see Chapter 18
PY	Payroll (HCM-PY)	Payroll; see Chapter 18
SCM	Supply Chain Management	Supply chain management; see Chapter 14
SD	Sales and Distribution	Sales and distribution; see Chapter 15
SRM	Supplier Relationship Management	Supplier relationship management; see Chapter 3

B   Glossary

ABAP   Advanced Business Application Programming. SAP-specific programming language.

Accounts payable accounting   Posts all business transactions that refer to vendors and receives its data from purchasing. It is supported by the FI-AP component from SAP ERP Financials.

Accounts receivable accounting
Records all business transactions that are customer-related. A lot of this information originates from sales and distribution. In the SAP system, accounts receivable accounting is supported by the FI-AR component from SAP ERP Financials.

Activity type   Categorizes the activities that are rendered within a controlling area (in time or quantity units).

Asset accounting   Records all business transactions that refer to a business's assets. The FI-AA component is used for the management of assets with regard to accounting (for example, for their evaluation).

Authentication   Process that checks the identity of a computer user to allow access to the system or data.

Authorization   The user's right to carry out a specific action in the SAP system.

Background job   Task that runs via background processing in the SAP system without user intervention.

Business Add-in   (BAdI) SAP enhancement technology; locations predefined by SAP where you can link custom developments (your own program code). See User exit.

Business Application Programming Interface   (BAPI) interface in the SAP system to which specific business rules are linked.

Business area   Organizational unit in the SAP system; in financial accounting, it corresponds to a defined area of responsibility to which the recorded value movement can be assigned.

Business Explorer   (BEx) part of SAP NetWeaver BW, contains reporting tools that you can use to map data from the data warehouse in various reports. See SAP NetWeaver BW and Data warehouse.

Business Intelligence   (BI) collective term for processes that evaluate data that is available across the enterprise. These evaluations are provided to users in order to support them in decision-making processes. BI data is often stored in a data warehouse. See Data warehouse.

Business partner   Natural or legal person or a group of persons outside the business with which the enterprise collaborates at business level.

Business process   Sequence of linked steps that are supposed to have a defined result and are carried out in a business environment. SAP applications support typical business processes, such as invoicing.

Business Workplace   A work environment within the SAP system that supports the user with functions for managing messages, documents, and appointments.

Chart of accounts   List of all accounts of an enterprise and integral part of double-entry accounting in which the accounts are systematically structured. Usually, a standard chart of accounts is used in the business.

Client   Topmost organizational unit in the SAP system; an entire enterprise can be mapped by client, for example. All organizational units within a client (for instance, company code) follow a standard chart of accounts and are managed together. You always log on to a SAP system in a specific client.

Client-server architecture   System architecture that enables you to distribute tasks across clients and servers within a network. The server provides services that the clients (user PCs) use. SAP R/3, and later SAP ERP, is based on a three-layer concept: database, server, and client.

Company code   Part of the organizational structure in the SAP system; the smallest organizational unit for which a complete, self-contained set of accounts can be drawn up for the purposes of financial accounting.

Compliance   Procedure for compliance with laws and guidelines, such as the Sarbanes-Oxley Act or Occupational Safety and Health Act.

Consolidation   In financial accounting, merging individual financial statements of various subsidiary companies into a consolidated financial statement. In the general context: merging data, information, and so on.

Controlling area   Organizational unit in the SAP system for controlling. Expenses and revenues are managed and allocated at this level. One or more company codes can be assigned to a controlling area.

Controlling   Managerial accounting. The controlling controlling component in SAP ERP Financials serves to monitor, plan, and control business costs and revenues.

Cost center   Enterprise-specific account assignment object to which costs are posted. In the SAP system, it is an organizational unit within a controlling area that presents a defined location of cost incurrence.

Cost element   Cost elements are G/L accounts that are relevant for controlling. Primary cost elements have the respective G/L accounts in financial accounting and are directly transferred to controlling as actual costs. Secondary cost elements are only used for cost management in controlling and do not have any effects on financial accounting.

Cross-Application Time Sheet   (CATS) SAP self-service application for employees and external service providers that enable time recording using the time sheet.

Customer Relationship Management See SAP Customer Relationship Management.

Customer Service   Component in SAP ERP that supports the processes in service processing (for example, the processing of returns, spare part deliveries, and repair processing, and the installation of devices) as well as the management of service contracts and maintenance.

Customizing   Customization of standard SAP software to fit the customer's requirements. In Customizing (in contrast to custom developments), the software is adapted to the business's processes without programming. See Implementation Guide.

Data warehouse   A centralized database whose data come from various sources (SAP ERP, for instance) and can be provided for analysis and reporting. It also contains historical data. The data warehouse in the SAP system is SAP NetWeaver BW.

Database   System for electronic data management in which large data volumes are stored and required data is made available in the appropriate display format for users and application programs. The most commonly used databases for SAP systems are MaxDB by SAP, Oracle, and DB2 by IBM.

Debits and credits   Basic principle of double-entry accounting, according to which expenses (debits = disposition of funds) and revenues (credits = source of funds) are posted separately. Every business transaction is posted on the debit and on the credit side to different accounts.

Distribution channel   Organizational unit in the SAP system in which various sales channels (for example, wholesale) are mapped in SAP SD. You can assign any number of distribution channels to a sales organization.

Division   Organizational unit in the SAP system that is mainly used for sales and distribution. The products of a business are assigned to a division in order to map the responsibility in sales or the responsibility for profits from products.

Document principle   Financial accounting principle that states that there must be a document for every posting.

Double-entry accounting   Accounting procedure that lists value changes in two different locations: debits and credits are posted in the posting record. See Debits and credits.

Electronic Data Interchange   (EDI) electronic data exchange procedure.

Employee Self-Service   (ESS) SAP function that enables employees to access data and execute processes using their user roles (for example, to submit leave requests or register for employee training, for example). See Manager Self-Service.

Enterprise Controlling   (EC) SAP ERP component for business controlling; contains functions for consolidation and profit center accounting.

Enterprise Resource Planning   (ERP) solution for human resources, logistics, and accounting that supports all core business transactions in an enterprise. See SAP ERP.

ERP Central Component   (ECC) technical core of SAP ERP.

Financial accounting   External accounting. SAP FI is used to manage and map all accounting data according to the document principle. It covers general ledger accounting as well as accounts payable accounting, accounts receivable accounting, asset accounting, and bank accounting.

Financial statement   Maps the payables (outside capital) and net assets (stockholders' equity) of an enterprise at a specific time. See Profit and loss statement.

Financial Supply Chain Management (FSCM) deals with the optimization of cash flows within the business in order to improve liquidity. SAP FSCM includes receivables management, for example.

G/L account   Account in the general ledger that is directly included in the financial statement or profit and loss statement.

General ledger accounting   Records all accounting-relevant business transactions using G/L accounts (accounts in the chart of accounts) . In SAP ERP Financials, mapped by the FI-GL component.

Governance, Risk, and Compliance (GRC) guiding principles for responsible and successful business management in which risks are identified and avoided and internal standards are met.

Graphical User Interface   (GUI) the application interface on the computer screen that the user uses to communicate with the computer.

HR area   Organizational unit in SAP ERP HCM; helps to generate default values during the entry of data, serves as a selection criterion for evaluations, and is critical for authorization checks.

Human Capital Management   See SAP ERP Human Capital Management.

Human Resources   See SAP ERP Human Capital Management.

IDES   Internet Demonstration and Education System; model enterprise whose business processes are implemented in the SAP system for training purposes. All business areas are already configured and mapped in an integrative manner.

Implementation Guide   (IMG) menu for the Customizing of the SAP system. The Implementation Guide has a hierarchical structure based on the hierarchy of the SAP components.

Industry solution   (IS) SAP software solution tailored to a specific industry (for example, to utilities, retail, automotive, banking, etc.). A total of 24 industry solutions is currently available.

Infotype   Information unit in SAP ERP HCM. Groups of related data fields are joined in infotypes in order to structure information, facilitate its entry, and enable time-dependent data storage.

Integration   Linking various applications and merging data in one software application with the aim of making processes more efficient and improving data quality.

Internal order   Enables the planning, collection, and monitoring of costs regarding specific transactions and tasks in the SAP system.

Inventory management   Deals with the quantity-based and value-based management of material stocks, the management of goods movements, and the physical inventory. In the SAP system, inventory management is supported by MM-IM.

Investment Management   The IM component in SAP ERP supports the planning and financing of tangible assets, investments in research and development, further training, and maintenance tasks in your business. For financial assets, see Treasury.

Invoice verification   Comparison of vendor invoices with purchase order and goods receipt. In the MM component of SAP ERP, MM-IV is used for invoice verification.

Key Performance Indicator   (KPI) quantitative information that is mapped in compressed (aggregated) form and reflects the success or failure of a business.

Knowledge Management   SAP solution that enables you to create, classify, and present information as well as distribute it across the entire business.

Ledger   In accounting, framework for the recording of value or quantity transactions for a specific subarea of financial accounting. See General ledger accounting.

Logistics Execution System   (LES) SAP ERP component which supports transport and distribution. This includes the transport of goods of all kinds using various means of transport.

Logistics Information System   (LIS) tool in SAP ERP for the evaluation of data from purchasing, production, sales and distribution, warehouse, plant maintenance, quality and transport management.

Manager Self-Service   Lets managers access data and carry out tasks in the SAP system using their roles in the enterprise (for example, hiring employees or planning budgets). See Employee Self-Service.

Master Data Management   See SAP NetWeaver Master Data Management.

Master data   Information that remains unchanged over a longer period of time and is repeatedly required in business processes. Examples of master data include name, address, and date of birth of an employee.

Material requirements planning   Umbrella term for the planning and distribution of orders as well as for the assignment/provision of resources in order processing.

Materials Management   The MM component in SAP ERP supports the entire purchasing process from purchasing management, to inventory management, to invoice verification. See Purchasing.

Mobile applications   See SAP NetWeaver Mobile.

One-time account   Collective account for various vendors in financial accounting that is used for one-time invoices and payments.

Online Service System   (OSS) See SAP Service Marketplace.

Operating concern Central element in Profitability Analysis.

Organizational structure Mapping of the enterprise structure in the SAP system in which every enterprise area (for example, financial accounting) is structured via organizational units.

Overhead cost controlling Overhead Management; CO-OM in SAP ERP Financials, encompasses all tasks that support the coordination, monitoring, and optimization of indirect costs (costs that cannot be directly assigned to a product or service).

Payroll Component in SAP ERP HCM that determines the remuneration for an employee. This includes preparation, settlement, transfer, social security contributions as well as the transport of the data to financial accounting. Payroll processes are subject to numerous legal regulations, such as taxes.

Personnel Administration SAP ERP HCM component that supports all activities that have to be carried out within the scope of employee management in the business. Particularly critical are the creation, maintenance, and assignment of employee data.

Personnel Development Component in SAP ERP HCM for strategic HR work in order to train and motivate employees. Today it is known as Talent Management.

Personnel Time Management Component in SAP ERP HCM for recording working times (attendance times, breaks, business trips, extra shifts, reduced hours, absences, etc.).

Plant Maintenance SAP PM supports the planning, implementation, and settlement of maintenance tasks. SAP now markets this component as SAP Enterprise Asset Management (EAM).

Plant Organizational unit of the SAP system in logistics; structures the business from the production, MRP, and plant maintenance perspective. Each plant is assigned to a company code, which can contain multiple plants.

Product cost controlling Product Costing; the CO-PC component in SAP ERP Financials supports product cost planning and basically uses data from production planning (SAP PP) and purchasing (SAP MM).

Production Planning and Control The PP component from SAP ERP covers the planning and control of the logistics processes within production (that is, the provision of raw materials and supplies, production processes, and the transport of the manufactured products).

Profit and loss statement Part of the year-end closing, which has to be created according to country-specific legal requirements. The profit and loss statement includes a list of all expenses and revenues for the fiscal year.

Profit center accounting A separate period result is determined for a part of an enterprise, for example, a subsidiary or branch store. Profit centers collect revenues and costs for the cost center for which they are responsible, like an independent business. In the SAP system, profit center accounting is supported by the CO-PCA component.

Profitability Analysis Controlling approach. The CO-PA component from SAP ERP Financials relates revenues from sales and distribution with costs from overhead cost controlling and product cost controlling.

Purchase requisition (PReq) initiates the procurement process. The user department creates a purchase requisition based on a requirement for goods or services and forwards it to the purchasing department.

Purchase Procuring goods and services at an optimum cost/performance ratio with the goods being available at the right place at the right time. In contrast to procurement, which consists of strategic tasks, purchasing mainly deals with operational tasks. The purchase process is managed with SAP MM. See Materials Management.

Purchasing group Organizational unit in the SAP MM component. The purchasing group is responsible for the procurement of specific materials or service providers and is the point of contact for certain vendors.

Purchasing organization Organizational unit in SAP MM. The purchasing organization is responsible for all purchasing processes. In legal terms, it is the procuring unit. Purchasing organizations are assigned to company codes and plants, and determine the purchase type (group-related, enterprise-related, or plant-related).

Quality Management The SAP QM component controls quality planning and checks and supports problem management and issue quality certificates. It

meets the requirements for QM systems according to ISO 9000.

Real Estate Management SAP ERP RE consists of the management of real estate, contract and area management, and financial mapping (control of cash flows, postings and evaluations, controlling, etc.).

Reconciliation account G/L account that can be used to update the subledger accounts in parallel to the general ledger. There is a reconciliation account for every subledger.

Recruitment Component in SAP ERP HCM that is used to manage applicant data and thus facilitate the search for and selection of appropriate candidates.

Return on investment (ROI) key figure that enables you to measure the yield of the capital employed.

Sales and distribution Refers to all processes that are necessary for selling a product or service to a customer. SAP SD supports sales processes as well as delivery and transport processes, and is a part of SAP ERP.

Sales organization Organizational unit in the SAP system that is the most critical element in sales and distribution. In legal terms, it refers to a selling unit. Complete sales business transactions are managed here. A company code can have several sales organizations, but a sales organization can only belong to one company code.

SAP Advanced Planning & Optimization (SAP APO) part of SAP SCM; software for the management and integration of sales, distribution and production planning, production control and external procurement, and vendor cooperation.

SAP Business All-in-One   Integrated software system by SAP that is based on SAP Best Practices for small and medium-sized enterprises.

SAP Business ByDesign   On-demand solution for customers in medium-sized businesses; a completely integrated solution with an easy configuration hosted at SAP.

SAP Business One   SAP software for small and medium-sized businesses; like SAP ERP, it covers all core business requirements.

SAP Business Suite   Comprehensive enterprise solution by SAP containing the following solutions: SAP ERP, SAP Customer Relationship Management, SAP Product Lifecycle Management, SAP Supply Chain Management, SAP Supplier Relationship Management. See these entries.

SAP Business Workflow   SAP component that is used to facilitate business processes. In the SAP system, a workflow controls the flow of documents, which are usually processed by several people and have to be handled according to a defined pattern.

SAP Customer Relationship Management   (SAP CRM) SAP solution for the management of business contacts and customer relationships; contains functions for marketing, sales and distribution, and customer service.

SAP Easy Access menu   User menu in the SAP system that is displayed as a tree structure on the left side of the screen after you have logged on to the system. It can be used for the user-specific navigation in the SAP system.

SAP ERP Financials   Part of SAP ERP that supports managerial and external accounting (financial accounting and controlling) as well as receivables management. See SAP FSCM, Treasury, Consolidation, etc.

SAP ERP Human Capital Management (SAP ERP HCM) part of SAP ERP for the management of human resources, such as personnel administration, time management, payroll, travel management.

SAP ERP   Software solution that covers the core business requirements of medium-sized and large businesses. Among other things, it includes human resources (SAP ERP HCM), financial accounting (SAP ERP Financials), sales and distribution (SAP SD), and logistics (SAP ERP Operations). See Enterprise Resource Planning.

SAP NetWeaver Application Server Formerly SAP Web Application Server; technical basis for most of the SAP products. It consists of an ABAP application server (formerly SAP R/3 Basis) and a Java EE application server which can be used together or separately.

SAP NetWeaver Business Warehouse (SAP NetWeaver BW) See Data warehouse of SAP.

SAP NetWeaver Exchange Infrastructure (SAP NetWeaver XI) obsolete name for See SAP NetWeaver Process Integration.

SAP NetWeaver Master Data Management (SAP NetWeaver MDM) component for master data management.

SAP NetWeaver Mobile   SAP NetWeaver component that allows the user to access data and applications on the go (for example, using a cell phone).

SAP NetWeaver Portal   SAP NetWeaver component; can be used to merge information and applications centrally in an enterprise portal and provide them in a uniform way.

SAP NetWeaver Process Integration (SAP NetWeaver PI) SAP NetWeaver component that enables the integration of processes and thus the communication between applications.

SAP NetWeaver   SAP technology platform; technical basis for most of the SAP solutions.

SAP Product Lifecycle Management (SAP PLM) SAP software solution that provides support for product development, project management, product plan management, and quality management.

SAP Project System   The SAP PS component supports the technical and commercial part of a project and ensures the structuring, workflow planning, and cost accounting of a complex project.

SAP R/3   Software that is based on the client-server architecture by SAP. It was introduced in 1992 and was the predecessor of SAP ERP.

SAP Service Marketplace   Online help system by SAP in which customers can enter (error) messages that are then processed by SAP employees (*http://service.sap.com*, logon required). SAP notes (formerly OSS notes) provide support for various topics.

SAP Solution Manager   An SAP support tool that supports SAP customers in the implementation and operation of SAP software.

SAP Strategic Enterprise Management (SAP SEM) part of SAP ERP Financials that contains functions for enterprise planning and consolidation.

SAP Supplier Relationship Management (SAP SRM) SAP solution from the logistics area which supports businesses in managing procurement processes and vendor communication.

SAP Supply Chain Management   (SAP SCM) SAP solution from the logistics area; used to coordinate supply and demand, monitor the supply chain, manage distribution, transport and other logistics tasks, and provide collaboration and analysis tools.

Scalability   The system's ability to be enhanced and extended.

Service-Oriented Architecture   (SOA) a software architecture that enables the use of exchangeable web services for the creation of business processes.

Solution Manager   See SAP Solution Manager.

Storage location   Organizational unit for logistics in the SAP system that allows for the differentiation of stocks within a plant. A plant can have several storage locations. In a complex warehouse, storage locations can be further divided into warehouse numbers, storage type, and storage bins.

Supply Chain Management   See SAP Supply Chain Management.

Time Management   Personnel Time Planning; is used to record and manage time data in human resources (PT component in SAP ERP HCM).

Training and Event Management Component in SAP ERP HCM for planning, implementing, and managing events, such as trainings.

Transaction code   Alphanumeric code that is used to navigate via the command field in the SAP system. It lets you enter the required functions directly.

Transaction data   Data that can be changed and is usually valid for a defined period of time for a specific transaction only. It is created during business processes and is edited by users or other applications for a limited period of time. See Master data.

Treasury   Manages financial transactions on the money and capital market.

The Treasury functions in SAP ERP Financials support businesses analyze and monitor financial risks on the money and capital market.

User exit   Predefined points in the SAP system for custom developments (custom program code), similar to Business Add-ins.

Warehouse Management   The WM component in SAP ERP controls and manages internal goods movements, goods receipt, and goods issue as well as all warehouse processes.

Web service   Module that consists of program code that provides a business function and is made available via the Internet. Usually, together with other web services, it forms a business process and can, once created, be reused in other business processes.

C   Menu Paths and Transaction Codes

General

Batch Input System, Transaction SM35

Maintain User-Specific Data, Transaction SU3

Business Workplace, Transaction SBWP

Define Job, Transaction SM36

QuickViewer, Transaction SQVI SAPMS38R

Role Assignment, Transaction SU01

SAP Query: User Group Maintenance, Transaction SQ03

SAP Query: Maintain InfoSet, Transaction SQ02

SAP Query: Maintain Queries, Transaction SQ01

Materials Management

Request for Quotation, Transaction ME41, ME42, ME43: Logistics ▶ Materials Management ▶ Purchasing ▶ RFQ/Quotation ▶ Create/ Change/Display

Maintain Quotation, Transaction ME47: Logistics ▶ Materials Management ▶ Purchasing ▶ RFQ/Quotation ▶ Quotation ▶ Maintain

Display Quotation, Transaction ME48: Logistics ▶ Materials Management ▶ Purchasing ▶ RFQ/Quotation ▶ Quotation ▶ Display

Stock Overview, Transaction MMBE: Logistics ▶ Materials Management ▶ Inventory Management ▶ Environment ▶ Stock ▶ Stock Overview

Add Incoming Invoice, Transaction MIRO: Logistics ▶ Materials Management ▶ Logistics Invoice Verification ▶ Document Entry ▶ Enter Invoice

Purchasing Info Record, Transaction ME11, ME12, ME13: Logistics ▶ Materials Management ▶ Purchasing ▶ Master Data ▶ Info Record ▶ Create/ Change/Display

Enjoy Purchase Requisition, Transaction ME51N, ME52N, ME53N: Logistics ▶ Materials Management ▶ Purchasing ▶ Purchase Requisition ▶ Create/Change/Display

Enjoy Purchase Order, Transaction ME21N: Logistics ▶ Materials Management ▶ Purchasing ▶ Purchase Order ▶ Create ▶ Vendor/Supplying Plant Known

Info Library: Logistics ▶ Logistics Controlling ▶ Logistics Information System ▶ Info Library

Enter Storage Locations, Transaction MMSC: Logistics ▶ Materials Manage Logistics ▶ Materials Management ▶ Material Master ▶ Other ▶ Enter Storage Locations

Delete Single Purchasing Info Record, Transaction ME15: Logistics ▶ Materials Management ▶ Purchasing ▶ Master Data ▶ Info Record ▶ Flag for Deletion

Delete Multiple Purchasing Info Records: Logistics ▶ Materials Management ▶ Purchasing ▶ Master Data ▶ Info Record ▶ Follow-On Functions ▶ Deletion Proposals

Mass Maintenance, Transaction MASS: Logistics ▶ Central Functions ▶ Mass Maintenance ▶ Mass Maintenance

Material Master Record, Transaction MM01, MM02, MM03: Logistics ▶ Materials Management ▶ Material Master ▶ Create/Change/Display

Output Message—Request for Quotation/Quotation, Transaction ME9A: Logistics ▶ Materials Management ▶ Purchasing ▶ RFQ/Quotation ▶ Request for Quotation ▶ Messages ▶ Print/Transmit

Output Message—Purchase Order, Transaction ME9F: Logistics ▶ Materials Management ▶ Purchasing ▶ Purchase Order ▶ Messages ▶ Print/Transmit

Price Comparison List, Transaction ME49: Logistics ▶ Materials Management ▶ Purchasing ▶ Request for Quotation/Quotation ▶ Quotation ▶ Price Comparison List

Goods Movement, Transaction MIGO: Logistics ▶ Materials Management ▶ Inventory Management ▶ Goods Movement ▶ Goods Movement (MIGO)

Sales and Distribution

Change Quotation, Transaction VA22: Logistics ▸ Sales and Distribution ▸ Sales ▸ Quotation ▸ Change

Create Quotation, Transaction VA21: Logistics ▸ Sales and Distribution ▸ Sales ▸ Quotation ▸ Create

Display Quotation, Transaction VA23: Logistics ▸ Sales and Distribution ▸ Sales ▸ Quotation ▸ Display

Outbound Delivery Monitor, Transaction VL06O: Logistics ▸ Sales and Distribution ▸ Shipping and Transportation ▸ Outbound Delivery ▸ Lists and Logs ▸ Outbound Delivery Monitor

Stock Overview, Transaction MMBE: Materials Management ▸ Inventory Management ▸ Environment ▸ Stock ▸ Stock Overview

Change Customer, Transaction VD02: Sales and Distribution ▸ Master Data ▸ Business Partner ▸ Customer ▸ Change (Sales and Distribution)

Create Customer, Transaction VD01: Sales and Distribution ▸ Master Data ▸ Business Partner ▸ Customer ▸ Create (Sales and Distribution)

Display Customer, Transaction VD03: Sales and Distribution ▸ Master Data ▸ Business Partner ▸ Customer ▸ Display (Sales and Distribution)

Change Invoice, Transaction VF02: Logistics ▸ Sales and Distribution ▸ Billing ▸ Billing Document ▸ Change

Create Invoice, Transaction VF01: Logistics ▸ Sales and Distribution ▸ Billing ▸ Billing Document ▸ Create

Display Invoice, Transaction VF03: Logistics ▸ Sales and Distribution ▸ Billing ▸ Billing Document ▸ Display

Output Invoice, Transaction VF31: Logistics ▸ Sales and Distribution ▸ Billing ▸ Output ▸ Issue Billing Documents

Billing Due List, Transaction VF04: Logistics ▸ Sales and Distribution ▸ Billing ▸ Billing Document ▸ Process Billing Due List

Condition Record: Change Pricing, Transaction VK12: Sales and Distribution ▸ Master Data ▸ Conditions ▸ Selection Using Condition Type ▸ Change

Condition Record: Create Pricing, Transaction VK11: Sales and Distribution ▸ Master Data ▸ Conditions ▸ Selection Using Condition Type ▸ Create

Condition Record: Display Pricing, Transaction VK13: Sales and Distribution ▸ Master Data ▸ Conditions ▸ Selection Using Condition Type ▸ Display

Change Sales Order, Transaction VA02: Sales and Distribution ▸ Sales ▸ Order ▸ Change

Create Sales Order, Transaction VA01: Sales and Distribution ▸ Sales ▸ Order ▸ Create

Display Sales Order, Transaction VA03: Sales and Distribution ▸ Sales ▸ Order ▸ Display

Change Delivery, Transaction VL02N: Logistics ▸ Sales and Distribution ▸ Shipping and Transportation ▸ Pack ▸ Outbound Delivery

Create Delivery: Logistics ▸ Sales and Distribution ▸ Shipping and Transportation ▸ Outbound Delivery ▸ Create ▸ Single Document

Display Delivery, Transaction VL03N: Logistics ▸ Sales and Distribution ▸ Shipping and Transportation ▸ Outbound Delivery ▸ Change ▸ Display

List of Quotations, Transaction VA25: Logistics ▸ Sales and Distribution ▸ Sales ▸ Information System ▸ Quotations ▸ Quotations List

List of Orders, Transaction VA05: Logistics ▸ Sales and Distribution ▸ Sales ▸ Information System ▸ Orders ▸ List of Sales Orders

List of Invoices, Transaction VF05: Logistics ▸ Sales and Distribution ▸ Billing ▸ Information System ▸ Billing Documents ▸ List Billing Documents

Change Material, Transaction MM02: Logistics ▸ Sales and Distribution ▸ Master Data ▸ Products ▸ Material ▸ Other Material ▸ Change

Create Material, Transaction MM01: Logistics ▸ Sales and Distribution ▸ Master Data ▸ Products ▸ Material ▸ Other Material ▸ Create

Display Material, Transaction MM03: Logistics ▸ Sales and Distribution ▸ Master Data ▸ Products ▸ Material ▸ Other Material ▸ Display

Financial Accounting

Due Date Analysis for OI, Transaction S_ALR_87012078: Accounting ▶ Financial Accounting ▶ Accounts Payable ▶ Information System ▶ Reports for Accounts Payable Accounting ▶ Vendors: Items ▶ Due Date Analysis for Open Items

Recurring Entries, Transaction F.14: Accounting ▶ Financial Accounting ▶ General Ledger (or Customers/or Vendors) ▶ Periodic Processing ▶ Recurring Entries ▶ Execute

Create/Change/Display Customer, Transaction FD01/FD02 /FD03: Accounting ▶ Financial Accounting ▶ Accounts Receivable ▶ Master Records ▶ Create/Change/Display

Block Customer, Transaction FD05: Accounting ▶ Financial Accounting ▶ Accounts Receivable ▶ Master Records ▶ Block/Unblock

Create/Change/Display Customer Centrally, Transaction XD01/XD02/XD03: Accounting ▶ Financial Accounting ▶ Accounts Receivable ▶ Master Records ▶ Maintain Centrally ▶ Create/Change/Display

Block Customer Centrally, Transaction XD05: Accounting ▶ Financial Accounting ▶ Accounts Receivable ▶ Master Records ▶ Maintain Centrally ▶ Block/Unblock

Customer Line Item List, Transaction VD01: Accounting ▶ Financial Accounting ▶ Accounts Receivable ▶ Account ▶ Display/Change Line Items

Clear Customer Account, Transaction F-32: Accounting ▶ Financial Accounting ▶ Accounts Receivable ▶ Account ▶ Clear

Customer Credit Memo: Single-Screen Transaction, Transaction FB75: Accounting ▶ Financial Accounting ▶ Accounts Receivable ▶ Document Entry ▶ Credit Memo

Customer Credit Memo, enter Transaction F-27: Accounting ▶ Financial Accounting ▶ Accounts Receivable ▶ Document Entry ▶ Credit Memo General

Customer Information System, Transaction F.30: Accounting ▶ Financial Accounting ▶ Financial Accounting ▶ Accounts Receivable ▶ Information System ▶ Tools ▶ Configure ▶ Display Evaluations

Customer Balances, Transaction S_ALR_87012172: Accounting ▶ Financial Accounting ▶ Accounts Receivable ▶ Information System ▶ Reports for

Accounts Receivable Accounting ▶ Customer Balances ▶ Customer Balances in Local Currency

Customer List, Transaction S_ALR_87012179: Accounting ▶ Financial Accounting ▶ Accounts Receivable ▶ Information System ▶ Reports for Accounts Receivable Accounting ▶ Master Data ▶ Customer List

Add Incoming Invoice, Transaction MIRO: Logistics ▶ Materials Management ▶ Logistics Invoice Verification ▶ Document Entry ▶ Enter Invoice

Customer (Vendor or G/L Account) Line Items, Transaction FBL3N: Accounting ▶ Financial Accounting ▶ General Ledger ▶ Account ▶ Display/Change Items (New)

Define Job/Update Information System, Transaction F.29: Accounting ▶ Financial Accounting ▶ Accounts Payable ▶ Information System ▶ Tools ▶ Configure ▶ Create Evaluations

Manage Cash Journal, Transaction FBCJ: Accounting ▶ Financial Accounting ▶ Banks ▶ Incomings ▶ Cash Journal

Create/Change/Display Vendor, Transaction FK01/FK02/FK03: Accounting ▶ Financial Accounting ▶ Accounts Payable ▶ Master Records ▶ Create/Change/Display

Vendor: Single-Screen Transaction, Transaction FB60: Accounting ▶ Financial Accounting ▶ Accounts Payable ▶ Document Entry ▶ Invoice

Create/Change/Display Vendor Centrally, Transaction XK01/XK02/XK03: Accounting ▶ Financial Accounting ▶ Accounts Payable ▶ Master Records ▶ Create/Change/Display

Block Vendor Centrally, Transaction XK05: Accounting ▶ Financial Accounting ▶ Accounts Payable ▶ Master Records ▶ Block/Unblock

Post Vendor Document, Transaction F-43: Accounting ▶ Financial Accounting ▶ Accounts Payable ▶ Document Entry ▶ Invoice General

Vendor Line Item List, Transaction FBL1N: Accounting ▶ Financial Accounting ▶ Accounts Payable ▶ Account ▶ Display/Change Line Items

Vendor Information System, Transaction F.46: Accounting ▶ Financial Accounting ▶ Accounts Payable ▶ Information System ▶ Tools ▶ Display Evaluations

Flag for Deletion, Transaction FD06: Accounting ▶ Financial Accounting ▶ Accounts Receivable ▶ Master Records ▶ Set Deletion Indicator

Dunning Program, Transaction F150: Accounting ▶ Financial Accounting ▶ Accounts Receivable ▶ Periodic Processing ▶ Dunning

Manual Outgoing Payments, Transaction F-53: Accounting ▶ Financial Accounting ▶ Accounts Payable ▶Outgoing Payment ▶ Post

G/L Account Posting, Transaction F-02: Accounting ▶ Financial Accounting ▶ General Ledger ▶ Posting ▶ General Posting

Payment Program, Transaction F110: Accounting ▶ Financial Accounting ▶ Accounts Payable ▶ Periodic Processing ▶ Payments

Outgoing Payments with Form Printout, Transaction F-58: Accounting ▶ Financial Accounting ▶ Accounts Payable ▶ Document Entry ▶ Outgoing Payment ▶ Post + Print Form

Controlling

Create Material Cost Estimate, Transaction CK11N: Accounting ▶ Controlling ▶ Product Cost Controlling ▶ Product Cost Planning ▶ Material Costing ▶ Product Cost Planning ▶ Material Costing ▶ Cost Estimate with Quantity Structure ▶ Create

Customer Sales, Transaction S_ALR_87012186: Accounting ▶ Financial Accounting ▶ Accounts Receivable ▶ Information System ▶ Reports for Accounts Receivable Accounting ▶ Customer Balances ▶ Customer Sales

Enter Direct Activity Allocation, Transaction KB21N: Accounting ▶ Controlling ▶ Cost Center Accounting ▶ Actual Postings ▶ Activity Allocation ▶ Enter

Profitability Analysis, Transaction KE30: Accounting ▶ Controlling ▶ Profitability Analysis ▶ Information System ▶ Execute Report

Create Internal Order, Transaction KO01: Accounting ▶ Controlling ▶ Internal Orders ▶ Master Data ▶ Specific Functions ▶ Order ▶ Create

Actual Settlement: Order, Transaction KO88: Accounting ▶ Controlling ▶ Internal Orders ▶ Period-End Closing ▶ Single Functions ▶ Settlement ▶ Individual Processing

Create Cost Center, Transaction KS01: Accounting ▸ Controlling ▸ Cost Center Accounting ▸ Master Data ▸ Cost Center ▸ Individual Processing ▸ Create

Cost Centers: Planning Overview, Transaction KSBL: Accounting ▸ Controlling ▸ Cost Center Accounting ▸ Information System ▸ Reports on Cost Center Planning ▸ Planning Reports ▸ Cost Centers: Planning Overview

Cost Center Planning, Set Planner Profile, Transaction KP04: Accounting ▸ Controlling ▸ Cost Center Accounting ▸ Planning ▸ Set Planner Profile

Cost Center Planning, Set Planner Profile, Transaction KP46: Accounting ▸ Controlling ▸ Cost Center Accounting ▸ Planning ▸ Statistic Key Figures ▸ Change

Vendor Balances, Transaction S_ALR_87012082: Accounting ▸ Financial Accounting ▸ Accounts Payable ▸ Information System ▸ Reports for Accounts Payable Accounting ▸ Vendor Balances ▸ Vendor Balances in Local Currency

Activity Types: Change Plan Data, Transaction KP26: Accounting ▸ Controlling ▸ Cost Center Accounting ▸ Planning ▸ Activity Output/Prices ▸ Change

Manual Transfer Posting, Enter Costs, Transaction KB11N: Accounting ▸ Controlling ▸ Cost Center Accounting ▸ Actual Postings ▸ Manual Reposting of Costs ▸ Enter

Open Customer Items, Transaction S_ALR_87012173: Accounting ▸ Financial Accounting ▸ Accounts Receivable ▸ Information System ▸ Reports for Accounts Receivable Accounting ▸ Customer: Items ▸ List of Customer Open Items for Printing

Maintain Period Lock, Transaction OKP1: Accounting ▸ Controlling ▸ Cost Center Accounting ▸ Environment ▸ Period Lock ▸ Change

Change Planning for Cost Element/Activity Input, Transaction KP06: Accounting ▸ Controlling ▸ Cost Center Accounting ▸ Planning ▸ Cost and Activity Inputs ▸ Change

Change Planning for Cost Element/Activity Input, Transaction KPF6: Accounting ▸ Controlling ▸ Internal Orders ▸ Planning ▸ Cost and Activity Inputs ▸ Change

Product Costing with Quantity Structure, Transaction S_P99_41000111: Accounting ▸ Controlling ▸ Product Cost Controlling ▸ Product Cost Planning ▸ Information System ▸ Object List ▸ For Material ▸ Analyze/Compare Material Cost Estimates

Change Standard Hierarchy, Transaction OKEON: Accounting ▸ Controlling ▸ Cost Center Accounting ▸ Master Data ▸ Standard Hierarchy ▸ Change

Display Standard Hierarchy, Transaction OKENN: Accounting ▸ Controlling ▸ Cost Center Accounting ▸ Master Data ▸ Standard Hierarchy ▸ Display

Comparison Between Current and Previous Year, Transaction S_ALR_87010779: Information Systems ▸ General Report Selection ▸ Controlling ▸ Operating Concern S001: Costing-Based ▸ Comparison: Current Year/Previous Year

Human Resources

Start Settlement, Transaction PC00_M01_CALC: Personnel ▸ Payroll ▸ Europe ▸ Germany ▸ Payroll ▸ Start Payroll

Settlement Simulation, Transaction PC00_M01_CALC_SIMU: Personnel ▸ Payroll ▸ Europe ▸ Germany ▸ Payroll ▸ Simulation

Payroll Status of an Employee, Transaction PU03: Human Resources ▸ Time Management ▸ Tools ▸ Tools Selection ▸ Payroll Status ▸ Change Payroll Status

Maintain Payroll Control Record, Transaction PA03: Human Resources ▸ Payroll ▸ Europe

Work Center: Time Management, Transaction PTMW: Human Resources ▸ Time Management ▸ Administration ▸ Time Manager's Workplace

Worklist: Time Management, Transaction PT40: Human Resources ▸ Time Management ▸ Administration ▸ Time Evaluation ▸ Time Management Pool

User-Specific Settings, Transaction PSVI: Human Resources ▸ Training and Event Management ▸ Settings ▸ User-Specific Settings

Remuneration Statement, Transaction PC00_M01_CEDT: Human Resources ▸ Payroll ▸ Europe ▸ Germany ▸ Payroll ▸ Remuneration Statement

Approval of Travel Requests and Travel Expenses/Overview: Accounting ▸ Financial Accounting ▸ Travel Management ▸ Travel Expenses ▸ Periodic Processing ▸ Approve Trips

Information System: Human Resources ▸ Training and Event Management ▸ Resources ▸ Information System ▸ Information Menu

Maintain Organizational Objects, Transaction PP01: Logistics ▶ Customer Service ▶ Service Processing ▶ Environment ▶ Organization ▶ Expert Mode ▶ General

Display Organizational Structure, Transaction PPOSE: Logistics ▶ Customer Service ▶ Service Processing ▶ Environment ▶ Organization ▶ Organizational Plan ▶ Organization and Staffing ▶ Display

Maintain Organizational Structure, Transaction PPOME: Collaboration Projects ▶ Master Data ▶ Organizational Model ▶ Change Organization and Staffing

Carry out Personnel Actions, Transaction PA40: Personnel ▶ Personnel Management ▶ Administration ▶ HR Master Data ▶ Personnel Actions

Display HR Master Data, Transaction PA20: Personnel ▶ Personnel Management ▶ Administration ▶ HR Master Data ▶ Display

Maintain HR Master Data, Transaction PA30: Personnel ▶ Personnel Management ▶ Administration ▶ HR Master Data ▶ Maintain

Planning Manager: Accounting ▶ Financial Accounting ▶ Accounting ▶ Financial Accounting ▶ Travel Management ▶ Travel Planning ▶ Planning Manager

Travel Expense Form (Standard Form), Transaction PRF0 _PDF: Accounting ▶ Financial Accounting ▶ Travel Management ▶ Travel Expenses ▶ Periodic Processing ▶ Print Forms ▶ Standard Form

Travel Expense Manager: Accounting ▶ Financial Accounting ▶ Travel Management ▶ Travel Expenses ▶ Travel Expense Manager

Travel Manager: Accounting ▶ Financial Accounting ▶ Travel Management ▶ Travel Manager

Settle Travel Expenses: Accounting ▶ Financial Accounting ▶ Travel Management ▶ Travel Expenses ▶ Periodic Processing ▶ Settle Trips

Resource Menu: Human Resources ▶ Training and Event Management ▶ Resources ▶ Resource Menu

Fast Entry of Time Data: Human Resources ▶ Time Management ▶ Administration ▶ Time Data ▶ Fast Entry

Attendance Menu: Human Resources ▶ Training and Event Management ▶ Attendance ▶ Attendance Menu

Training and Event Management: Human Resources ▶ Training and Event Management ▶ Business Events ▶ Business Event Menu

Time Evaluation: Human Resources ▶ Time Management ▶ Administration ▶ Time Evaluation ▶ Time Evaluation

Display Time Data: Human Resources ▶ Time Management ▶ Shift Planning ▶ Environment ▶ Display time data

Maintain Time Data: Human Resources ▶ Time Management ▶ Shift Planning ▶ Environment ▶ Maintain time data

Time Statement: Human Resources ▶ Time Management ▶ Administration ▶ Time Evaluation ▶ Time Statement

D Buttons, Key Combinations, and Function Keys

Key Combinations

Action	Key Combination
Cancel actions step-by-step	`Esc`
Select all	`Ctrl`+`A`
Activate selected element	`↵` or space bar
Cut	`Ctrl`+`X`
Paste	`Ctrl`+`V`
Activate entry in list	`↵`
Replace	`Ctrl`+`H`
Navigate in list of entries which can be selected	`←`, `↓`, `↑`, `→`
Copy	`Ctrl`+`C`
Delete	`Del` (numeric keypad)
Find	`Ctrl`+`F`
Repeat	`Ctrl`+`Y`
Cut line	`Ctrl`+`⇧`+`X`
Duplicate line	`Ctrl`+`D`
Copy line	`Ctrl`+`⇧`+`T`
Delete line	`Ctrl`+`⇧`+`1`
Move line upward	`Ctrl`+`Alt`+`8` (numeric keypad)
Move line downward	`Ctrl`+`Alt`+`2` (numeric keypad)
Change lines	`Ctrl`+`Alt`+`T`

Action	Key Combination
Go to menu	[Alt]
Navigate to next element	[⇥]
Navigate to previous element	[⇧]+[⇥]
Navigate to next group	[Ctrl]+[⇥]
Navigate to previous group	[⇧]+[Ctrl]+[⇥]
Undo	[Ctrl]+[Z]
Refresh SAP Easy Access menu	[Ctrl]+[F1]

Function Keys

Function Key	Explanation
[F1]	Help
[F3]	Back
[F4]	Display search list
[F5]	Overview
[F6]	Copy to personal value list
[F12]	Cancel

Buttons

Standard Toolbar

Button	Key Combination	Function
	[↵]	Enter
	[Ctrl]+[S]	Save
	[F3]	Back

Button	Key Combination	Function
	⌂ + F3	Exit
	F12	Cancel
	Ctrl + P	Print
	–	New session
	F1	Help
	Ctrl + F	Find
	Ctrl + G	Find next
	Ctrl + Page ↑	First page
	Ctrl + Page ↓	Last page
	Page ↑	Next page
	Page ↓	Previous page
	–	Desktop link
	Alt + F1	Customize local layout

General Functions

Button	Key Combination	Function
	F8	Execute
	F6	Create
	–	Copy
	Ctrl + ⌂ + F3	Change favorites
	Ctrl + F6	Display

Button	Key Combination	Function
	F7	Switch: display/change
	F7	Select all lines
	F8	Deselect
	—	Retrieve variant
	F5	Display document overview
	⇧ + F6	Screen help
	—	Multiple selection
	—	Refresh
	⇧ + F2	Delete
	—	Lock
	—	Unlock
	Ctrl + ⇧ + F6	Release
	F12	Cancel
	Ctrl + ⇧ + F6	Add favorite
	⇧ + F2	Delete favorite
	—	Object services
	⇧ + F5	Display next document
	F6	Display document header
	—	Selection variant

F4 Help

Button	Function
✔	Execute search
✖	Close
◈	Multiple selection
ℹ	Documentation
🖨	Print hit list
▦	Copy value to personal hit list
▦	Delete value from personal hit list
◉	Change to personal value list
◉	Display all values

Reports

Button	Key Combination	Function
🖨	Ctrl + F4	Sort in ascending order
🖨	Ctrl + ⇧ + F4	Sort in descending order
▼	Ctrl + F5	Set filter
Σ	Ctrl + F6	Total
▦	Ctrl + ⇧ + F6	Subtotals
▦	Ctrl + F8	Change layout
▥	Ctrl + ⇧ + F11	Create diagram

Button	Key Combination	Function
	–	Mass change
	Ctrl + F7	Send message
	Ctrl + ⇧ + F9	Local file
	Ctrl + ⇧ + F7/F8	Export to word processing/ spreadsheet
	Ctrl + F1	ABC analysis
	Ctrl + ⇧ + F3	Display details

E   Bibliography

- Bomann, Stefan; Hellberg Torsten: Rechnungsprüfung mit SAP MM. Galileo Press 2008.
- Brück, Uwe: Praxishandbuch SAP-Controlling. 3rd, updated edition, Galileo Press 2009.
- Forsthuber, Heinz; Siebert, Jörg: Praxishandbuch SAP-Finanzwesen. 4th, extended edition, Galileo Press 2010.
- Hellberg, Torsten: Einkauf mit SAP MM. 2nd, updated and extended edition, Galileo Press 2009.
- Junold, Anja; Buckowitz, Christian; Cuello, Nathalie; Möller, Sven-Olaf: Praxishandbuch SAP-Personalwirtschaft. Galileo Press 2011.
- Kappauf, Jens; Koch, Matthias; Lauterbach, Bernd: Discover Logistik mit SAP. Galileo Press 2010.
- Scheibler, Jochen; Maurer, Tanja: Praxishandbuch Vertrieb mit SAP. 3rd, updated and extended edition, Galileo Press 2010.
- Then, Tobias: Einkauf mit SAP. Der Grundkurs für Für Einsteiger und Anwender. Galileo Press 2011.

Index

J

K

L

P

Q

R

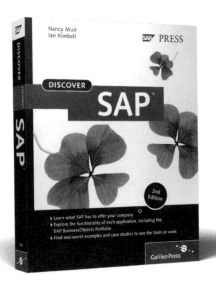

Learn what SAP has to offer your company

Explore the functionality of each application, including the SAP BusinessObjects portfolio

Find real-world examples and case studies to see the tools at work

Nancy Muir, Ian Kimbell

Discover SAP

Discover SAP, second edition will teach anyone new to SAP, decision makers just considering SAP, and consultants getting started with SAP the practical details you need to really understand what the SAP solution is and how it can benefit your company. As part of the Discover series, the, the book is written in practical language to clearly explain what SAP is in layman's terms, while providing practical insights into the applications that make up the SAP complete solution. The book is filled with interesting examples, case studies, marginal notes, and tips for readers to glean insights into how SAP can benefit their organization.

440 pp., 2. edition 2010, 39,95 Euro / US$ 39.95
ISBN 978-1-59229-320-9

>> www.sap-press.com

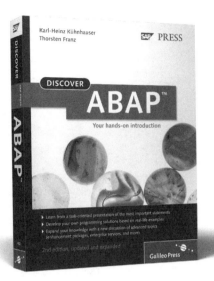

Learn from a task-oriented
presentation of the most important
statements

Develop your own programming
solutions based on real-life examples

Expand your knowledge with a new
discussion of advanced topics

Karl-Heinz Kühnhauser, Thorsten Franz

Discover ABAP

If you're new to ABAP and want practical programming guidance,
look no further. <i>Discover ABAP</i> offers a clear and concise
introduction to SAP's main programming language, giving you the
information you need to immediately start writing code. Based on
a real-life example that is carried throughout the book, you'll quickly
develop your own programming solutions, right from page one. This
revised edition is updated for SAP NetWeaver 7.2/02, and is exactly
the tool you need to begin your ABAP experience.

approx. 540 pp., 2. edition, 49,95 Euro / US$ 49.95
ISBN 978-1-59229-402-2, Nov 2011

>> www.sap-press.com

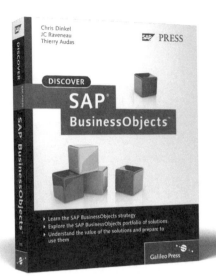

Learn the SAP BusinessObjects Strategy

Explore the SAP BusinessObjects portfolio of solutions

Understand the value for SAP customers and prepare to get started or transition to the new solutions

Chris Dinkel, JC Raveneau, Thierry Audas, Chris Dinkel

Discover SAP BusinessObjects

Discover SAP BusinessObjects will answer the many questions that you, as a decision maker or current SAP or BusinessObjects customer, may have about the new BI strategy from SAP. You'll learn about the business value of the new SAP BusinessObjects solutions and learn how to get started or transition to these solutions. And, throughout the book, you'll find an emphasis on how to position all of the key solutions in the new SAP BusinessObjects portfolio, and see how they fit together into existing SAP customer landscapes.

380 pp., 2011, 39,95 Euro / US$ 39.95
ISBN 978-1-59229-315-5

>> www.sap-press.com

Explore the features and functionality of SAP SCM 7.0

Find detailed coverage of core functional areas, including DP, SNP, PP/DS, etc.

Learn how to maximize your return on investment

Shaun Snapp

Discover SAP SCM

This text offers general overview of the SAP SCM application, which provides broad functionality for enabling responsive supply networks and integrates seamlessly with both SAP and non-SAP software. This text provides detailed coverage of all the functional areas within SAP SCM.

384 pp., 2010, 39,95 Euro / US$ 39.95
ISBN 978-1-59229-305-6

>> www.sap-press.com